SPECTRUM MULT

BIBLICAL

HERMENEUTICS

FIVE VIEWS

EDITED BY STANLEY E. PORTER
and BETH M. STOVELL

CONTRIBUTIONS BY
Craig L. Blomberg, Richard B. Gaffin Jr.,
F. Scott Spencer, Robert W. Wall, *and* Merold Westphal

IVP Academic
An imprint of InterVarsity Press
Downers Grove, Illinois

InterVarsity Press
P.O. Box 1400, Downers Grove, IL 60515-1426
ivpress.com
email@ivpress.com

InterVarsity Press® is the book-publishing division of InterVarsity Christian Fellowship/USA®, a movement of students and faculty active on campus at hundreds of universities, colleges and schools of nursing in the United States of America, and a member movement of the International Fellowship of Evangelical Students. For information about local and regional activities, visit intervarsity.org.

Cover design: David Fassett
Interior design: Beth McGill
Images: Geometric background: © Rogotanie / iStockphoto/ Getty Images
  gray grunge background: © Vladimirovic / iStock / Getty Images
  wood grain pattern: © ambassador806 / iStock / Getty Images Plus
  connecting lines: © ambassador806 / iStock / Getty Images Plus
  graphic eye: © vasabii / iStock / Getty Images Plus
  book icon: © pay404 / iStock /Getty Images Plus

ISBN 978-0-8308-3963-6

Printed in the United States of America ∞

InterVarsity Press is committed to ecological stewardship and to the conservation of natural resources in all our operations. This book was printed using sustainably sourced paper.

Library of Congress Cataloging-in-Publication Data

Biblical hermeneutics: five views / edited by Stanley E. Porter and
Beth M. Stovell; with contributions by Craig L. Blomberg . . . [et
al.].
    p. cm.—(Spectrum multiview book)
  Includes bibliographical references and index.
  ISBN 978-0-8308-3963-6 (pbk.: alk. paper)
  1. Bible—Hermeneutics. I. Porter, Stanley E., 1956- II. Stovell,
Beth M., 1978- III. Blomberg, Craig.
  BS476.B4945 2012
  220.601—dc23

                                                                2012005238

| **P** | 23 | 22 | 21 | 20 | 19 | 18 | 17 | 16 | 15 | 14 | 13 | 12 | 11 | 10 | 9 | 8 | 7 | 6 |
| **Y** | 33 | 32 | 31 | 30 | 29 | 28 | 27 | 26 | 25 | 24 | 23 | 22 | 21 | 20 | 19 | 18 | 17 | |

Contents

Abbreviations   5

Preface   7

Introduction: Trajectories in Biblical Hermeneutics   9
  Stanley E. Porter and Beth M. Stovell

PART ONE: FIVE VIEWS OF BIBLICAL HERMENEUTICS

1. THE HISTORICAL-CRITICAL/GRAMMATICAL VIEW . . . 27
  Craig L. Blomberg

2. THE LITERARY/POSTMODERN VIEW 48
  F. Scott Spencer

3. THE PHILOSOPHICAL/THEOLOGICAL VIEW 70
  Merold Westphal

4. THE REDEMPTIVE-HISTORICAL VIEW 89
  Richard B. Gaffin Jr.

5. THE CANONICAL VIEW 111
  Robert W. Wall

PART TWO: RESPONSES

6. THE HISTORICAL-CRITICAL/GRAMMATICAL RESPONSE 133
  Craig L. Blomberg

7. THE LITERARY/POSTMODERN RESPONSE 146
  F. Scott Spencer

8. THE PHILOSOPHICAL/ THEOLOGICAL RESPONSE. 160

Merold Westphal

9. THE REDEMPTIVE-HISTORICAL RESPONSE 174

Richard B. Gaffin Jr.

10. THE CANONICAL RESPONSE 188

Robert W. Wall

Interpreting Together: Synthesizing Five Views of
Biblical Hermeneutics. 201

Stanley E. Porter and Beth M. Stovell

List of Contributors 211

Name and Subject Index 213

Scripture Index 223

Abbreviations

ABRL	Anchor Bible Reference Library
AJT	*Asia Journal of Theology*
BETL	Bibliotheca ephemeridum theologicarum lovaniensium
BECNT	Baker Exegetical Commentary on the New Testament
BSac	*Biliotheca sacra*
CBQ	*Catholic Biblical Quarterly*
CTM	*Concordia Theological Monthly*
EstBib	*Estudios biblicos*
ExpTim	*Expository Times*
GBS	Guides to Biblical Scholarship
ICC	International Critical Commentary
JBL	*Journal of Biblical Literature*
LXX	Septuagint
MT	Masoretic text
NAC	New American Commentary
NGS	New Gospel Studies
NIGTC	New International Greek Testament Commentary
NIVAC	NIV Application Commentary
NovT	*Novum Testamentum*
NTL	New Testament Library
NTS	*New Testament Studies*
PAST	Pauline Studies
PNTC	Pillar New Testament Commentary
SBLSymS	Society of Biblical Literature Symposium Series
TrinJ	*Trinity Journal*
WBC	Word Biblical Commentary
WTJ	*Westminster Theological Journal*

Preface

We would like to extend our thanks to all of our contributors, Craig Blomberg, Richard Gaffin, Scott Spencer, Robert Wall and Merold Westphal, for sharing their time and insight on this project. We realize that producing a volume such as this is in some ways more difficult than others, because it requires not only that the contributors write to particular specifications but also that they do so to specific deadlines, and that they do this twice, once in submitting their major position paper and again in response to the work of their fellow contributors. We appreciate their attention to deadlines and details. We also wish to thank Dan Reid at InterVarsity Press for his editorial supervision on this project in the Spectrum series. We believe that InterVarsity Press has done an excellent job in promoting a series that addresses important issues in serious ways, admitting to the existence and encouraging discussion of disparate and challenging viewpoints.

Stan would like to thank his wife, Wendy, for her extraordinary support and encouragement during the completion of this project. Those who know us will know that this project was being completed at a time when it was uncertain how not only this project but also life itself would unfold. God has proven himself to be faithful, gracious and loving throughout—not that he needed to prove himself to us or to anyone else. God certainly made the truth of 1 Corinthians 10:13 come to life in a vivid and affirming way. Stan would also like to thank Beth Stovell for being willing to undertake this project together and for her carrying the major burden of correspondence with the authors and organizing the electronic paperwork as it came together. It has been a pleasure to work together, and Stan wishes her congratulations on her new position at St. Thomas University. Stan finally wishes to thank his colleagues, as well as his excellent Ph.D. students (of whom Beth began as one),

at McMaster Divinity College not only for providing a unique and re-
warding environment for serving as president and dean of the college but
also for allowing him to indulge his love for the study of God's Word as
revealed in the New Testament.

Beth would like to thank her husband, Jon, for his encouragement over
the four-year process of envisioning and coordinating this volume. His
humor and insight have been an ever-present help and support. She would
also like to thank Stan for the opportunity to work together on this project. This experience has been a great joy. The way he has shared his guidance and experience with her along this journey has been beneficial to her
professional development, meaningful to her personally and, of course,
invaluable to this project. Finally Beth would like to thank her colleagues
at McMaster Divinity College and St. Thomas University for their insights and support.

We finally wish to thank our readers of this volume. We hope and pray
that this volume will provide new insights into biblical hermeneutics and
how such interpretive models might aid in biblical understanding and
interpretation.

Introduction

Trajectories in Biblical Hermeneutics

Stanley E. Porter and Beth M. Stovell

The issue of interpreting the Bible has a long history and vast complexity,[1] even if the term *hermeneutics*, which is often used in conjunction with biblical interpretation, is of more recent vintage.[2] Students and scholars alike struggle to differentiate between the meaning of terms like *biblical exegesis, interpretation* and *hermeneutics*.[3] This very tension in defining the concepts of biblical interpretation, hermeneutics and exegesis leads to one of the major questions influencing the debates in this book, which in turn justifies its creation. Anthony Thiselton, one of the leading figures in biblical hermeneutics, especially in evangelical circles, provides a helpful distinction among these important terms:

> Whereas *exegesis* and *interpretation* denote the *actual processes* of interpreting texts, *hermeneutics* also includes the second-order discipline of asking

---

[1]For major histories of Old Testament and New Testament interpretation, see Henning Graf Reventlow, *History of Biblical Interpretation*, 4 vols., trans. Leo G. Perdue and James O. Duke (Atlanta: SBL, 2009–2010); William Baird, *History of New Testament Research*, 2 vols. (Minneapolis: Fortress, 1992–), with the third volume for the period after Bultmann still forthcoming.

[2]Recent treatments of hermeneutics with a focus on the Bible include Anthony C. Thiselton, *Hermeneutics: An Introduction* (Grand Rapids: Eerdmans, 2009); Petr Pokorný, *Hermeneutics as a Theory of Understanding*, trans. Anna Bryson Gustová (Grand Rapids: Eerdmans, 2010); Stanley E. Porter and Jason C. Robinson, *Hermeneutics: An Introduction to Interpretive Theory* (Grand Rapids: Eerdmans, 2011).

[3]Some scholars use *interpretation* and *hermeneutics* interchangeably (see W. Randolph Tate, *Biblical Interpretation: An Integrated Approach*, 3rd ed. [Peabody, Mass.: Hendrickson, 2008], p. 1), while others differentiate between exegesis, interpretation and hermeneutics (see Merold Westphal, *Whose Community? Which Interpretation? Philosophical Hermeneutics for the Church* [Grand Rapids: Baker Academic, 2009], esp. "Hermeneutics 101," pp. 17-26).

critically *what exactly we are doing when we read, understand, or apply*
texts. Hermeneutics explores *the conditions and criteria* that operate to
try to ensure responsible, valid, fruitful, or appropriate interpretation.[4]

This book thus focuses on the question of what hermeneutics is specifically as it applies to biblical interpretation. While other books have
addressed this issue in the past, this book uses a new format to address the
question of biblical hermeneutics. One can broadly classify most books on
the topics of biblical hermeneutics or biblical interpretation according to
two major types.[5] The first type of book presents students with step-by-
step instructions on how one should interpret the biblical text; in other
words, hermeneutics is an exegetical procedure.[6] These books may provide
some explanation of the variety of methods available, but their goal is primarily the practical application of a specific method as a tool for biblical
interpretation. A second type of book provides an introduction to the variety of different methods of biblical interpretation. These books may
move historically through the various methods, or they may discuss the
strategies, goals and outcomes of these methods in synchronic perspective.
In either case the authors of these books frequently display (whether intentionally or unintentionally) their own preference through their presentations of the various views, or sometimes they present the range of positions

---

[4]Thiselton, *Hermeneutics*, p. 4.
[5]For a more detailed overview of the issues, see Stanley E. Porter, "What Difference Does
Hermeneutics Make? Hermeneutical Theory Applied," *Jian Dao* 34/*Pastoral Journal* 27 (2010):
1-50, esp. 13-21.
[6]Examples include Otto Kaiser and Werner G. Kümmel, *Exegetical Method: A Student Handbook,* trans. E. V. N. Goetschius and M. J. O'Connell (New York: Seabury, 1981); John H.
Hayes and Carl R. Holladay, *Biblical Exegesis: A Beginner's Handbook,* 3rd ed. (Atlanta: John
Knox, 2007); Tate, *Biblical Interpretation*; Gordon D. Fee, *New Testament Exegesis: A Handbook
for Students and Pastors,* rev. ed. (Louisville: Westminster John Knox, 1993); Douglas Stuart,
Old Testament Exegesis: A Handbook for Students and Pastors, 3rd ed. (Louisville: Westminster
John Knox, 2001); Werner Stenger, *Introduction to New Testament Exegesis,* trans. Douglas W.
Stott (Grand Rapids: Eerdmans, 1993); Scot McKnight, ed., *Introducing New Testament In-
terpretation* (Grand Rapids: Baker, 1989); Craig C. Boyles, ed., *Interpreting the Old Testament:
A Guide for Exegesis* (Grand Rapids: Baker Academic, 2001); Mary H. Schertz and Perry B.
Yoder, *Seeing the Text: Exegesis for Students of Greek and Hebrew* (Nashville: Abingdon, 2001);
Richard J. Erickson, *A Beginner's Guide to New Testament Exegesis: Taking the Fear out of Critical
Method* (Downers Grove, Ill.: InterVarsity Press, 2005); Darrell L. Bock and Buist M. Fan-
ning, eds., *Interpreting the New Testament Text: Introduction to the Art and Science of Exegesis*
(Wheaton, Ill.: Crossway, 2006); Craig L. Blomberg with Jennifer Foutz Markley, *A Handbook
of New Testament Exegesis* (Grand Rapids: Baker Academic, 2010).

in a historical fashion rather than directly engaging the debate.[7] Both types of book tend to overlook the larger hermeneutical issues involved in biblical interpretation and often do not do justice to the diverse range of opinions in biblical hermeneutics. In other words, they fail to raise and address questions regarding the nature of interpretation itself: what it involves, what its presuppositions and criteria are, what its foundations need to be, and how it affects the practice of interpretation and its results. We are not saying that there are no books on biblical hermeneutics that present hermeneutics as hermeneutics,[8] only that it is difficult to capture the diversity of the discipline from a vantage point that focuses on procedure, history, or even the perspective of a single viewpoint or author.

This book represents a new way of presenting several of the major views within biblical hermeneutics. Rather than introducing the individual hermeneutical approaches in survey fashion or providing a step-by-step instruction guide to interpretation, this book provides a forum for discussion

---

[7]Examples include Milton S. Terry, *Biblical Hermeneutics: A Treatise on the Interpretation of the Old and New Testaments* (repr., Eugene, Ore.: Wipf and Stock, 1999); A. Berkeley Mickelsen, *Interpreting the Bible* (Grand Rapids: Eerdmans, 1963); Christopher Tuckett, *Reading the New Testament: Methods of Interpretation* (Philadelphia: Fortress, 1987); Stephen Neill and Tom Wright, *The Interpretation of the New Testament, 1861-1986*, new ed. (Oxford: Oxford University Press, 1988); Gerhard Maier, *Biblical Hermeneutics*, trans. Robert Yarbrough (Wheaton, Ill.: Crossway, 1994); Dan McCartney and Charles Clayton, *Let the Reader Understand: A Guide to Interpreting and Applying the Bible* (Wheaton, Ill.: BridgePoint, 1994); David S. Dockery, Kenneth A. Mathews and Robert B. Sloan, eds., *Foundations for Biblical Interpretation* (Nashville: Broadman & Holman, 1994); John Barton, *Reading the Old Testament: Method in Biblical Study*, rev. ed. (Louisville: Westminster John Knox, 1997); David Alan Black and David S. Dockery, eds., *Interpreting the New Testament: Essays on Methods and Issues* (Nashville: Broadman & Holman, 1994); Bruce Corley, Steve W. Lemke and Grant I. Lovejoy, eds., *Biblical Hermeneutics: A Comprehensive Introduction to Interpreting Scripture*, 2nd ed. (Nashville: Broadman & Holman, 2002); Grant R. Osborne, *The Hermeneutical Spiral: A Comprehensive Introduction to Biblical Interpretation*, rev. ed. (Downers Grove, Ill.: IVP Academic, 2006); William W. Klein, Craig L. Blomberg and Robert L. Hubbard Jr., *Introduction to Biblical Interpretation*, rev. ed. (Nashville: Thomas Nelson, 2004); Graeme Goldsworthy, *Gospel-Centered Hermeneutics: Foundations and Principles of Evangelical Biblical Interpretation* (Downers Grove, Ill.: IVP Academic, 2006); Henry A. Virkler and Karelynne Gerber Ayayao, *Hermeneutics: Principles and Processes of Biblical Interpretation*, 2nd ed. (Grand Rapids: Baker Academic, 2007); Jeannine K. Brown, *Scripture as Communication: Introducing Biblical Hermeneutics* (Grand Rapids: Baker Academic, 2007); Joel B. Green, ed., *Hearing the New Testament: Strategies for Interpretation*, 2nd ed. (Grand Rapids: Eerdmans, 2010).

[8]Besides the volumes in notes 2 and 3 above, see also Anthony C. Thiselton, *The Two Horizons: New Testament Hermeneutics and Philosophical Description with Special Reference to Heidegger, Bultmann, Gadamer, and Wittgenstein* (Grand Rapids: Eerdmans, 1980); Thiselton, *New Horizons in Hermeneutics: The Theory and Practice of Transforming Biblical Reading* (Grand Rapids: Zondervan, 1992); as well as other of his works.

by including contributions from several of the major advocates of these diverse models.[9] Each contributor provides a position essay describing the traits that characterize his perspective and a response essay describing his position in comparison to the other approaches.[10] By using this format, this book allows the reader to assess the strengths and weaknesses of each position by listening in on a scholarly debate over the major hermeneutical stances and issues. This introduction and the conclusion of the book, prepared by the editors, are designed to orient the discussion and set it within the wider history of biblical hermeneutics. Toward this goal of orientation, this introduction will survey many of the key issues of biblical hermeneutics by tracing their context within the history of traditional and modern biblical interpretation, using the literary categories of "behind the text," "within the text" and "in front of the text."[11] This survey will highlight some of the key questions and issues in debates surrounding the subject of biblical hermeneutics. It will then place the particular views represented in this book in that broader context and explain the structure of the book.

A BRIEF HISTORY OF THE DEVELOPMENT OF BIBLICAL HERMENEUTICS

This is not the place to offer a full or complete history of biblical hermeneutics. Such histories are offered in a number of works and in more detail than we can present here.[12] Nevertheless, our threefold orientation to the text provides a useful framework for capturing the major issues in biblical

---

[9]A. K. M. Adam, Stephen E. Fowl, Kevin J. Vanhoozer and Francis Watson, *Reading Scripture with the Church: Toward a Hermeneutic for Theological Interpretation* (Grand Rapids: Baker Academic, 2006), includes the written opinions of the four authors, but they all represent similar viewpoints.

[10]We consciously use the masculine singular pronoun because each of the advocates is a man.

[11]This triad develops a pattern in the approach of Paul Ricoeur, who pointed to what was "in front of the text" over what was "behind the text." As Ricoeur explains, "The sense of the text is not behind the text, but in front of it. It is not something hidden, but something disclosed." Ricoeur, *Interpretation Theory: Discourse and the Surplus of Meaning* (Fort Worth: Texas Christian University Press, 1976), pp. 87-88. The apparent correlation with the hermeneutical triad of author–text–reader is not accidental. See now also Joel B. Green, "The Challenge of Hearing the New Testament," in *Hearing the New Testament: Strategies for Interpretation*, ed. Joel B. Green, 2nd ed. (Grand Rapids: Eerdmans, 2010), pp. 1-14, esp. 10-13.

[12]Besides Thiselton, *Hermeneutics*, and Porter and Robinson, *Hermeneutics*, see Manfred Oeming, *Contemporary Biblical Hermeneutics: An Introduction*, trans. Joachim F. Vette (Aldershot, U.K.: Ashgate, 2006). Cf. Kurt Mueller-Vollmer, ed., *The Hermeneutics Reader* (New York: Continuum, 1989).

hermeneutics as they have unfolded. As a result of the shape of this volume, we will orient our comments specifically, though not exclusively, to New Testament hermeneutics on interpretation, but without neglecting the Old Testament.

Behind the text. In some ways, the history of biblical hermeneutics begins as early as the biblical account itself. In the Old Testament, the latter writings, like the Psalms and the Prophets, reinterpret the story of Israel presented in the Torah, and the New Testament continues to reinterpret this continuing story in light of the life, death and resurrection of Jesus Christ (an approach that later redemptive-historical scholars would appropriate).[13] Some scholars trace the beginnings of historical exegesis to the historically based exegesis of the Antiochene school, which was responding to the allegorical methods of the Alexandrian school.[14] The majority of scholars, however, point to the Enlightenment as a critical turning point in the field of biblical interpretation.[15] Through the influences of Cartesian thought, Pyrrhonian skepticism and English deism, Enlightenment scholars began to question the historicity of miracles,[16] to search for the historical Jesus,[17] to explore different types of texts and sources[18] and

---

[13]For an example of biblical allusions within the Old Testament corpus, see Mark J. Boda and Michael H. Floyd, eds., *Bringing out the Treasure: Inner Biblical Allusion and Zechariah 9–14*, JSOTSup 370 (Sheffield: Sheffield Academic Press, 2003). Scholars focusing on intrabiblical interpretation often discuss the role of New Testament interpretation of the Old Testament. For discussion on rabbinic models of interpretation and their impact on the early church, see Richard N. Longenecker, *Biblical Exegesis in the Apostolic Period*, 2nd ed. (Grand Rapids: Eerdmans, 1999).

[14]Kurt Anders Richardson rightly points to problems with this approach; our modern perspectives tend to skew the methods of the Antiochene school. Richardson, "The Antiochene School," in *Dictionary of Biblical Criticism and Interpretation*, ed. Stanley E. Porter (New York: Routledge, 2007), pp. 14-16.

[15]See Anthony C. Thiselton, "New Testament Interpretation in Historical Perspective," in *Hearing the New Testament: Strategies for Interpretation*, ed. Joel B. Green (Grand Rapids: Eerdmans, 1995), pp. 10-36 (one of the articles deleted in the second edition).

[16]For further discussion, see R. M. Burns, *The Great Debate on Miracles: From Joseph Glanvill to David Hume* (Lewisburg, N.Y.: Bucknell University Press, 1981).

[17]For a fuller discussion of the various quests for the historical Jesus, see N. T. Wright, *Jesus and the Victory of God*, Christian Origins and the Question of God 2 (Minneapolis: Fortress, 1996), pp. 3-124. This depiction of the quests has been strongly criticized by several scholars. See Walter P. Weaver, *The Historical Jesus in the Twentieth Century: 1900-1950* (Harrisburg, Penn.: Trinity Press International, 1999), pp. xi-xii; Dale C. Allison, "The Secularizing of the Historical Jesus," *Perspectives in Religious Studies* 27, no. 1 (2000): 135-51; Stanley E. Porter, *The Criteria for Authenticity in Historical-Jesus Research: Previous Discussion and New Proposals*, JSNTSup 191 (Sheffield: Sheffield Academic Press, 2000), pp. 31-62.

[18]For example, Johannes Albrecht Bengel (1687–1752) and Johann Jakob Griesbach (1745–1812)

generally to ask the kinds of historical questions we see in contemporary Old and New Testament introductions.[19]

Responding to this Enlightenment tradition, Friedrich Schleiermacher—often said to be the founder of modern hermeneutics—introduced a form of interpretation frequently described as romantic hermeneutics.[20] This form of hermeneutics focused on the mind of the author, along with the impact of his or her sociohistorical setting, as the means of gaining meaning from a given text. Wilhelm Dilthey followed in Schleiermacher's footsteps in focusing on the relationship between author and text in interpretation.[21]

These various developments had a formative influence on the hermeneutical model that we will broadly call "traditional criticism," which is still frequently associated with biblical exegesis. One can delineate three salient features that distinguish traditional criticism: evolutionary models of biblical texts, historical reconstructions, original meaning[22]—although not all traditional critics would accept all of them or emphasize them in the same way.

As Norman Petersen explains, "Essential to the historical-critical theory of biblical literature is the evolutionary model upon which it is constructed."[23] This feature of traditional criticism points to the desire to determine the backgrounds of our biblical texts and to develop theories

---

are two important figures in the field of textual study. See Robert Morgan with John Barton, *Biblical Interpretation* (Oxford: Oxford University Press, 1988), pp. 44-129; F. F. Bruce, "The History of New Testament Study," in *New Testament Interpretation: Essays on Principles and Methods*, ed. I. Howard Marshall (Grand Rapids: Eerdmans, 1977), pp. 21-59. For a more detailed description of many of these important advances of the Enlightenment period, see Baird, *History of New Testament Research*, 1:3-195.

[19]See Edgar Krentz, *The Historical-Critical Method* (Philadelphia: Fortress, 1975), p. 19; Thiselton, "New Testament Interpretation," pp. 12-14.

[20]See J. R. Hustwit, "Open Interpretation: Whitehead and Schleiermacher on Hermeneutics," in *Schleiermacher and Whitehead: Open Systems in Dialogue*, ed. Christine Helmer et al. (Berlin: De Gruyter, 2004), p. 185; Richard Crouter, *Friedrich Schleiermacher: Between Enlightenment and Romanticism* (Cambridge: Cambridge University Press, 2005); and Porter and Robinson, *Hermeneutics*, pp. 23-33.

[21]Rudolf A. Makkreel, *Dilthey: Philosopher of the Human Studies*, 3rd ed. (Princeton: Princeton University Press, 1992); Porter and Robinson, *Hermeneutics*, pp. 33-45.

[22]These categories reflect those of John Barton for historical criticism: genetic questions, original meaning, historical reconstruction, and disinterested scholarship. See Barton, "Historical-Critical Approaches," in *The Cambridge Companion to Biblical Interpretation*, ed. John Barton (Cambridge: Cambridge University Press, 1998), pp. 9-20.

[23]Norman R. Petersen, *Literary Criticism for New Testament Critics* (Philadelphia: Fortress, 1978), p. 11.

tracing how we gained our current text from that background.[24] For example, form criticism—often a tool employed in traditional criticism—uses the theories of the *religionsgeschichtliche Schule* ("history of religions school") to differentiate the individual units of the oral tradition that evolved into our biblical text.[25] This form-critical analysis is usually based on source-critical analysis; thus this evolutionary model begins with the existence and relationship of sources as part of their evolution. Redaction criticism—another of the tools of traditional criticism, and usually dependent on source and form criticism—seeks the context within the church that caused the editing of the biblical text to be tailored to meet the theological needs of the community at hand.[26]

Often the goal of traditional criticism is to access the authenticity of the biblical texts or the stories behind the texts. We can see this trend in the source-critical attempts to identify the earliest sayings of Jesus and stories within the biblical accounts.[27] The various levels of authenticity in form criticism serve a similar function. At times biblical scholars have followed the philosopher Baruch Spinoza in bracketing out aspects of the biblical text to create a historical reconstruction of the background of the Bible.[28]

Seeking the original meaning of the text sounds somewhat similar to the goals of scholars looking "within the text" (see the next section below), yet the traditional search for the original meaning of the text not only

---

[24]For example, scholars within the *religionsgeschichtliche Schule* sought the prehistory of Jewish and Christian religious concepts and practices using anthropology, ethnology, and the newly made discoveries in archaeology and ancient languages. See Neill and Wright, *Interpretation of the New Testament*, pp. 175-77.

[25]For discussion on some of the key players in form criticism, see Edgar V. McKnight, *What Is Form Criticism?* (Philadelphia: Fortress, 1969).

[26]*Redaktionsgeschichte* ("redaction criticism") came to the fore in the 1950s in New Testament studies with three major German scholars: Günther Bornkamm, Hans Conzelmann, and Willi Marxsen (although they were preceded by other scholars, such as R. H. Lightfoot). Each suggested a different theological situation for the churches of the individual Evangelists, pointing to the life of the Evangelist as the third *Sitz im Leben* ("situation in life," or "context"), in addition to that of the early church and Jesus. See David R. Catchpole, "Tradition History," in *New Testament Interpretation: Essays on Principles and Methods,* ed. I. Howard Marshall (Grand Rapids: Eerdmans, 1977), pp. 181-95; and Robert H. Stein, *Studying the Synoptic Gospels: Origin and Interpretation,* 2nd ed. (Grand Rapids: Baker Academic, 2001), pp. 238-39.

[27]Barton, "Historical-Critical Approaches," p. 11.

[28]Roy A. Harrisville and Walter Sundburg, *The Bible in Modern Culture: Baruch Spinoza to Brevard Childs,* 2nd ed. (Grand Rapids: Eerdmans, 2002), pp. 30-45; Richard H. Popkin, "Spinoza and Bible Scholarship," in *The Cambridge Companion to Spinoza,* ed. Don Garrett (Cambridge: Cambridge University Press, 1996), pp. 383-407.

looks at linguistic and philological questions but also locates the text within its context among earlier texts and locates the original readers within their historical context.[29] Modern scholars have recently joined traditional scholars in this quest. Modern practitioners of forms of traditional criticism include social-scientific critics such as Bruce Malina and Jerome Neyrey, and sociorhetorical approaches such as that of Ben Witherington.[30] Composition criticism, similar to redaction criticism, also follows traditional methods to varying degrees, even if it reflects newer developments.[31]

Within the text. In response to perceived weaknesses of the traditional approach, which looks behind the text, many biblical scholars began to look for new hermeneutical orientations and excitedly embraced approaches that looked within the text itself, such as forms of literary criticism prominent in the 1970s.[32] A form of phenomenological biblical literary interpretation emerged from several of these types of literary criticism, which New Testament scholars dubbed "narrative criticism."[33] One of the proponents of this shift, the New Testament scholar Norman Petersen, argues that this approach was the answer to the historical and literary questions that redaction criticism raised.[34] Narrative criticism has its literary and theoretical basis in what was known in secular literary criticism as New Criticism, a form of literary reading that dominated literary theory from at least the 1950s to the 1970s.[35] These methods, with their

---

[29]See Barton, "Historical-Critical Approaches," pp. 10-11.

[30]See, for example, Bruce J. Malina, *Christian Origins and Cultural Anthropology: Practical Models for Biblical Interpretation* (Atlanta: John Knox Press, 1986); Malina, *The New Testament World: Insights from Cultural Anthropology* (Louisville: Westminster John Knox, 1993); Bruce Malina and Jerome H. Neyrey, *Portraits of Paul: An Archaeology of Ancient Personality* (Louisville: Westminster John Knox, 1996); and Ben Witherington, *The Acts of the Apostles: A Socio-Rhetorical Commentary* (Grand Rapids: Eerdmans, 1998).

[31]See Norman Perrin, *What Is Redaction Criticism?* (Philadelphia: Fortress, 1969), pp. 65-67.

[32]For a history of this development, see Stanley E. Porter, "Literary Approaches to the New Testament: From Formalism to Deconstruction and Back," in *Approaches to New Testament Study*, ed. Stanley E. Porter and David Tombs, JSNTSup 120 (Sheffield: Sheffield Academic Press, 1995), pp. 77-128.

[33]Stephen D. Moore traces the label "narrative criticism" to David Rhoads's appraisal of the nonstructuralist literary studies of the 1970s in Mark, in an article titled "Narrative Criticism and the Gospel of Mark" (*Journal of the American Academy of Religion* 50 [1982]: 411-34). Moore, *Literary Criticism and the Gospels: The Theoretical Challenge* (New Haven: Yale University Press, 1989), p. 7.

[34]Petersen, *Literary Criticism*, pp. 18-19.

[35]For the history of narrative criticism, see Moore, *Literary Criticism and the Gospels*, pp. 3-68;

philosophical roots in Anglo-American logical positivism, developed out of a hermeneutical tradition that focused on the text as the autonomous means of transmitting meaning. Many of these approaches also had interpretive roots in elements of the all-embracing interpretive movement of the twentieth century, structuralism, as well as connections to the New Hermeneutic.[36]

By accepting this form of literary theory, biblical scholars shifted their focus from behind the text to within the text, moving from an evolutionary model to a communications model of hermeneutics.[37] With this shift, many biblical scholars inadvertently (or sometimes intentionally) removed both authorial intent and historical background from the equation, replacing these with an emphasis on poetics, narrative and textual unity. Poetics includes an emphasis on the literary or even rhetorical means by which texts are constructed and convey their literary quality, such as the use of character, setting, irony, metaphor, symbolism and other literary tropes. Narrative—in part because the New Testament does not contain much if any genuinely poetic material—is the dominant genre or textual type of the New Testament, as well as constituting much of the Old Testament. Scholars came to emphasize and interpret elements of narrative, such as plot (motivated events) and the literary opening, closing and development. Emphasis on the autonomous text also led to a focus on textual unity, in which all of the elements of the text, even those in tension, contributed to its overall sense.

In front of the text. Stephen Moore argues that narrative criticism naturally moves into more reader-oriented (in front of the text) hermeneutical models, such as reader-response criticism, because critics often discuss the effect the text has on the reader, whether original or contemporary.[38] The movement to consider the factors in front of the text includes both focus on the formation and hence reception and interpretation of the biblical canon in the scholarship of canonical criticism,[39] and the reader-centered

---

cf. Porter and Robinson, *Hermeneutics*, pp. 274-96.

[36]See Thiselton, *New Horizons in Hermeneutics*, pp. 471-515; cf. Porter and Robinson, *Hermeneutics*, pp. 154-67, 237-39.

[37]Petersen, *Literary Criticism*, p. 33.

[38]Moore, *Literary Criticism and the Gospels*, p. 73; cf. Porter and Robinson, *Hermeneutics*, pp. 285-87.

[39]See Robert W. Wall and Eugene Lemcio, *The New Testament as Canon: A Reader in Canonical Criticism*, JSNTSup 76 (Sheffield: JSOT Press, 1992).

approaches often associated with poststructuralism, which reacted against an arid structuralism and embraced the role of the subject in interpretation. While canonical criticism is concerned with the impact of the shape of the canon on its readers and thus has been described as a "mediating position" among author, text and reader,[40] poststructuralism is closely associated with the heavily reader-oriented deconstructionism of Jacques Derrida. The term *poststructuralism* describes a literary-philosophical movement beginning in the late 1960s, which is still having some effect today.[41]

Poststructuralism developed in response to the assumption, common in structuralism, that meaning resides within texts themselves, or at least within their deep linguistic structures. Besides deconstruction and the work of Derrida, philosophical and phenomenological hermeneutics deeply affected the continuing influence of structuralism and helped lead to the emergence of poststructuralism. Philosophers like Hans-Georg Gadamer, with his philosophical hermeneutics, and Paul Ricoeur, with his hermeneutic phenomenology, questioned the epistemological neutrality of any given interpreter, especially foundationalists who grounded their hermeneutics in supposedly neutral deep structures, by focusing on the interplay between the assumptions of the interpreter and their interpretation and by demonstrating the interpretive gap between the reader and the original context in ancient texts.[42]

Poststructuralism was only one of the developments within the broader scope of postmodernism, which encompassed a variety of theories having an impact on understanding meaning. In the resulting developments of postmodernism, whereas previous traditional and modern hermeneutical models suggested that meaning was to be found by searching behind and within the text, postmodern hermeneutical theories offered no such guar-

---

[40]Osborne, *Hermeneutical Spiral,* pp. 492-93.
[41]For discussion of poststructuralism in relation to postmodern hermeneutics, see Thiselton, *New Horizons in Hermeneutics,* pp. 495-99; Thiselton, *Hermeneutics,* pp. 201-3, 327-49; Porter and Robinson, *Hermeneutics,* pp. 190-213.
[42]See Hans-Georg Gadamer, *Truth and Method,* 2nd rev. ed., trans. Joel Weinsheimer and Donald Marshall (New York: Continuum, 1989); Paul Ricoeur, *The Conflict of Interpretations: Essays in Hermeneutics,* ed. Don Ihde (Evanston, Ill.: Northwestern University Press, 1974); Ricoeur, *Interpretation Theory*; Ricoeur, *Figuring the Sacred: Religion, Narrative, and Imagination,* trans. David Pellauer, ed. Mark Wallace (Minneapolis: Fortress, 1995). See also Porter and Robinson, *Hermeneutics,* pp. 74-104, 105-30.

antee, and in some instances reveled in the resultant interpretive and hermeneutical uncertainty. Postmodern theorists rejected as a fallacy the epistemological neutrality claimed by the proponents of traditional methods, as one could no more easily discover an objective reading of a text than divine the intention of the author. These theorists further rejected the claim to have unmediated access to history and replaced this claim with subjective interpretations standing in opposition to power, hierarchy and other foreseen evils within the text. These questions of power and hierarchy have been influenced by the thinking of Friedrich Nietzsche, Michel Foucault, Karl Marx and Sigmund Freud—each of whom has been interpreted in very different ways.[43]

Poststructuralism began to significantly influence biblical scholars in the late 1980s, and some today still use it.[44] While some biblical scholars, like Moore, have hailed these new theories as joyous tidings and liberation from authorial and textual captivity,[45] others have been more cautious or negative in their response. The mixed response among biblical scholars is largely related to the implications of various postmodern/poststructuralist approaches, as we have noted above.

As one can see, biblical hermeneutics is a complex field—one might even venture to say, a minefield—of potentially competing orientations, assumptions and foundations for determining meaning. As a field, it is highly dependent on developments in hermeneutics not primarily concerned with the Bible, such as the romantic hermeneutics of Schleiermacher and Dilthey, structuralism, literary hermeneutics, the philosophical hermeneutics of Gadamer, the phenomenological hermeneutics of Ricoeur, and the poststructuralist hermeneutics of Derrida and others. Nevertheless, biblical hermeneutics also brings with it, naturally, its primary focus on the Bible, with its own lengthy and complex traditions of interpretation, from biblical times through the rise of the Enlighten-

---

[43]A. K. M. Adam, *Handbook of Postmodern Biblical Interpretation* (St. Louis: Chalice, 2000), p. 92.

[44]For a more detailed description of poststructuralism and deconstruction, see Stephen D. Moore, *Poststructuralism and the New Testament: Derrida and Foucault at the Foot of the Cross* (Minneapolis: Fortress, 1994); Jonathan Culler, *On Deconstruction: Theory and Criticism After Structuralism* (Ithaca, N.Y.: Cornell University Press, 1982).

[45]Moore concludes his book on literary criticism and the Gospels with praise of poststructuralist theories and a suggestion that this is the way forward for biblical studies. Moore, *Literary Criticism and the Gospels*, pp. 171-78.

ment—with its historical methods such as form, source and redaction criticism—to modern and postmodern interpretation. The result for biblical hermeneutics is a varied and intertwined mix of models and fundamental orientations, each competing with the others to establish itself as the basis for biblical interpretation.

ORIENTING QUESTIONS AND ISSUES IN BIBLICAL HERMENEUTICS

Due to the variety and complexity of the field of biblical hermeneutics, it is helpful to point to some of the orienting questions that the contributors to this volume will discuss either directly or indirectly. Some of the contributors tackle these questions head-on, often in response to other hermeneutical positions, while others address them more circumspectly by incorporating them into (or even rejecting them from) their hermeneutical framework. These questions include:

1. Where does meaning happen? Is meaning to be located in the author's intent? What about the reader's engagement? What is the role of the ancient believing community, the continuing community or the modern community in reading the text today?

2. What is the basis or foundation of meaning? Is it to be found in grounded substance, such as the text or the mind of the author? What if there is no foundation for meaning? Are texts simply constructs created by readers? How does one know?

3. Is meaning limited to the author's original intent (if we can in fact be certain of finding the author's original intent)? What about the use of the Old Testament in the New Testament (as in our example[46])? Does meaning change from one context to another (whether from Old Testament to New Testament or from biblical text to reader)?

4. Who or what arbitrates a "correct" reading or at the very least a "helpful" or "harmful" reading?

5. What is the role of theology in biblical interpretation? Is it assumed, primary or merely derivative?

---

[46]We asked the contributors both to define their particular assigned hermeneutical stance and to apply it to a common passage, Mt 2:7-15, which quotes Hos 11:1.

6. What role do events occurring after the original composition play in interpretation? For example, the Christ event, the process of canonization, the experience of a given reader and so on.

7. What other disciplines should be used to help provide greater clarity to biblical studies? Philosophy? Theology? Literary studies?

Each of the contributors to this volume attempts in some way to answer these (and other) questions in different ways. While some of their answers may at times overlap, the differences in these answers provide aspects of each contributor's unique position on biblical hermeneutics.

FIVE VIEWS OF BIBLICAL HERMENEUTICS

The five views of biblical hermeneutics both capture this diversity and depict many of the major shifts within biblical hermeneutics. Craig Blomberg, professor of New Testament at Denver Seminary in Colorado and author of two books on biblical interpretation,[47] represents the historical-critical/grammatical view. This category brings together the major emphases of traditional criticism noted above, including the rise of the historical-critical method during the Enlightenment, as well as placing emphasis on the grammar of the biblical text, which goes back to the time of the Reformers. Scholars do not usually refer to this traditional hermeneutical model by this name,[48] but it is often the most common in evangelical circles. The historical-critical/grammatical view seeks insight for interpretation from taking a critical view of the history behind the text, on the one hand, and utilizing a grammatical analysis of the text, on the other. This approach includes various forms of critical analysis such as source, form, redaction, tradition and textual criticism. Blomberg functions with a conservative form of this criticism, basing his assumptions on what might be termed "maximalist" views of historical and biblical evidence. Other historical critics might be much more "minimalist" in their approach, while practicing in many ways a similar biblical hermeneutic.

Influenced by intellectual movements in literary and social-scientific

---

[47]See Blomberg with Markley, *Handbook of New Testament Exegesis;* Klein, Blomberg and Hubbard, *Introduction to Biblical Interpretation.*

[48]Scholars often refer to their approach as historical-critical or grammatical-critical, but each often uses the tools of the other, as Blomberg's essay makes clear, even if not accepting all of the same interpretive presuppositions.

studies, Scott Spencer, who is professor of New Testament and preaching at Baptist Theological Seminary at Richmond, Virginia, and an avid practitioner of the literary/postmodern approach that he demonstrates here in this volume,[49] views the biblical text as relevant to today's reader. Spencer draws these connections through his focus on the role of both ancient and modern readers in interpretation. In light of this perspective, literary/postmodern interpreters use a synchronic approach instead of the diachronic approach more common in traditional criticism,[50] and they are attuned to literary questions of style, character and narrative, as well as to hermeneutical issues raised by poststructuralism, postcolonialism and reader-response theories.

Richard Gaffin, emeritus professor of biblical and systematic theology at Westminster Theological Seminary in Philadelphia and a well-known Reformed theologian,[51] presents the redemptive-historical approach. Proponents of a redemptive-historical view, following the theological interpretation of the Reformers as well as scholars such as Geerhardus Vos,[52] argue that the role of Christ in his redemptive work is central to interpreting the whole of Scripture, whether the Old or the New Testament. Gaffin offers a very concise and straightforward exposition of the redemptive-historical approach. His emphasis that the theme of redemption explains the Old Testament in light of the New, as one might expect, influences Gaffin's interpretation of the biblical text that was assigned to each contributor. Due to his redemptive-historical view, Gaffin is particularly attuned to the impact of the redemptive work of Christ in reading Hosea in relation to Matthew's depiction of Christ.

Following in the footsteps of Brevard Childs,[53] the Old Testament

---

[49]See F. Scott Spencer, *Dancing Girls, "Loose" Ladies, and Women of "the Cloth": The Women in Jesus' Life* (London: Continuum, 2004); Spencer, *Journeying Through Acts: A Literary-Cultural Reading* (Peabody, Mass.: Hendrickson, 2004).

[50]Synchronic and diachronic approaches (terms growing out of structuralism) contrast an approach that examines all phenomena on the same (temporal) plane versus one that views them through the course of (temporal) development and succession.

[51]See Richard B. Gaffin Jr., *The Centrality of the Resurrection: A Study in Paul's Soteriology* (Grand Rapids: Baker, 1978; reissued as *Resurrection and Redemption: A Study in Paul's Soteriology* [Phillipsburg, N.J.: P & R, 1978]); Gaffin, *By Faith, Not by Sight: Paul and the Order of Salvation* (Milton Keynes, U.K.: Paternoster, 2006).

[52]For example, Geerhardus Vos, *Biblical Theology: Old and New Testaments* (Grand Rapids: Eerdmans, 1948).

[53]Among many works, see Brevard Childs, *Introduction to the Old Testament as Scripture* (Phil-

scholar known for his view of the importance of canon for interpretation, Robert Wall, who is professor of New Testament and Wesleyan studies at Seattle Pacific University in Washington State and well-known for his own canonical studies,[54] represents canonical criticism well by arguing for the necessity of reading the entire canon in relationship to each part of the canon. Thus the Old Testament should be read in light of the New Testament and the New Testament in light of the Old Testament. More than this, however, even the parts of the canon should be read in light of each other, such as the placement of Acts within various canonical groupings and how this determines interpretation of the Gospels, the Pauline Epistles, or the Catholic Epistles. This framework influences the goals, procedures and results of a canonical approach to biblical hermeneutics.

Representing the philosophical/theological approach, Merold Westphal, who is emeritus professor of philosophy at Fordham University in New York City and author of a number of philosophical and hermeneutical works,[55] addresses the question of biblical hermeneutics through the insights of scholars who can be very broadly labeled as following a form of philosophical hermeneutics, such as Paul Ricoeur, Hans-Georg Gadamer and Wilhelm Dilthey.[56] Westphal's approach is certainly highly philosophical in its focus (understandable for a well-known career philosopher), but philosophically oriented biblical hermeneutics provides an awareness of many of the major issues also influencing what might be called theological hermeneutics as it addresses questions in biblical hermeneutics through a philosophical lens. Westphal cannot be expected to address all of the questions for a philosophical *and* theological hermeneutics, but his philosophical reflections raise important issues that must be addressed.[57]

---

adelphia: Fortress, 1979), and *The New Testament as Canon: An Introduction* (Valley Forge, Penn.: Trinity Press International, 1994).

[54]See Wall and Lemcio, *New Testament as Canon;* Wall, "The Acts of the Apostles," in *New Interpreter's Bible,* ed. Leander E. Keck (Nashville: Abingdon, 2002), 10:3-370.

[55]See Westphal, *Whose Community? Which Interpretation?;* Westphal, *God, Guilt, and Death: An Existential Phenomenology of Religion* (Bloomington: Indiana University Press, 1984).

[56]Along with Westphal, we here lump together these philosophers who are also hermeneuts. For the distinctions among them on the basis of the type of hermeneutics they practice, see Porter and Robinson, *Hermeneutics,* pp. 7-8, 10-12. For an even more expansive view of philosophical hermeneutics, see Donald G. Marshall, "Philosophical Hermeneutics," in *Dictionary of Biblical Criticism and Interpretation,* ed. Stanley E. Porter (New York: Routledge, 2007), pp. 275-77.

[57]This of courses raises but does not answer the question not only of the relationship of theological hermeneutics to philosophical hermeneutics but also, perhaps even more importantly, the

CONCLUSION

A volume such as this cannot raise or answer all questions regarding biblical hermeneutics. No volume is able to ascend to such lofty and intellectually satisfying heights. However, we believe that the essays included within this volume go a long way toward asking the right questions, differentiating the major issues involved, proposing possible answers and then attempting to show how various biblical hermeneutical stances have practical results in biblical interpretation. We expect that some readers will come away from contemplating these essays having at least as many questions afterward as they had beforehand. Others may simply find in these essays evidence and arguments to reinforce hermeneutical positions that they already hold, now greatly strengthened. Our preferred hope, however, is that these essays will challenge all of our readers, even those who are the most firmly entrenched in their hermeneutical position, to reexamine and rethink their approach to biblical hermeneutics. This volume offers a snapshot of five such approaches reflective of current interpretive practice. We are optimistic that examination and engagement with their arguments will lead to further developments in this field crucial for the interpretation of Scripture.

relationship of theological (philosophical) hermeneutics to what is readily known as theological interpretation. Our impression is that theological interpretation is less a hermeneutic than it is a theological vantage point that utilizes various hermeneutical models in subservience or in relation to the theological tradition of especially premodern biblical interpretation. Theological hermeneutics, therefore, is probably better characterized as distinct from theological interpretation and in closer relation to philosophical hermeneutics as a hermeneutical position. Hence philosophical/theological hermeneutics, whereas theological interpretation, whatever its relation to theological hermeneutics and other hermeneutical models, is not a hermeneutical approach itself per se. See Porter and Robinson, *Hermeneutics*, pp. 245-73, on Thiselton and Kevin J. Vanhoozer, who despite their formative roles in theological interpretation are better seen as proponents of a theological hermeneutics grounded in deep philosophical thought, what we are calling here philosophical/theological hermeneutics (as opposed to philosophical hermeneutics as represented by Gadamer; see Porter and Robinson, *Hermeneutics*, pp. 74-104).

PART ONE

FIVE VIEWS
OF BIBLICAL
HERMENEUTICS

1

The Historical-Critical/Grammatical View

Craig L. Blomberg

It is my task in this essay to describe a "historical-critical/grammatical" position, but such a description is by no means straightforward. On the one hand, some would describe the "historical-critical method" as a method founded on Ernst Troeltsch's three principles of criticism, analogy and correlation. The principle of criticism, also known as methodological doubt, affirms that the study of history arrives at only probable, never indisputable, conclusions. The principle of analogy highlights the similarities among historical events and postulates that nothing can happen that hasn't already had an analogy somewhere in history. The principle of correlation argues for a closed continuum of cause and effect in a naturalist universe, excluding the possibility of the supernatural and therefore of God, as traditionally conceived.[1]

The grammatico-historical method, on the other hand, refers to studying the biblical text, or any other text, in its original historical context, and seeking the meaning its author(s) most likely intended for its original audience(s) or addressees based on the grammar and syntax.[2]

---

[1]Many of Troeltsch's key works have never been translated into English. Of those that have, see esp. his "Historical and Dogmatic Method in Theology," in *Religion in History*, ed. James L. Adams (Minneapolis: Fortress, 1991), esp. pp. 13-14. Edgar Krentz uses the expression "historical-critical" in his work *The Historical-Critical Method* (1975; repr., Eugene, Ore.: Wipf & Stock, 2002).

[2]Milton S. Terry (*Biblical Hermeneutics: A Treatise on the Interpretation of the Old and New Testaments* [1883; repr., Eugene, Ore.: Wipf & Stock, 1999], p. 203), offered perhaps the most com-

The grammatico-historical method does not adjudicate on what can or cannot happen in history; indeed, its purpose is not one of critique but of interpretation. Believers with a high view of Scripture will presumably want to respond to a grammatico-historical interpretation of a biblical text by seeking to apply it in methodologically responsible ways to their contemporary lives and world. They will look for examples to imitate, commands to obey, promises to claim, dangers to avoid, truths to believe, and praises or prayers to offer to God.[3]

Thus anyone describing a "historical-critical/grammatical" approach must carefully articulate what it includes and does not include, particularly in light of the other positions presented in this volume. Toward this end, it is helpful to address the broader taxonomies of hermeneutics possible and place this approach among them. Various taxonomies of hermeneutical methods today divide higher criticism into three broad categories: historical, theological and literary approaches.[4] My mandate is to discuss the importance of the historical group of hermeneutical methods. This does not mean that I reject theological and literary analyses; indeed, I find them crucial. However, they can be engaged in legitimately only when built on the appropriate historical foundations. Readers, then, who are looking for a polemical "either-or-or-or-or" approach from me to the five approaches discussed in this volume will be disappointed. What they will discover instead is an appreciative "both-and-and-and-and" position. However, if any of the other contributors should wish to make their approach the foundational one (or, worse still, the only one), then we will have some interesting disagreement, because I am convinced that all of the other approaches must build on the historical-critical/grammatical approach in order to function legitimately.[5]

---

monly cited definition: "The grammatico-historical sense of a writer is such an interpretation of his language as is required by the laws of grammar and the facts of history." Terry distinguished the method from "the allegorical, mystical, naturalistic, mythical, and other methods, which have more or less prevailed."

[3]For full details on application, see Craig L. Blomberg with Jennifer F. Markley, *Handbook of New Testament Exegesis* (Grand Rapids: Baker Academic, 2010), pp. 239-68.

[4]E.g., Graeme Goldsworthy, *Gospel-Centered Hermeneutics: Foundations and Principles of Evangelical Biblical Interpretation* (Downers Grove, Ill.: InterVarsity Press, 2006), pp. 199-272.

[5]Cf. esp. Donald A. Hagner, "The State of the Bible in the Twenty-First Century," *CTM* 35 (2008): 6-18; and idem, "The Bible: God's Gift to the Church of the Twenty-First Century," *CTM* 35 (2008): 19-31.

LOWER CRITICISM VS. HIGHER CRITICISM

Analysis of ancient documents has typically distinguished between lower criticism and higher criticism. *Lower criticism* is synonymous with *textual criticism* and refers to the exercise of collating all known manuscripts of an ancient work to see if there are any differences in wording among the manuscripts that scribal copying produced and then using established principles to determine which text, if any, most likely preserves the original reading at each point where there are differences. The results of these individual decisions are then combined to produce a document that comes as close as possible to reflecting what the lost original most likely contained from start to finish. The more independent copies of a given text that we have, the fewer the number of differences among those copies, the more minor the nature of those differences, and the closer to the original that the existing manuscripts can be dated, the greater the degree of confidence we have that we have closely approximated the original document.[6]

Obviously, lower or textual criticism has to be foundational, even among the historical methods. If we lack the confidence that we have anything close to what an original document contained, there is little point in engaging in theological or literary analyses except to shed light on what a group of people at one given time or place in the past may have believed about a text and their resulting application of it. Christians who are looking for a normative Bible from which to derive theology that makes a difference in their lives today will be interested only in that which is highly likely to approximate closely the original words that they believe God guided the biblical authors and editors to write. To the extent that part of literary criticism analyzes the establishment of a *collection* of authoritative books[7]—one of the objects of study of canon or canonical criticism in particular—then textual criticism is foundational for literary study as well.

THE PRINCIPLES OF THIS POSITION

Historical criticism as historical-cultural analysis. If the historical-critical

---

[6]A good primer for the textual criticism of both testaments is Paul D. Wegner, *A Student's Guide to Textual Criticism of the Bible: Its History, Methods and Results* (Downers Grove, Ill.: InterVarsity Press, 2006).

[7]Not to be confused with an *authoritative* collection of texts. See Bruce M. Metzger, *The Canon of the New Testament: Its Origin, Development and Significance* (Oxford: Oxford University Press, 1987), pp. 282-88.

method imposes an antisupernaturalist worldview onto the interpretation of texts, then one might expect a historical-critical/grammatical method to do so as well, while simply adding a study of grammar. Rather, by *historical-critical,* some scholars refer to the study of "the history behind the text." Scholars will sometimes distinguish the two enterprises by referring to this latter task not as historical-critical but as "historical criticism" or simply "historical analysis" or "historical background."[8] With the booming industry of the social-scientific criticism of Scripture—understanding the sociological and anthropological values and customs of a given culture in which a text is written—it is probably worth adding another word to our descriptor and speaking of "historical-*cultural*" analysis.

At one level, this involves little more than what historians and interpreters have agreed on or intuited for centuries. The better one wants to understand any communicative act, the more one needs to know who spoke or wrote it, when, where and under what circumstances. If it is possible to recover or surmise the original addressees, one can discern even further limits on possible meanings.[9] It is very unlikely that the originally intended meaning of the message, whether written or oral, could be something that an original audience couldn't possibly have conceived.[10] The same is true with cultural analysis. Unless contemporary interpreters of ancient texts consciously remind themselves that they are reading documents from very different cultures, they can envision all too easily the activities those texts depict as if they were taking place today, or at least they may evaluate the thoughts and motives of individuals from other cultures by anachronistic, modern analogies.[11]

One objection put forward against historical approaches has come from twentieth-century hermeneutical conversations concerning "the intentional fallacy"—the inability of interpreters to recover the mental actions

---

[8]See further Blomberg with Markley, *Handbook of New Testament Exegesis,* pp. 63-92.

[9]It may not always be possible to be sure of original meaning, but one can at least rule out many unlikely possibilities. See esp. Umberto Eco et al., *Interpretation and Overinterpretation* (Cambridge: Cambridge University Press, 1992).

[10]Gordon D. Fee and Douglas Stuart, *How to Read the Bible for All Its Worth,* 3rd ed. (Grand Rapids: Zondervan, 2003), p. 254.

[11]An excellent introduction, recognizing the link with historical study, is Stephen C. Barton, "Historical Criticism and Social-Scientific Perspectives in New Testament Study," in *Hearing the New Testament: Strategies for Interpretation,* ed. Joel B. Green, 2nd ed. (Grand Rapids: Eerdmans, 2010), pp. 34-64.

of dead speakers or writers.[12] Critics argue that all we have to interpret is the text an author left behind. However, with documents for which we have reason to believe that communicative intentions were largely successful, this proves much less of a problem. What is described as discerning "authorial intent," moreover, is often really shorthand for discerning the most likely meaning of a given text in light of all that we can recover about its original author(s), audience(s) and the historical and cultural milieus in which they lived.[13] We are not seeking irrecoverable mental processes. Rather, we seek what has been disclosed of those processes by virtue of the very texts still in existence, along with any additional information we may have about the circumstances surrounding the production of those texts.

More complicated is the question of a "fuller meaning" that goes beyond an author's historical intention but which remains consistent with it. Speakers and writers have regularly had the experience of receiving feedback from addressees along the lines of, "It seems to me from what you have said that you intend . . . [or "you mean . . ."]," when in fact what comes next is something the speaker or writer had never thought of at all. But upon reflection one can reply, "I see where you get that from and I think I'd be happy to affirm that."[14] This forms still one more dimension of historical criticism, though it can overlap with theological or literary analysis. It examines a reader's response, but it is an *authorial* reader's response—the intended audience's interpretation. This phenomenon proves especially important when we assess New Testament authors' use of Old Testament texts.[15]

Historical criticism as tradition-critical analysis. Biblical cultures and modern cultures differ in their production of texts. With the advent of the printing press, the production of written documents became dramatically

---

[12]The classic articulation was William K. Wimsatt and Monroe C. Beardsley, "The Intentional Fallacy," in Wimsatt, *The Verbal Icon: Studies in the Meaning of Poetry* (Lexington: University of Kentucky Press, 1950), pp. 3-18.

[13]See further William W. Klein, Craig L. Blomberg and Robert L. Hubbard Jr., *Introduction to Biblical Interpretation*, rev. ed. (Nashville: Thomas Nelson, 2004), pp. 185-88.

[14]Or, as D. A. Carson ("Matthew," in *The Expositor's Bible Commentary*, ed. Tremper Longman III and David E. Garland, rev. ed. [Grand Rapids: Zondervan, 2010], 9:119) puts it, "Had [Hosea] been able to see Matthew's use of 11:1, he would not have disapproved, even if messianic nuances were not in his mind when he wrote that verse."

[15]See esp. Douglas J. Moo and Andrew D. Naselli, "The Problem of the New Testament's Use of the Old Testament," in *But My Words Will Never Pass Away: The Enduring Authority of the Christian Scriptures*, ed. D. A. Carson, 2 vols. (Grand Rapids: Eerdmans, forthcoming).

simplified; in the digital age, it has become easier still. In contrast, in the biblical cultures, writing materials were costly, scrolls were cumbersome, and even some fairly bright and well-born individuals were not skilled at reading or writing.[16] Thus writers might memorize an outline in considerable detail of what they wanted to say before beginning to dictate to their scribes.[17] Ancient orators might commit to memory the entire wording of a lengthy speech before delivering it, so that the contents and the desired effects would be as precise as possible.[18] In short, the biblical cultures were oral cultures.

What this meant for the production of historical and biographical literature, which constitutes almost half of Scripture, was that groups of people who particularly valued the preservation of accounts of the people's lives and events important to them would commit to memory narratives of the significant teachings or actions of those individuals and their times. The more sacred or valuable the narratives became, the greater the care taken in their preservation. Yet, as long as stories and traditions circulated entirely by word of mouth, they could be retold with a fair amount of flexibility. Any given public recitation could abbreviate, omit, explain, expand, paraphrase, interpret and highlight as the speaker saw fit. Still, there were fixed points, known to the audiences, that had to be told certain ways, and it was the right and responsibility of the listeners to interrupt and correct a speaker if these fixed points were left out or not recounted accurately.[19]

For the most part, disciples of ancient philosophers or rabbis did not take notes but memorized their masters' words. Nevertheless, various forms of ancient shorthand did develop, while students did sometimes write down some of their teachers' words *after* a given period of instruction.[20] As time elapsed, collections of such teachings might be committed

---

[16]E. Randolph Richards, *The Secretary in the Letters of Paul* (Tübingen: Mohr, 1991), p. 19.

[17]For the diversity of practice, including more flexible *and* more inflexible models, see throughout Werner H. Kelber and Samuel Byrskog, eds., *Jesus in Memory: Traditions in Oral and Scribal Perspectives* (Waco, Tex.: Baylor University Press, 2009).

[18]For this and other approaches, see Thomas H. Olbricht, "Delivery and Memory," in *Handbook of Classical Rhetoric in the Hellenistic Period (330 B.C.-A.D. 400)*, ed. Stanley E. Porter (Boston: Brill, 1997), pp. 159-67.

[19]See esp. Kenneth E. Bailey, "Informal Controlled Oral Tradition and the Synoptic Gospels," *AJT* 5 (1991): 34-54 (reprinted in *Themelios* 20 [1995]: 4-11); and James D. G. Dunn, "Altering the Default Setting: Re-envisaging the Early Transmission of the Jesus Tradition," *NTS* 49 (2003): 139-75.

[20]E. Earle Ellis, "New Directions in Form Criticism," in *Jesus Christus in Historie und Theologie,*

to writing. A significant majority of ancient histories or biographies refer to earlier written sources, now lost, as well as to oral tradition or eyewitness interviews, as the backdrop for their compilations.[21] It is a modern myth that the ancients were seldom concerned with historical accuracy in the narratives they compiled or that they could not distinguish between fact and fiction the way we do. Of course the Mediterranean world of old had writers who were either unable or unwilling to write accurate history, just as we do. However, people understood the difference between good and bad history, had established criteria for distinguishing between fact and fiction, and recognized a time and place for each genre.[22]

A bigger difference between ancient and modern historiography involves ideological spin. The idea of preserving a dispassionate chronicle of events for posterity—with no necessary lessons to be learned from it—*is* largely a modern invention.[23] But deriving morals, supporting a political or religious viewpoint or improving society as purposes for history (or biography) writing are not inherently related to the question of how accurately events are recounted. It is possible to be a poor chronicler with no particular ideological bias or a good chronicler who believes that there is a pattern to the events chronicled that supports a particular perspective. As modernity increasingly gives way to postmodernity, the whole notion of historiography for the sake of advocacy is again taking a large and deserved place at the scholarly table, as long as authors candidly acknowledge their presuppositions and the causes that they are supporting.[24]

This discussion thus sets the stage for a definition of the historical-critical/grammatical method that includes source, form, redaction and tradition criticism. Source, form and redaction criticism form a natural triad

---

ed. Georg Strecker (Tübingen: Mohr, 1975), pp. 299-315; and Alan Millard, *Reading and Writing in the Time of Jesus* (Sheffield: Sheffield Academic Press, 2000), pp. 175-76, 202-4, 227-29.

[21]See the impressive summary of primary and secondary literature for this point, as well as for the last two points documented in nn. 19 and 20, in Craig S. Keener, *The Historical Jesus of the Gospels* (Grand Rapids: Eerdmans, 2009), pp. 144-52.

[22]Keener, *Historical Jesus of the Gospels*, pp. 95-108. Cf. Ben Witherington III, *The Acts of the Apostles: A Socio-Rhetorical Commentary* (Grand Rapids: Eerdmans, 1998), pp. 2-39.

[23]See Colin J. Hemer, *The Book of Acts in the Setting of Hellenistic History*, ed. Conrad H. Gempf (Tübingen: Mohr, 1989), pp. 63-100; Keener, *Historical Jesus of the Gospels*, pp. 109-25.

[24]See Klein, Blomberg and Hubbard, *Introduction to Biblical Interpretation*, pp. 87-101, and the literature there cited.

of disciplines that are often treated together.[25] This order of listing the three methods corresponds to the sequence in which each had its heyday in late-nineteenth- through late-twentieth-century scholarship. In terms of analyzing the composition of ancient documents, including biblical narratives, the chronological sequence in which to consider them is form, source and redaction criticism. Form criticism studies the period of time between the composition of the first written sources about a given individual(s) or event(s) and the occurrence of the original event(s) or life of the original individual(s). Source criticism then analyzes the written sources that were later utilized to produce the actual document being analyzed. Redaction criticism, finally, studies the theological or ideological distinctives that the final author(s) introduced into the text—both by what they added to their sources and by what they highlighted from those sources.[26]

Luke 1:1-4 contains important biblical precedent for all three of these forms of historical analysis, at least with respect to a Gospel. There we read,

> Many have undertaken to draw up an account of the things that have been fulfilled among us, just as they were handed down to us by those who from the first were eyewitnesses and servants of the word. With this in mind, since I myself have carefully investigated everything from the beginning, I too decided to write an orderly account for you, most excellent Theophilus, so that you may know the certainty of the things you have been taught. (NIV)

Because Luke was not present for any of the events of the Gospel that bears his name, he interviewed eyewitnesses and "servants of the word"— those who "have not only quoted and reported what they had heard and seen but have also been active as ministers of the word as well, which must mean that they have preached, taught, expounded the scripture,

---

[25]E.g., Craig A. Evans, "Source, Form and Redaction Criticism: The 'Traditional' Methods of Synoptic Criticism," in *Approaches to New Testament Study*, ed. Stanley E. Porter and David Tombs (Sheffield: Sheffield Academic Press, 1995), pp. 17-45; and David R. Catchpole, "Source, Form and Redaction Criticism of the New Testament," in *A Handbook to the Exegesis of the New Testament*, ed. Stanley E. Porter (Boston: Brill, 1997), pp. 167-88.

[26]For New Testament studies, see the works listed in n. 25 above. For Old Testament studies, see esp. Paul E. Hughes, "Compositional History—Source, Form and Redaction Criticism," in *Interpreting the Old Testament: A Guide for Exegesis*, ed. Craig C. Broyles (Grand Rapids: Baker Academic, 2001), pp. 221-44.

and so on."[27] This handing down is part of the process of oral tradition, as information was preserved by word of mouth. Luke also knows of "many" who had already put information about Jesus into writing. The most common meaning of the Greek word behind "account" *(diēgēsis)* is a written narrative of some kind.[28] These documents may have included the Gospel of Mark, a compilation of sayings found in both Matthew and Luke but not in Mark (often designated as "Q" from the German *Quelle,* meaning "source"), a collection of traditions written in one or more sources used only by Luke ("L"), and a similar collection used only by Matthew ("M").[29]

What can be deduced with any level of confidence from Old Testament narratives suggests a similar tripartite undertaking. Ancient Near Eastern cultures transmitted epic narratives by word of mouth, sometimes for centuries, and often with remarkable care and accuracy. The Old Testament itself refers to other sources, now lost, which contain fuller accounts of the events it depicts. Among the most famous are the recurring references in 1-2 Kings to the "book of the annals of the kings of Israel" and the "book of the annals of the kings of Judah" (see, e.g., 1 Kings 14:19, 29). The canonical books of 1-2 Kings and 1-2 Chronicles also offer an excellent example of an Old Testament "Synoptic Problem," with Chronicles most likely having used Kings in numerous places, while omitting material that did not fit its theological emphases and adding details that did.[30] Form, source and redaction criticism again all come into play. We may extrapolate to other biblical genres, even if on a smaller scale, and observe similar developments. Examples include the oral traditions present behind the Prophets, Proverbs and Psalms;[31] the

---

[27]Birger Gerhardsson, *The Reliability of the Gospel Tradition* (Peabody, Mass.: Hendrickson, 2001), p. 112.

[28]Joseph A. Fitzmyer, *The Gospel according to Luke I-IX* (Garden City, N.Y.: Doubleday, 1981), p. 292.

[29]Reflecting the classic four-source solution to the Synoptic Problem by B. H. Streeter, *The Four Gospels: A Study of Origins* (1924; repr., Eugene, Ore.: Wipf & Stock, 2008).

[30]See esp. Sara Japhet, *The Ideology of the Book of Chronicles and Its Place in Biblical Thought*, 2nd ed. (Winona Lake, Ind.: Eisenbrauns, 2009).

[31]See, e.g., throughout the chapters "Israelite Prophets and Prophecy," by David W. Baker; "Wisdom Literature," by Bruce K. Waltke and David Diewert; and "Recent Trends in Psalms Study," by David M. Howard Jr. in *The Face of Old Testament Studies: A Survey of Contemporary Approaches,* ed. David W. Baker and Bill T. Arnold (Grand Rapids: Baker Academic, 1999), pp. 266-94, 295-328 and 329-68, respectively.

hymnic elements found in the New Testament letters;[32] the literary relationship between 2 Peter and Jude;[33] and the use of other historical background materials in the book of Revelation.[34]

Tradition criticism is a term that has not had as fixed a referent as any of the members of the triad of source, form and redaction criticism. Some scholars have preferred to apply *tradition criticism* to the study of the oral period that form criticism as a whole focuses on, while reserving *form criticism* for the analysis of the distinct literary forms that make up an entire biblical book, along with their respective interpretive principles.[35] Others have applied the label of tradition criticism to the study of the historical trustworthiness of any portion of a book of the Bible, and especially of the Gospels.[36] To this end, various "criteria of authenticity" have been devised to determine the likelihood of a given saying or deed attributed to Christ actually corresponding to what the historical Jesus said or did.[37] Still others have preferred to make *tradition criticism* the umbrella term that embraces source, form and redaction criticism, as in the heading for this subsection of this chapter.[38]

Unlike historical criticism as historical-cultural background analysis, which emphasizes the adjective *historical* more than the noun *criticism*, historical criticism as tradition-critical analysis in this overarching sense inverts these two components. In source, form and redaction criticism, we are no longer just accumulating data or utilizing methods that best enable us to *interpret* a biblical text. Instead, we are employing approaches to the

---

[32]The fullest collection of suggestions for the locations of such material appears in E. Earle Ellis, *The Making of the New Testament Documents* (Boston: Brill, 2002), pp. 53-141, 183-200.

[33]Peter H. Davids, *The Letters of 2 Peter and Jude*, PNTC (Grand Rapids: Eerdmans, 2006), pp. 136-43; Gene L. Green, *Jude and 2 Peter*, BECNT (Grand Rapids: Baker Academic, 2008), pp. 159-62.

[34]See esp. David E. Aune, *Revelation 1-5*, WBC (Dallas: Word, 1997), pp. cv-cxxxiv, although Aune's proposals probably impose more precision on the data than they actually permit.

[35]E.g., Bruce Chilton, "Traditio-Historical Criticism and the Study of Jesus," in *Hearing the New Testament: Strategies for Interpretation*, ed. Joel B. Green (Grand Rapids: Eerdmans, 1995), pp. 37-60.

[36]Classically, Robin S. Barbour, *Traditio-Historical Criticism of the Gospels: Some Comments on Current Methods* (London: SPCK, 1972).

[37]For the fullest survey and critique, see Stanley E. Porter, *The Criteria for Authenticity in Historical-Jesus Research: Previous Discussion and New Proposals* (Sheffield: Sheffield Academic Press, 2000).

[38]E.g., Holly J. Carey, "Traditio-Historical Criticism," in *Hearing the New Testament: Strategies for Interpretation*, ed. Joel B. Green, 2nd ed. (Grand Rapids: Eerdmans, 2010), pp. 102-21.

text that allow us to adjudicate its origin, the nature of its transmission, the probability of its historical trustworthiness and the like. For some very conservative biblical interpreters, it is always wrong to embark on such activities because it seems to place the interpreter above Scripture and inevitably leads to historical verdicts that contradict the inerrancy of Scripture.[39] The latter objection is simply mistaken; thousands of evangelical scholars worldwide use chastened forms of historical criticism and remain well within the rubric of inerrancy.[40] As for the former complaint, if all we do is take the Bible's claims at face value without examination, plenty of other people will render very different verdicts on the nature of its formation and its resulting credibility (or incredibility) and we will have no reply! For this reason, what we are calling the historical-critical/grammatical method must have this "critical" dimension to it—that is, a dimension that is both analytical and evaluative, based on common ground shared with the skeptic. If our faith cannot withstand historical inquiry, it does not merit retention.[41] If it does, then we must subsequently subject ourselves to Scripture.

Grammatical methods. The final adjective in this hybrid combination of methods is *grammatical.* This is the piece of interpretation that focuses on the meanings of words; the analysis of grammar; and the structure of phrases, clauses, sentences, paragraphs and increasingly larger units of thought up to the level of an entire book. At its most basic level, grammatical analysis is necessary because the biblical text does not come to us in our own native tongue. Instead, the first step to understanding any given biblical text is correctly translating the text. Because words can have more than one meaning at a given time in the history of a language,[42] one must turn to the immediate context of any given use of a word to deter-

---

[39]See esp. throughout *The Jesus Crisis: The Inroads of Historical Criticism into Evangelical Scholarship*, ed. Robert L. Thomas and F. David Farnell (Grand Rapids: Kregel, 1998). Cf. also Eta Linnemann, *Historical Criticism: Methodology or Ideology?* (1990; repr., Grand Rapids: Kregel, 2001).

[40]Most notably, many are members of the Evangelical Theological Society, which contains belief in inerrancy in its doctrinal basis.

[41]See the excellent survey of those who think historical criticism leads to a skeptical approach to Scripture, those who think it is unrelated to belief in the Bible and those who (correctly, in my opinion) see it as supportive of Scripture, in N. T. Wright, *Jesus and the Victory of God* (Minneapolis: Fortress, 1996), pp. 3-124. The rest of Wright's volume is a further demonstration of his conviction that this last option is the right one.

[42]This is usually the case with all but the most specialized of terms.

mine what makes the most sense in that context. If a particular author has
his or her own idiolect—distinctive meanings for certain words—that
must also be taken into account. Biblical interpreters in particular must
beware of committing a variety of lexical fallacies when engaging in word
studies. Most notably, they must recall that etymologies do not necessarily
produce meanings that people consciously reflected on centuries later.
They must avoid both semantic anachronism—giving words meanings
they would have *later* in the history of the language but didn't yet have—
and semantic obsolescence—giving words meanings from an *earlier* time
in the history of the language that had fallen out of use.[43]

Not only words can be ambiguous but likewise multiword expressions.
Does "the love of God" mean "someone's love for God" (an objective genitive) or "God's love for someone else" (a subjective genitive)? Only the
immediate context in the writing in question can help us determine the
answer. Even taking context into account, ambiguities sometimes remain
because we are not given enough information to conclusively exclude all
options but one. Does an adverbial participle introducing a dependent
clause function temporally, causally, conditionally or instrumentally, to
mention just four possibilities? In Greek, the same form of a given participle could function in any of these ways.[44]

Subordinate phrases and clauses may be adverbial or adjectival. Often
it is clear which is which, and which word from the main clause each
modifies. But ambiguities may arise here too. How do sentences relate to
each other and where should paragraph breaks, subsection breaks and
section breaks be placed? All of these grammatical decisions can make a
difference as to how a passage is interpreted. In short, any text under
scrutiny must be analyzed in view of the narrative flow of thought in
which it is embedded.[45]

PROVISIONAL SUMMARY AND COMPARISONS

What does all this add up to? The historical-critical/grammatical method,

---

[43]See further D. A. Carson, *Exegetical Fallacies,* 2nd ed. (Grand Rapids: Baker, 1996), pp. 28-37
and passim.

[44]Any responsible intermediate Greek grammar will provide the major categories for the various
parts of speech that the exegete needs to master. See, e.g., Stanley E. Porter, *Idioms of the Greek
New Testament* (Sheffield: Sheffield Academic Press, 1992).

[45]Cf. further Blomberg with Markley, *Handbook of New Testament Exegesis,* pp. 93-102.

as opposed to the other four methods presented in this volume, analyzes the *historical* setting in which a given communicative act occurs. This involves general information about who is speaking to whom, where, when and under what circumstances, as well as specific information concerning what is sometimes called a shared "presuppositional pool"—whatever knowledge the author and audience share about past or present events, customs and practices, culture and society, and so on, that might be important for interpreting particular details of the communication at hand.[46] The historical-critical/grammatical method is *critical* as well as historical because it seeks to analyze the formation of documents, including earlier written sources, oral forms of communication and whatever distinctive emphases the author of the document may have added to the tradition he or she inherited. Such analysis can also lead to judgments about the reliability of the document being assessed. Finally, the historical-critical/grammatical method is *grammatical* because it insists on a careful study of words, grammatical forms, sentence parts, sentences and multisentence structures as they relate to each other.

What does this method *not* do that one or more of the other four methods do? It differs from literary and postmodern methods in that it does not treat the document from an ahistorical perspective, seeking merely to understand the literary elements of plot, theme, motifs, characterization, narrative time and the like. It does not stop with the narrative world internal to a document that focuses only on implied authors or narrators and implied readers or narratees, wanting instead to know whatever is possible to recover about real authors, original audiences and real readers.[47] It does not embrace those forms of postmodernism that so revel in diversity in the interpretation of texts that they reject the constraints of limiting meaning to what was first intended and/or likely to have been understood in those texts' original settings.[48]

---

[46]E.g., Peter Cotterell and Max Turner, *Linguistics and Biblical Interpretation* (Downers Grove, Ill.: InterVarsity Press, 1989), pp. 90-97, 257-59.

[47]On the meanings of these various terms and the distinctions among them, see Mark A. Powell, *What Is Narrative Criticism?* (Minneapolis: Fortress, 1990), pp. 29-31; or James L. Resseguie, *Narrative Criticism of the New Testament: An Introduction* (Grand Rapids: Baker Academic, 2005), pp. 30-33.

[48]As, e.g., throughout A. K. M. Adam, *What Is Postmodern Biblical Criticism?* (Minneapolis: Fortress, 1998); and idem, ed., *Postmodern Interpretations of the Bible: A Reader* (St. Louis: Chalice, 2001).

Our method differs from philosophical and theological approaches in that it stops short of making syntheses like those that characterize *systematic* theology. Our method is very interested in the theological emphases of one specific biblical book but leaves the task of comparing and contrasting these emphases with those found elsewhere in Scripture to the systematic or biblical theologians. Our task is not to synthesize all of one writer's (or testament's or the whole Bible's) perspective on a given topic or to sum up all of the major themes of one particular part of Scripture, as in *biblical* theology.[49] The historical-critical/grammatical method does not typically study the "afterlife" of texts via the history of their interpretation through the centuries, nor is it particularly interested in the "history of the effects" of the passage on other disciplines.[50] It does not analyze a text to see if it can contribute to the creation of some overall philosophical or theological system of thought or because it fits in a preexisting philosophical or theological system held by the analyst.[51]

Our method is not the same as the redemptive-historical method because it treats each passage in each testament as part of the biblical book in which it appears and seeks the meaning it most likely held when that book was completed. It does not read New Testament meanings back into Old Testament texts. It may use meanings of Old Testament texts that were most likely known by the author of a New Testament text, but then only because they form part of the *historical* background for that New Testament text. It does not try to make all of Scripture "preach Christ" unless there is historical and contextual warrant for doing so. It tends not to raise questions of contemporary significance, application or contextualization, or locate a biblical passage in the flow of redemptive history (that is, in the unfolding story of God's dealings with humanity).[52]

---

[49]For proper distinctions and overlaps, see esp. D. A. Carson, "Unity and Diversity in the New Testament: The Possibility of Systematic Theology," in *Scripture and Truth*, ed. D. A. Carson and John D. Woodbridge (1983; repr., Grand Rapids: Baker, 1992), pp. 65-95.

[50]For the value of which, see esp. Markus Bockmuehl, *Seeing the Word: Refocusing New Testament Study* (Grand Rapids: Baker Academic, 2006).

[51]In circles in which the historical-critical method, as defined by Krentz and Troeltsch (see n. 1 above), precluded all theological synthesis or personal appropriation, a healthy pendulum swing is today often occurring that at times avoids these traps, though not always. See Daniel J. Treier, *Introducing Theological Interpretation of Scripture: Recovering a Christian Practice* (Grand Rapids: Baker Academic, 2008).

[52]Tasks nicely addressed throughout Zondervan's NIV Application Commentary series in their "Bridging Contexts" and "Contemporary Significance" sections, but only after first addressing "Original Meaning."

The historical-critical/grammatical method, finally, is not the same as the canonical method in that it focuses on the final form of individual books within the canon rather than later stages of canonical development, when interpreters read those books alongside other canonized books.[53] Canonical criticism intentionally asks different questions like, "What happened to the interpretation of Luke and Acts when John was inserted in between them?"[54] Such questions are legitimate, but if some of the answers to those questions contradict the interpretation of texts in their own integrity, the former must be eschewed in favor of the latter.

I said at the outset of this chapter that I was *not* trying to defend the historical-critical/grammatical method as the sole legitimate approach among the five hermeneutical approaches that this book presents but that I *would* argue for its logical priority. Without an anchor in the historical context and the original meanings of words and grammatical structures, literary/postmodern methods have few checks and balances. As some have insisted, the only two criteria for a good interpretation (for there are then no longer any "correct" interpretations) then become creativity or cleverness and consistency or coherence. In other words, one seeks an interpretation that is fun to read and worthy of admiration and that does not contradict itself internally at any point. Whether or not it corresponds to any external reality becomes irrelevant.[55]

Without a foundation in history and grammar, philosophical/theological methods too easily twist meanings of texts to fit desired or preexisting syntheses or to address issues for which these texts were never designed. Without an appreciation of the integrity of each biblical book in its original setting, redemptive-historical methods and canonical methods too often appeal uncritically to the principle of Scripture interpreting Scripture (or "the rule of faith") and come up with meanings that no one could have ever imagined (including the book's original audience). At best, these conclusions represent what has been called "the right doctrine from the wrong

---

[53] Again, Old Testament works already accepted as canonical by New Testament authors are an exception.

[54] See, classically, Brevard S. Childs, *Introduction to the Old Testament as Scripture* (Philadelphia: Fortress, 1979); idem, *The New Testament as Canon: An Introduction* (Philadelphia: Fortress, 1984).

[55] Summarized as the concept of "freeplay" by John Dominic Crossan, *Cliffs of Fall: Paradox and Polyvalence in the Parables of Jesus* (1980; repr., Eugene, Ore.: Wipf & Stock, 2008), pp. 25-104.

texts."[56] At worst, they lead to wrong doctrine altogether. *With* the historical and grammatical checks and balances provided by the method we have discussed, however, all of these other approaches may move forward in a responsible fashion.

APPLICATION TO MATTHEW 2:7-15

Space forbids anything like a comprehensive application of our method to our assigned text. However, we can give illustrations and highlights of each step of the process.

Dealing with issues of textual criticism first, we can note that the Nestle-Aland Greek New Testament lists six textual variants. In four cases, the manuscript evidence for the preferred text is so overwhelming they do not offer external evidence.[57] In the other two instances, the textual variants involve minor differences in verb forms with little change to the meaning of the text. Clearly we have a secure text and can proceed to the remaining tasks before us.

Commentators differ over the dating of Matthew but are largely agreed that it is the most Jewish-Christian of the Synoptics (and perhaps of all four Gospels) and is addressing a primarily Jewish-Christian church or collection of churches, probably in either Syrian Antioch or Jerusalem, in a setting in which both Christian Judaism and the beginnings of rabbinic Judaism are vying for the role of being the only legitimate spiritual heir of Israelite religion.[58] Not surprisingly, then, one common way of outlining Matthew's birth narrative (Mt 1–2) is according to its references to the Hebrew Scriptures. First, Matthew stresses Jesus' legitimate messianic genealogy in Matthew 1:1-17, and then he shows the Christ child fulfilling five key Old Testament prophecies in Matthew 1:18–2:23 (see Mt 1:23; 2:6, 15, 18, 23).[59] These two chapters have been called the "who" and "whence" of Jesus' birth, with Matthew 1 showing Jesus as the son of David, the son of Abraham (both in Mt 1:1) and Emmanuel (Mt 1:23) and

---

[56]G. K. Beale, ed., *The Right Doctrine from the Wrong Texts? Essays on the Use of the Old Testament in the New* (Grand Rapids: Baker, 1994).

[57]The UBS text lists no variants.

[58]For a good survey of the options, see Donald A. Hagner, *Matthew 1–13*, WBC (Dallas: Word, 1993), pp. lxiv-lxxv.

[59]R. T. France (*The Gospel of Matthew* [Grand Rapids: Eerdmans, 2007], pp. 40-45), e.g., defends his label for Mt 1:18-2:23 as "A Demonstration that Jesus of Nazareth is the Messiah: Five Scriptural Proofs" (40).

Matthew 2 detailing key events surrounding Bethlehem (Mt 1:1, 5-6, 8), Egypt (Mt 1:13-15), Ramah (Mt 1:18) and Nazareth (Mt 1:23).[60] Matthew 2:7-15 spans the last six verses of the story about the magi (Mt 2:1-12) and all three of the verses about the flight to Egypt (Mt 2:13-15).

Various questions of historical background typically surround a discussion of the magi's visit to Bethlehem. We will focus only on factors related to Matthew 2:9-13. Under Caesar Augustus, Herod the Great, of Idumean ancestry, became the client king over Israel and ruled from 37-4 B.C. Near the end of his life he became increasingly paranoid about real or imagined attempts on his life and would have been greatly threatened if he believed that one legitimately in line to be Israel's king had been born.[61] The magi were most likely a cross between what we would today call astronomers and astrologers, coming from either Persia or Arabia.[62] Seeing a new heavenly body in the sky above a particular land was often believed to portend the birth of a new king in that region.[63] The magi may well have assumed that Israel's current ruler, of all people, would know who this child was. In Matthew 2:9, they have just come from meeting with Herod. But he had to consult his personal, indigenous, religious advisors to learn about the prophecy from Micah 5:2 that predicted the birth of the Messiah in Bethlehem, a scant five to six miles south of Jerusalem.

The magi were overjoyed. They headed for the tiny village,[64] and the "star" began to move in some fashion that guided them to the very house they were looking for. Several factors suggest that their visit occurred at least several months after the baby's birth and was not part of the "manger scene" from Luke 2:1-20: the time preceding the trip deciding their course

---

[60]Krister Stendahl, "Quis et Unde? An Analysis of Matthew 1–2," in *Judentum, Urchristentum, Kirche*, ed. Walther Eltester (Berlin: Töpelmann, 1960), pp. 94-105.

[61]For a full, critical study of Herod's life, see Peter Richardson, *Herod: King of the Jews and Friend of the Romans* (Columbia: University of South Carolina Press, 1996).

[62]Mark A. Powell, "The Magi as Wise Men: Re-examining a Basic Supposition," *NTS* 46 (2000): 1-20; Tony T. Maalouf, "Were the Magi from Persia or Arabia?" *BSac* 156 (1999): 423-42.

[63]Craig S. Keener, *The Gospel of Matthew: A Socio-Rhetorical Commentary* (Grand Rapids: Eerdmans, 2009), pp. 98-102.

[64]On what little information archaeologists have uncovered from this period, and for help distinguishing the authentic from the "traditional" among the tourist sites, see Bargil Pixner, *Wege des Messias und Stätten der Urkirche*, ed. Rainer Riesner, 3rd ed. (Giessen: Brunnen, 1996), pp. 29-41; and Joaquín González Echegaray, *Arqueología y evangelios*, 2nd ed. (Estella, Navarra: Verbo Divino, 1999), pp. 99-101.

of action, the length of their journey from its inception and their arrival at a private home.[65] The gifts of gold, frankincense and myrrh were appropriate for royalty.[66] Initially, the magi may have had no reason to doubt Herod's sincerity in also wanting to do obeisance to the new king (Mt 2:8), but one or more of them had a dream that convinced them not to report back to Jerusalem, but rather head immediately back to their homeland.

Danger from Herod turns out to be real, as Matthew 2:13-15 depicts Joseph, the adoptive father of the young Jesus, also experiencing a dream, this time explicitly involving an angel, who warned him to take his family and flee to Egypt. South and southwest of the land under Herod's jurisdiction was largely desert; it was not until one had crossed the Sinai Peninsula that there would be good, safe places to stay. Egypt had a significant minority of Jews living in it in the first century; undoubtedly Joseph and Mary headed to a community with a settlement of their own kinfolk. Because they had to escape *to* Egypt, they would later have to return *from* Egypt, which makes Matthew recall an Old Testament passage that, in its original context, referred to Israel, collectively, as God's son, coming out of Egypt at the time of the exodus and the giving of the *Mosaic* covenant (Hos 11:1). Matthew, however, finds it too remarkable to be pure coincidence that the Messiah who would represent Israel also had to come out of Egypt at the time of the fulfillment of the prophecies about God's *new* covenant. Thus he employs the well-established Jewish interpretive method of typology to speak of this text being "fulfilled" (in the sense of "filled full") in Jesus' life as well.[67]

Grammatically, there is little of controversy in these verses. Older translations rendered *en tē anatolē* as "in the east" in Matthew 2:9 (and also in Mt 2:2), but that would make magi seeing a star in the opposite direction from which they traveled! Of course, the magi were themselves from

---

[65]Combined with other evidence for the date of Jesus' birth, it may have been up to two years afterward. See David L. Turner, *Matthew*, BECNT (Grand Rapids: Baker Academic, 2008), p. 86; and cf. John Nolland, *The Gospel of Matthew: A Commentary on the Greek Text*, NIGTC (Grand Rapids: Eerdmans, 2005), p. 122.

[66]Cf. Ben Witherington III, *Matthew*, Smyth & Helwys Bible Commentary (Macon, Ga.: Smyth & Helwys, 2006), pp. 66-67.

[67]Michael J. Wilkins, *Matthew*, NIVAC (Grand Rapids: Zondervan, 2004), p. 78. See further Craig L. Blomberg, "Interpreting Old Testament Prophetic Literature in Matthew: Double Fulfillment," *TrinJ* 23 (2001): 17-33. A fuller study of this passage as typology, after reviewing other proposals, is Tracy L. Howard, "The Use of Hosea 11:1 in Matthew 2:15: An Alternative Solution," *BSac* 143 (1986): 314-28.

the East (Mt 2:1), so perhaps that is all that the phrases in Matthew 2:2, 9 mean. But, if so, the prepositional phrases are unusually placed, by being linked more closely in both verses to the verbs for seeing than to the magi themselves. The ESV, GWN, NAB, NET, NJB, NRSV and NIV are thus probably correct to translate this phrase as "when it rose" (i.e., when they first saw it near the time of dawn—which occurs in the east).[68] The verb *proskyneō*, usually translated "worship" in Matthew 2:8, can just mean to kneel, bow or lie prostrate in someone's presence. The magi themselves may not have thought that they were worshiping God or a god but simply paying appropriate homage to royalty (cf. NAB, NJB, NRSV).[69] At the redactional level, however, Matthew, who uses this verb more than any other Gospel writer (Mt 13×, Mk 2×, Lk 3×, Jn 11×), may well have seen deeper significance in their behavior.[70]

Source critically, our verses form uniquely Matthean material, which may or may not come from a distinct oral or written source M.[71] If the apostle Matthew did in fact write this Gospel, he may simply be reporting what Jesus or some other member of Jesus' family had told him.[72] Form critically, there are partial parallels between some of these events and certain details in the birth narratives of other great people in the ancient Mediterranean world, but they are scarcely close enough to make it plausible that Matthew was merely adopting a well-known fictitious genre to magnify his master.[73] Dream narratives appear scattered throughout Scripture; two constant factors are that they always prove prophetic and

---

[68]W. D. Davies and Dale C. Allison Jr., *A Critical and Exegetical Commentary on the Gospel according to Saint Matthew* (Edinburgh: T & T Clark, 1988-97), 1:236.

[69]Richard A. Horsley, *The Liberation of Christmas: The Infancy Narratives in Social Context* (New York: Crossroad, 1989), p. 58.

[70]Ulrich Luz, *Matthew 1-7: A Continental Commentary*, trans. Wilhelm Linss (Minneapolis: Augsburg, 1989), p. 137.

[71]The last full-length study in English of this putative document does not include Matthew 1-2 and postulates only a sayings source. See Stephenson H. Brooks, *Matthew's Community: The Evidence of His Special Sayings Material* (Sheffield: JSOT Press, 1987). For the view that Matthew merged and developed what were originally two independent sources for Mt 2:1-12, see John Nolland, "The Sources for Matthew 2:1-12," *CBQ* 60 (1998): 283-300.

[72]It has often been observed that Matthew's infancy narrative reflects more of what could have been Joseph's perspectives; and Luke's, what could have been Mary's perspectives.

[73]So also Davies and Allison (*A Critical and Exegetical Commentary*, 1:214-16), although they find important similarities to hagaddic material on Moses. Still definitive on the superficiality of the supposed Jewish or Greco-Roman parallels to the canonical birth narratives about Jesus is J. Gresham Machen, *The Virgin Birth of Christ* (1930; repr., London: James Clarke, 1987).

that the prophecies always come true. We need read only into the next three verses (Mt 2:16-18) to see that that is true here also.[74]

Redactionally, the emphasis on the fulfillment of prophecy stands out as Matthew's primary contribution to the episodes that constitute Matthew 1:18–2:23.[75] Though the form of typology employed might not seem as persuasive to us today as a straightforward prediction-fulfillment scheme, it should have had significant impact on a faithful first-century Jew. God's providence worked through recurring patterns in history, especially with respect to creative and redemptive events.[76] If Matthew was trying to convince more Jews to become followers of Jesus, he chose a very astute way to begin his narrative.

CONCLUSION

The historical-critical/grammatical approach is one way of referring to the method of interpreting the Scriptures (or any other communicative act) that seeks to recover an author's meaning as disclosed in a text or utterance designed for a specific audience or audiences. It is historical because it prioritizes acquiring as much information as possible, from both inside and outside of the text, about the historical and cultural circumstances in which the text was composed. It is critical in the sense of being analytical, not in the sense of criticizing. It is critical, too, in that it recognizes valid components within all of the subdisciplines developed by the historical-critical method more narrowly framed, despite the antisupernatural presuppositions that the framers of that method originally employed. Shorn of such presuppositions and the various corollaries they birthed, textual, source, form, tradition and redaction criticism are all essential tools for understanding the contents of an original document, its formation and origin, its literary genre and subgenres, the authenticity of the purportedly

---

[74]See Robert Gnuse, "Dream Genre in the Matthean Infancy Narratives," *NovT* 32 (1990): 97-120. More broadly, Derek S. Dodson (*Reading Dreams: An Audience-Critical Approach to the Dreams in the Gospel of Matthew* [New York: T & T Clark, 2009]) demonstrates that generic similarities from as far afield as Greco-Roman dream narratives would have likewise led Matthew's readers to expect the dreams he includes to disclose God's will for the characters they treat.

[75]Robert H. Gundry's thorough study (*The Use of the Old Testament in St. Matthew's Gospel: With Special Reference to the Messianic Hope* [Leiden: Brill, 1967]) has yet to be superseded.

[76]On typology in the New Testament more generally, see esp. Leonhard Goppelt, *Typos: The Typological Interpretation of the Old Testament in the New* (1982; repr., Eugene, Ore.: Wipf & Stock, 2002).

historical material it includes, and its theological or ideological emphases and distinctives. Finally, this approach is grammatical because it pays close attention to the meanings of words in their historical and cultural contexts as collocated in phrases, clauses, sentences, paragraphs and still larger units of thought. The historical-critical/grammatical approach is by no means the only legitimate approach to the biblical text. However, it is the necessary foundation on which all other approaches must build. As illustrated in Matthew 2:7-15, with Matthew's typological use of Hosea 11:1 in Matthew 2:15, it can even illuminate why, in certain contexts more than others, one might want to move on to other methods that focus more on the entire canon, the sweep of redemptive history, contemporary application and the like.

2

The Literary/Postmodern View

F. *Scott Spencer*

Literary approaches are varied and they are employed by scholars for many different reasons and in service of many different ends."[1] So says Mark Allan Powell at the end of a recent survey of literary-critical interpretations of Matthew's Gospel. Throw in "sociological" and "postmodern" ingredients—which scholars increasingly mix with their literary-rich stock—and the methodological stew becomes even thicker, spicier and harder to outline in recipe form. But those of us who happily and profitably dive into this interpretive smorgasbord would like to think there is some logic in the methodological madness. While this essay provides no foolproof recipe, perhaps it at least explains a few key ingredients.

Regarding the now familiar triad of author-, text- or reader-oriented approaches to biblical interpretation, current literary-focused critics concentrate on the latter two options. Generally frustrated with elusive excavations for authorial identity and intention, these interpreters prefer the more palpable company of texts and readers. Simply put, for example, we do not know for sure who wrote the first Gospel or what he intended. Its early attribution to Matthew the tax collector turned apostle may be correct, but the best available manuscripts remain anonymous. Likewise, we have no advance "book proposal" or statement of "goals and objectives" outlining "Matthew's" intended aims for his Gospel. But whatever we lack, we at least have in hand Matthew's text (more or less) as well as written responses from real readers—not the original ones, to be sure—but

---

[1]Mark Allan Powell, "Literary Approaches and the Gospel of Matthew," in *Methods for Matthew*, ed. Mark Allan Powell (Cambridge: Cambridge University Press, 2009), p. 82.

many others throughout Christian history.

Still, a text and readers in the hand hardly nullify an author in the bush. *Someone* wrote the first Gospel and did not do so willy-nilly, slapping traditions together in haphazard fashion. Judging from the final, polished narrative product—which recent literary analysis has particularly demonstrated—this "someone" was an intelligent, careful and purposeful writer. Literary-oriented criticism, chiefly concerned with narrative strategies in Matthew's case, thus offers a sample "index" of likely objectives the author had in mind.[2] And in turn, this narrative-based index provides a set of controls for assessing the multiplicity of reader responses.

In sum, I'm assuming considerable fluidity in the hermeneutical triad sketched above[3]—more like an interrelated "trinity." But if we must prioritize, I maintain that, in their best-practiced forms, literary/postmodern approaches cohere in giving prime attention to the *text* at the high point of the triangle, with *readers* especially (texts do not read and interpret themselves) and *authors* (texts do not produce themselves) providing vital base support. Thus I turn to describe briefly several *textual foci* of these approaches before applying these to the *focal text* of Matthew 2:7-15.

TEXTUAL FOCI

Final text. Historically oriented critics have typically treated the Gospels as archaeological tells underneath which they burrow to discover the foundational layers or building blocks of the "authentic" words and deeds of Jesus. Their concern is chiefly *diachronic:* to determine how the various sources, forms, traditions and redactions (edits) have developed *through time* toward the construction of final Gospel editions. The archaeological model breaks down, however, at the point of *material artifacts.* In place of hard coins, pottery shards and the like, which archaeologists actually dig up, historical Gospel critics base much of their work on reconstructed *hypothetical* documents and tradition units *theorized* from final texts.

More than questioning these shaky underpinnings of historical-evolutionary criticism, however, literary-centered interpreters have especially

---

[2]Mark Allan Powell, *Chasing the Eastern Star: Adventures in Biblical Reader-Response Criticism* (Louisville: Westminster John Knox, 2001), pp. 67-69.

[3]Cf. Joel B. Green, "Narrative Criticism," in *Methods for Luke*, ed. Joel B. Green (Cambridge: Cambridge University Press, 2010), p. 75: "Today, narratology increasingly blurs the lines between author, text, and reader."

lamented the relative neglect of the Gospels as *complete and compelling literary works* designed to be heard, read and viewed in one sitting, like a novella, play or painting.[4] Their concern is largely *synchronic:* to ascertain how various scenes, seams and segments *fit together in the time frame* of the overall narrative. It is best to appreciate and approach the Gospels as the finely textured works of theological art they are. We must carefully analyze and scrutinize their complex portraits of Jesus from every angle, but not claw through them to find some safe to crack in the wall behind, only to find it full of fool's gold.

However, unlike a certified Leonardo or Michelangelo piece we might view at the Louvre, we cannot contemplate a complete, *original* Gospel composition. The best we can do is to sift through myriad manuscript copies, none of which are identical. Fortunately, however, the situation is not that ominous: thanks to the painstaking work of textual critics, we possess a reconstructed Greek text of each New Testament Gospel, closely approximating the "autograph," or original document. Where questions remain, footnotes offer the most significant variants—which literary scholars must adjudicate if they really want to engage the *final text*. In this initial exercise of determining a final Gospel text, not to mention the basic work of *reading* it in a dead, ancient language, literary critics thus inescapably participate in historical-linguistic investigation *behind* as well as *within* the narrative.

Cotext. Using discourse analysis, Joel Green describes *cotext* as "the string of linguistic data within which a text is set, the relationship of, say, a sentence to a paragraph or a pericope in Luke's Gospel to the larger Lukan narrative."[5] As an interpretive strategy, attention to cotext "invites a close reading of the text for its structural elements and argumentative development."[6] Following on the holistic interest in final texts, cotextual analysis stresses the linear connectedness and logical coherence of plot, characters and themes across the narrative. As a final-text focus resists plowing up narratives, cotextual concerns resist pulling them apart into

---

[4]Of course, the more compelling the work, the more "sittings" it will invite; and each fresh encounter *with the entire product* will spark new insights.

[5]Joel B. Green, "Discourse Analysis and New Testament Interpretation," in *Hearing the New Testament: Strategies for Interpretation,* ed. Joel B. Green, 2nd ed. (Grand Rapids: Eerdmans, 2010), p. 226.

[6]Ibid., p. 228.

discrete units. Where form critics tend to treat the Gospels as a chain of variable individual pearls randomly strung together by juvenile artists, narrative critics appreciate the mature craftsmanship of the entire necklace. On a more popular level, this proclivity toward atomization is evident in much Sunday school curricula and congregational preaching, concentrating on "focal texts" from one to several verses, often with little or no connection to the biblical book from which they derive.

Exploring cotextual connections and patterns constitutes the bread and butter of *narrative criticism.*[7] In terms of *plot,* this approach assumes an orderly, step-by-step progression through the story,[8] one scene preparing for the next, and indeed for the balance of the entire work, by establishing a database of information for the (implied) reader and creating expectations for what follows. Likewise, *characters'* reported actions and words, which drive the plot, build over the course of the narrative into more or less static (flat) or dynamic (round) portraits. Such steady plot progression and character construction, however, do not proceed in complex narratives like the Gospels and Acts in a smooth, sanitized fashion. Serious conflicts, surprising twists and turns (the stuff of irony), and puzzling gaps and hiccups maintain suspense and dramatic interest. Yet the prime thrust of narrative criticism has been to negotiate and resolve these tensions in the interest of thematic coherence and unity.

Intertext. For all the value of narrative criticism's final and cotextual emphases, rigid devotion to such approaches runs the risk of myopically treating each Gospel narrative as "a hermetic and self-sufficient whole."[9] No text, however, as Mikhail Bakhtin and other literary theorists have stressed, is produced or, still less, interpreted in some pristine isolation chamber. All texts—indeed, all language and communication—are influenced by other texts and voices they answer, both directly and tacitly. The

---

[7]For standard monograph surveys, see Mark Allan Powell, *What Is Narrative Criticism?* GBS (Minneapolis: Fortress, 1990); James L. Resseguie, *Narrative Criticism of the New Testament: An Introduction* (Grand Rapids: Baker Academic, 2005).

[8]In the preface, Luke explicitly identifies the ensuing narrative as an "orderly [*kathexēs*] narrative" (Lk 1:3; cf. Lk 8:1; Acts 3:24; 11:4; 18:23).

[9]Patricia K. Tull, "Rhetorical Criticism and Intertextuality," in *To Each Its Own Meaning: An Introduction to Biblical Criticisms and Their Application,* ed. Steven L. McKenzie and Stephen R. Haynes, rev. and exp. ed. (Louisville: Westminster John Knox, 1999), pp. 166-67, citing Mikhail M. Bakhtin, *The Dialogic Imagination,* ed. Michael Holquist (Austin: University of Texas Press, 1991), pp. 273-74.

traffic does not run on a one-way racetrack, where new texts, as it were, simply load up cargo and baggage from prior texts and hurtle toward their destinations. Relationships between texts truly function *intertextually* or *dialogically*, mutually addressing and responding to each other. In the process, a welter of changes can occur: the traffic can cruise, race, skid, spin, bump or jam around the intertextual, interpretive oval.

At a fundamental level, the entire New Testament engages in thoughtful, respectful and intimate conversation with Israel's Scriptures, or what Christians call the Old Testament. This becomes clear from the opening words of Matthew's Gospel, in which the author identifies Jesus as "the Messiah, the son of David, the son of Abraham" and then unpacks his full genealogy over forty-two generations (Mt 1:1-17). This opening passage assumes readers' competent understanding of an extensive Old Testament literary repertoire beyond a fuzzy recognition of a few key names. More than simply acknowledging Matthew's conviction that these and other episodes in the literary-canonical stream of Israel's biblical story are "made right" and find their fulfillment in Jesus the Christ (as important as such a claim is), an intertextual approach urges readers to allow the accounts of Genesis's Tamar, for example, and of Matthew's Jesus to stand side-by-side—or better, face-to-face—and talk with each other, shape and reshape each other, illuminate and interpenetrate each other. Obviously, this interpretive strategy challenges reducing New Testament use of the Old Testament to a set of mechanical operations and random proof-texting.

Similarly, in Gospel study, intertextuality compels comparative analyses among Synoptic and Johannine narratives, but (1) *more* with a view to full-throated synchronic dialogue among these distinctive later first-century portraits of Jesus than to straight diachronic mapping of literary dependence;[10] and (2) *less* constrained by pressures toward harmonization and conformity with tightly defined "rules of faith."[11] Further, I follow

---

[10]Cf. Gail R. O'Day, "Intertextuality," in *Dictionary of Biblical Interpretation*, ed. John H. Hayes (Nashville: Abingdon, 1999), 1:548: "Intertextual studies provide a bridge between strictly diachronic and strictly synchronic approaches to biblical texts, challenging traditional notions of influence and causality while at the same time affirming that every biblical text must be read as part of a larger literary context."

[11]For reasons pertaining to both my theological and ecclesial commitments and my literary and historical judgments, I train my main attention on the interplay among the four canonical Gospels (and the Old Testament) rather than on later, "apocryphal" accounts of Jesus' life and teaching. See F. Scott Spencer, *What Did Jesus Do? Gospel Profiles of Jesus' Personal Conduct*

most scholars in mining the rich *contextual* resources of Hellenistic-Jewish and Greco-Roman literature to illuminate the cultural world of the New Testament Gospels. Here, as elsewhere, terms blur together; *intertexts* fund a major part of a work's *contexts*.

Context. Along with encompassing intertextual perspectives, *context* also relates closely to *cotextual* matters. Rather than simply referring to what comes before and after a given text, in this essay, *context* refers more to the wider "worlds" or surroundings in which texts are embedded, with special attention to their *temporal, spatial* and *social* coordinates.[12]

On a literary level, these categories map the settings or backdrops of scenes and their symbolic significance within the "story world."[13] For example, the "tax collectors" in Luke reflect a complex economic (rich milking the poor), political (quislings supporting foreign rule) and religious ("sinners" serving self rather than God and others) web of social relations.

On a historical level, context focuses on the shared temporal, spatial and social environments of the "cultural world" engulfing the Gospels. Although technically *outside* the narratives, such information is presumed by the narrator for all competent readers within the thick milieu of first-century life. For example, the barest of allusions to the destruction of Jerusalem and its temple evoked a painful cluster of memories for post-A.D.-70 Jews (including those confessing Jesus as Lord and Messiah) as poignant as those sparked by the mere mention of 9/11 for twenty-first-century Americans. Moreover, in addition to assuming knowledge of major group conflicts and watershed events of the era, Gospel narratives also take for granted, with little explanation, readers' deep awareness of pervasive ancient eastern Mediterranean cultural values concerning, for example, honor-shame codes, patron-client systems, and dyadic (versus individualistic) identities.[14] But as time marches on memories fade, and implied contexts must be made explicit through historical research. As

---

(Harrisburg, Penn.: Trinity Press International, 2003), pp. 1-24. But, of course, others may opt to stretch their intertextual nets much wider.

[12]For a sustained attempt to map the book of Acts according to this "trifocal cartography," see F. Scott Spencer, *Journeying Through Acts: A Literary-Cultural Reading* (Peabody, Mass.: Hendrickson, 2004).

[13]Cf. Powell, *What Is Narrative Criticism?* pp. 69-83.

[14]See Jerome H. Neyrey, ed., *The Social World of Luke-Acts: Models for Interpretation* (Peabody, Mass.: Hendrickson, 1991); David A. deSilva, *Honor, Patronage, Kinship and Purity: Unlocking New Testament Culture* (Downers Grove, Ill.: InterVarsity Press, 2000).

Green avers, without exaggeration, "Every reading of every New Testament text today is an exercise in intercultural communication and understanding."[15]

Accordingly, literary-oriented approaches that respect the integrity and distinctive presentations of the first-century Gospel narratives are by no means antihistorical or unconcerned with ancient materials outside the text.[16] Yet the historical interests of the narrative critic focus again more on the synchronic social, political and cultural environment surrounding and permeating the text than on the diachronic stages leading up to and generating the document.[17]

Open text. Having started with privileging the final text, recent literary approaches to biblical interpretation by no means end there. Or, put another way, the final text proves to be not so final after all—that is, not a closed, self-evident system of meaning that veritably leaps off the page and hits the reader in the face. Especially in the Protestant tradition, nothing is more basic than an *open Bible open for everyone's engagement.* Any evangelical sermon worth its salt begins with exhorting the congregation, "Open your Bibles to [such and such chapter and verse]," which introduces the focal text for explication and application. While the preacher then does all the talking from an elevated pulpit, the communication event is well out of his or her hands, because all those open Bibles in the pew are being concurrently read and interpreted by independent thinkers. Readers, even within shared cultural and theological traditions, bring their own perspectives, experiences and competencies to bear on the interpretive event. Open texts become open to multiple readings, rereadings and misreadings; not only the preacher but also the texts themselves lose a measure of control, as hearers/readers inevitably both create meaning from texts and are shaped by them. Here we are back to Bakhtinian "dialogism," but now, instead of focusing on interchange among comparative texts, we attend to conversation between texts and their diverse readers. The reader

---

[15]Joel B. Green, "The Challenge of Hearing the New Testament," in *Hearing the New Testament: Strategies for Interpretation,* ed. Joel B. Green, 2nd ed. (Grand Rapids: Eerdmans, 2010), p. 6.

[16]See F. Scott Spencer, "Acts and Modern Literary Approaches," in *The Book of Acts in Its First Century Setting,* vol. 1, *The Book of Acts in Its Ancient Literary Setting,* ed. Bruce W. Winter and Andrew D. Clarke (Grand Rapids: Eerdmans, 1993), pp. 381-414.

[17]Cf. Stephen C. Barton, "Historical Criticism and Social-Scientific Perspectives in New Testament Study," in *Hearing the New Testament: Strategies for Interpretation,* ed. Joel B. Green, 2nd ed. (Grand Rapids: Eerdmans, 2010), pp. 42-47.

factor pushes the notion of dialogue miles beyond a simple two-way variant on the singular "monologue" into an intricate communication network of "polyphonous" (multivoiced) and "heteroglot" (other-tongued) circuits.[18]

If this is true for more or less homogeneous groups, how much more for a highly diversified biblical readership, as increasingly confronts us in our global, Web-wired world? The last few decades have witnessed an explosion of distinctive New Testament readings from various grass-roots as well as academic Asian, Latin American and African perspectives, complementing—and often counterpointing—more traditional Western viewpoints. Such "other" readers tend to lay their social and ideological cards on the table and respectfully insist that others do the same, since we all bring our baggage, for good and ill, to the meaning-making experience. Hiding under a smug cloak of alleged objectivity is getting harder to justify, and it sometimes makes it harder to carry on a civil conversation.

With all these added voices, polyphony easily becomes cacophony, and counterpoint slides into discord. But that is what happens when voices that have been muffled and stifled finally get a hearing. It should not surprise us that nontraditional readers of the New Testament, who have not typically enjoyed access to ecclesiastical power structures, become *resistant readers*, exercising, to various degrees, a *hermeneutic of suspicion* toward texts that have been used to oppress them, but more than that, toward *dominant readers* who have twisted those texts for exploitative purposes.[19] At root the gospel of Christ heralds good news to the poor, the bound, the afflicted and the disenfranchised (cf. Lk 4:16-21). Many of these resistant ("protest-ant") voices are helping the global church rediscover this truth.

Two major strains of resistant New Testament reading have avowed *feminist* and *postcolonial* interests, the former stemming from women's equal rights movements of the 1960-1970s and the latter stoked by the pervasive multicultural, global-village, World Wide Web interfaces of the

---

[18]On the intersection of Bakhtin and biblical studies, see Carol A. Newsom, "Bakhtin," in *Handbook of Postmodern Biblical Interpretation*, ed. A. K. M. Adam (St. Louis: Chalice, 2000), pp. 20-27; and Barbara Green, *Mikhail Bakhtin and Biblical Scholarship: An Introduction* (Atlanta: Society of Biblical Literature, 2000).

[19]The classic work on resistant readers is by Judith Fetterly, *The Resisting Reader: A Feminist Approach to American Fiction* (Bloomington: Indiana University Press, 1978); for an application to New Testament narrative, see Robert M. Fowler, "Reader-Response Criticism: Figuring Mark's Reader," in *Mark and Method: New Approaches in Biblical Studies*, ed. Janice Capel Anderson and Stephen D. Moore, 2nd ed. (Minneapolis: Fortress, 2008), pp. 83-91.

1990s.[20] In biblical studies, both approaches share a *liberationist* agenda, seeking, through critical engagement with the text, to promote the flourishing of historically marginalized and colonized persons on the basis of gender (feminism) and geopolitical (postcolonialism) hierarchies. This big ideological tent covers a wide range of particular expressions, from virtually rejecting the Bible in whole or part as hopelessly oppressive to enthusiastically reclaiming it as an emancipation proclamation. For example, in Matthean studies, major voices have weighed in both (1) exposing the First Gospel as an insidious patriarchal and imperialist manifesto,[21] and (2) emphasizing Matthew's inclusive, egalitarian, *anti*imperial thrust.[22]

With this stress on polyglot perspectives and power dynamics among texts and readers, we jump full-square into the precarious world of postmodern criticism, which staunchly resists absolutist "claims about determinacy, universality, univocity, and legitimacy" in biblical interpretation.[23] In this worldview, an open Bible does not merely allow for multiple readings; it intrinsically demands them! Grand assumptions of narrative unity and coherence are *deconstructed* as interpretive power plays that smooth over contentious voices *within* the text as well as among readers. All texts carry the wild seeds of their own de(con)struction, loose threads of their own unraveling, and the postmodern, deconstructive critic loves to pull the dangling threads to see what happens, both seriously and playfully. Gaps, breaks and tensions in the text are appreciated and teased out more than negotiated and ironed out. Influenced by the French literary theorist Jacques Derrida, postmodern interpreters particularly eschew rigid dualistic, hierarchical, binary-oppositional analytical categories pertaining to

---

[20]These theories are often traced to Edward Said's trenchant analysis in 1978 of East-West political and cultural perceptions. See Edward W. Said, *Orientalism* (New York: Pantheon, 1978).

[21]See, for example, Musa W. Dube, *Postcolonial Feminist Interpretation of the Bible* (St. Louis: Chalice, 2000), pp. 144-55; for discussion and critique of Dube and other postcolonial feminist readings of New Testament texts, see F. Scott Spencer, "Feminist Criticism," in *Hearing the New Testament: Strategies for Interpretation*, ed. Joel B. Green, 2nd ed. (Grand Rapids: Eerdmans, 2010), pp. 303-4, 317-18.

[22]Warren Carter, *Matthew and the Margins: A Sociopolitical and Religious Reading* (Maryknoll, N.Y.: Orbis, 2000); idem, *Matthew and Empire: Initial Explorations* (Harrisburg, Penn.: Trinity Press International, 2001); see helpful discussion of both Dube's and Carter's positions in Fernando F. Segovia, "Postcolonial Criticism and the Gospel of Matthew," in *Methods for Matthew*, ed. Mark Allan Powell (Cambridge: Cambridge University Press, 2009), pp. 216-37.

[23]A. K. M. Adam, "Post-Modern Biblical Interpretation," in *Dictionary of Biblical Interpretation*, ed. John H. Hayes (Nashville: Abingdon, 1999), 1:307.

gender (male/female), ethnicity (native/foreign), government (ruler/subject), class (master/slave) and other sociopolitical relations.[24] Both sides—better, all sides—must be given their due and their say.

So where does all this openness lead us? Into "hermeneutical anarchy,"[25] where anything goes? It certainly runs that risk. Yet nothing requires us to be postmodern, deconstructive purists—pushing instability and indeterminacy to the brink. Common experience and seasoned exegetical practice confirm that meaningful communication happens despite propensities toward misunderstanding; texts support some readings more than others; some voices come through louder and clearer than others; and complex narratives struggle, with varying degrees of success, to arbitrate fairly between different viewpoints. David Seeley strikes a keynote in this regard:

> The point of deconstruction is not to make nonsense of a text, but to locate structural, systemic faultlines within it. . . . Deconstructionist or not . . . what I am suggesting . . . is not a Matthew who is foolish or devious, but rather one who is intelligent, and doing the best he can with materials that possess varying degrees of resistance to one another.[26]

In brief, amid all the panoply of readings an open Bible generates, there remain legitimate "limits of interpretation" constrained by the text itself and authorial intentions, however restricted our access to those might be. Kevin Vanhoozer cites an extreme example from literary critic Umberto Eco, but one that effectively scores its point. As Eco poses: "If Jack the Ripper told us that he did what he did on the grounds of his interpretation of the Gospel according to Saint Luke, I suspect that many reader-

---

[24]See Stephen D. Moore, "Deconstructive Criticism: Turning Mark Inside-out," in *Mark and Method: New Approaches in Biblical Studies*, ed. Janice Capel Anderson and Stephen D. Moore, 2nd ed. (Minneapolis: Fortress, 2008), pp. 95-110; idem, *Poststructuralism and the New Testament: Derrida and Foucault at the Foot of the Cross* (Minneapolis: Fortress, 1994).

[25]Adam, "Post-Modern Biblical Interpretation," 306.

[26]David Seeley, *Deconstructing the New Testament*, Biblical Interpretation Series 5 (Leiden: Brill, 1994), pp. 38-39; cf. Mark K. George, "Postmodern Literary Criticism: The Impossibility of Method," in *Method Matters: Essays on the Interpretation of the Hebrew Bible in Honor of David L. Petersen*, ed. Joel M. LeMon and Kent Harold Richards (Atlanta: Society of Biblical Literature, 2009), p. 467: "Deconstruction undertakes very close readings of texts; in fact, Derrida himself is a model of rigorous exegesis. . . . trac[ing] the logic of texts in order to reveal their instability, the result of inevitable jumps in logic, the surplus meanings of language, and other inconsistencies. The goal of such readings is not nihilism or the end of civilization, critics notwithstanding."

oriented critics would be inclined to think that he read Saint Luke in a pretty preposterous way." I certainly hope so. "There *is* such a thing as misinterpretation," as Vanhoozer concludes.[27]

FOCAL TEXT: MATTHEW 2:7-15

We now seek to apply the approaches sketched above to Matthew 2:7-15, a key text from Matthew's birth narrative; for clarity's sake, we reprise the same textual categories.

Final text. The lack of significant textual variants leaves us a consensus final Greek text. The unparalleled content might also suggest the futility of quests for underlying sources. Historical materials that influenced this text remain concealed in the final product. But that has not deterred scholars from trying to extract sources from it. A leading hypothesis isolates separate "Herod" and "magi" strands, which Matthew stitched together in Matthew 2:1-23, leaving certain breaks and seams as tell-tale markers of his patchwork.[28] As source critics turn redaction critics, asking why and how Matthew brought these two sources together (in not the smoothest fashion), answers typically highlight an aim to contrast sinister and sincere motives for seeking Christ on the part of different professional (royal-priestly/astrological) and ethnic (Jew/Gentile) groups.

Such juxtaposition of characters and viewpoints is quite transparent from a narrative analysis of the final text without proposed source divisions.[29] Thus, beyond grounding Matthew's work on more solid historiographical foundations,[30] we might ask what interpretive gain we derive

---

[27]Kevin J. Vanhoozer, "The Reader in New Testament Interpretation," in *Hearing the New Testament: Strategies for Interpretation,* ed. Joel B. Green, 2nd ed. (Grand Rapids: Eerdmans, 2010), pp. 284, citing Umberto Eco, "Interpretation and History," in Umberto Eco with Richard Rorty, Jonathan Culler, and Christine Brook-Rose, *Interpretation and Overinterpretation,* ed. Stefan Collini (Cambridge: Cambridge University Press, 1992), p. 24; cf. Vladimir E. Alexandrov, *Limits to Interpretation: The Meanings of Anna Karenina* (Madison: University of Wisconsin Press, 2004), p. 65: "I seek to work in the middle space between the impossible goal of complete objectivity and the chaos of unconstrained interpretation."

[28]See Raymond E. Brown, *The Birth of the Messiah: A Commentary on the Infancy Narratives in the Gospels of Matthew and Luke,* updated ed., ABRL (New Haven: Yale University Press, 1993), pp. 104-19, 188-96; John Nolland, "The Sources for Matthew 2:1-12," *CBQ* 60 (1998): 283-300.

[29]See David R. Bauer, "The Kingship of Jesus in the Matthean Infancy Narrative: A Literary Analysis," *CBQ* 57 (1995): 306-23.

[30]Note the thoughtful defense of Matthew as "a creative innovator with conservative instincts" in Nolland, "Sources," p. 300 (cf. pp. 298-300).

from positing discrete Herod and magi traditions behind our text. More to the point, from more recent literary perspectives, we should ask what is potentially *lost* in treating Matthew 2 as a composite account rather than a single continuous story. A key difference surrounds the assessment of gaps and breaks noted above. While the source critic interprets these as patchwork sutures, the narrative critic negotiates them as creative tensions and complex connections. For example, the supposed inconsistencies of Herod's intelligence gathering serve a *narrative* interest of characterizing Herod as paranoid, unbalanced, out of control, flailing around for answers and ultimately exploding in maniacal rage (Mt 2:16). The awkward *seams* in the story thus show the *unraveling* of Herod's character and authority.

Cotext. Building on the narrative-critical viewpoints just offered regarding the seamless—or better, masterly woven—interconnectivity and literary integrity of Matthew 2:7-15 within its immediate cotext of Matthew 2:1-23, I briefly canvass some wider linkages of setting, plot and characters within the first Gospel. I pay particular attention to the coherence of our focal text with (1) the larger birth/infancy narrative (Mt 1–2), which sets the stage for the entire Gospel, and with (2) the closing death/passion narrative (Mt 26–28), which completes the *inclusio* framing the whole story.

First, in terms of geographic *setting*, Matthew 2:7-15 charts a path from Jerusalem to Bethlehem in Judea to Egypt within a longer journey in Matthew 2 commencing outside of Palestine somewhere in "the East" (Mt 2:1) and concluding in Nazareth of Galilee (Mt 2:23). While such a trek could be tracked on a map of the ancient Near East, literary-oriented critics are more concerned with the *symbolic relations* among these places. Ironically, the holy Jewish city of Jerusalem represents the center of opposition to the true Jewish king Jesus, who finds a welcome home in small outlying villages of Judean Bethlehem and Galilean Nazareth and even in the non-Jewish "East" and Egypt, both notorious regions of bitter exile in Israel's history. Matthew's narrative opens with a sweeping genealogy of Jesus Messiah structured around the Babylonian (Eastern) "deportation" (Mt 1:17). At the end of the Gospel, though Jesus enjoys an initial royal reception as he enters Jerusalem (Mt 21:1-9), it soon devolves into confused tumult over his lowly Nazareth origins (Mt 21:10-11), and, by week's end, the whole city clamors for his crucifixion (Mt 27:22-23). After this tragic ending is gloriously overcome by Jesus' resurrection, he launches a fresh plan to extend his mission through his followers. By design, Matthew sets this final episode in *Galilee;* and *from there* Jesus commissions his "worshiping"[31] Galilean deputies "to make disciples of all nations," thus appearing to bypass an inhospitable Jerusalem (Mt 28:16-20; cf. Mt 23:37-39).

Second, regarding *plot,* we may further unpack the *precarious journey* motif that dramatically propels Matthew's story through suspenseful conflict and resolution. The "hard time of it" the magi had on "such a long journey" to the Christ child,[32] though unique in many respects, echoes other excursions and pilgrimages. For example, tracking Jesus' lineage back to the great patriarch Abraham (Mt 1:1-2) and the mention of foremother Ruth (Mt 1:5) recall both of their challenging journeys. In Matthew's closing chapters, Jesus' *itinerant* ministry ends with his ill-fated trip to Jerusalem, as we have seen. In the final days before his crucifixion, he tells provocative parables featuring travel (Mt 21:33-46; 25:14-30); and following his resurrection, he dispatches his disciples as missionary journeymen (Mt 28:19-20). Matthew's plot thus moves along through the plotted movements of its characters.

Speaking of *characters,* the incumbent Judean King Herod, the visiting Eastern magi and the Bethlehem-born Christ child (and parents) resonate with Matthew's wider birth and death narratives, even though, except for Jesus, these figures drop out of the story after Matthew 2. The foreign magi follow in the train of the four foremothers spotlighted in the genealogy (Mt 1:3, 5-6), all of whom have Gentile connections and secure their own survival and preserve the messianic line through some form of divinely sanctioned "trickery" (cf. Mt 2:16).[33] Moreover, the magi pave the way for surprising foreign advocates for Jesus at his trial and death: Pilate's wife affirms Jesus' "innocence" and seeks to deter her husband's judgment

---

[31]The same verb *(proskyneō)* describes the "worship/homage" paid to Jesus by both the magi at the beginning of Matthew (Mt 2:2, 11) and the disciples, female and male, at the end (Mt 28:9, 17).

[32]T. S. Eliot, "Journey of the Magi," in *Collected Poems and Plays: 1909-1950* (Orlando: Harcourt Brace, 1952), p. 68.

[33]See F. Scott Spencer, "Those Riotous—Yet Righteous—Foremothers of Jesus: Exploring Matthew's Comic Genealogy," in *Are We Amused? Humour About Women in the Biblical Worlds,* ed. Athalya Brenner (London: T & T Clark, 2003), pp. 7-30; idem, *Dancing Girls, "Loose" Ladies and Women of "the Cloth": The Women in Jesus' Life* (New York: Continuum, 2004), pp. 24-46; on these ancestors' Gentile roots, see Richard Bauckham, *Gospel Women: Studies of the Named Women in the Gospels* (Grand Rapids: Eerdmans, 2002), pp. 17-46.

against him (Mt 27:19); and a Roman centurion and cohorts at the cross are ultimately stirred to certify Jesus' identity as "Son of God" (Mt 27:54). This major Christological *divine sonship* motif in Matthew—inextricably tied to *covenantal* and *royal* traditions associated with *Israel* as God's son/people (Ex 4:22; Jer 31:9; Hos 11:1) and *David* as God's anointed son/king (2 Sam 7:14; Ps 2:1-7)—reverberates in Matthew 2:7-15 and throughout the birth and death narratives.[34] Amazingly, this Jesus of Nazareth via Bethlehem, though targeted for extermination as an innocent "child" by a ruthless client ruler of Rome and in fact executed as an adult on a Roman cross, is the true viceroy of God's kingdom (not Caesar! not Herod!) and true representative of God's people.

Intertext. Dramatic tales featuring omen-signaled births of heroic figures and "persecution and preservation of a royal child" abound in the ancient world, providing a rich intertextual repertoire for our focal text.[35] Of course the Jewish Scriptures offer the clearest and deepest resonances for Matthew, evidenced in Matthew 2 not only in the four "fulfillment" citations (Mt 2:5-6, 15, 17-18, 23), three drawn from the Old Testament prophets, but also in various allusions to historical narratives surrounding Joseph, Moses, and Balaam, as well as David.[36] Current literary approaches encourage both telescopic (zoom lens) and panoramic (wide angle) engagement with these intertexts, expanding beyond strict chapter-and-verse boundaries of cited passages[37] and attending to points of divergence as much as correspondence. The goal is much less to itemize particular hermeneutical operations Matthew performs on Old Testament texts than to bring Matthew and the Old Testament into rigorous dialogue and debate

---

[34]See collocation of Davidic/messianic/Israelite/filial elements in Mt 1:1, 6, 17, 20; 2:4-6, 15 (birth narrative); 21:4-9, 15; 22:41-46; 26:63-68; 27:11-14, 17, 22, 29, 37, 39-43, 54 (passion narrative); and discussion in Bauer, "Kingship of Jesus"; and R. T. France, *The Gospel of Matthew*, NICNT (Grand Rapids: Eerdmans, 2007), pp. 61-62.

[35]The citation is from Ulrich Luz, *Matthew 1–7: A Commentary,* trans. James E. Crouch, Hermeneia (Minneapolis: Fortress, 2007), p. 119 (cf. pp. 119-20); cf. W. D. Davies and Dale C. Allison, *A Critical and Exegetical Commentary on the Gospel according to Saint Matthew,* ICC 29 (Edinburgh: T & T Clark, 1988), 1:233-34, 258-59.

[36]See Brown, *Birth of the Messiah,* pp. 104-19, 188-96; France, *Gospel of Matthew,* pp. 61-64; David Instone-Brewer, "Balaam-Laban as the Key to the Old Testament Quotations in Matthew 2," in *Built Upon the Rock: Studies in the Gospel of Matthew,* ed. Daniel M. Gurtner and John Nolland (Grand Rapids: Eerdmans, 2008), pp. 207-27.

[37]See Richard B. Hays, *Echoes of Scripture in the Letters of Paul* (New Haven: Yale University Press, 1989).

with each other for purposes of mutual illumination.

Regarding the quotation of Hosea 11:1 in our focal text, "Out of Egypt have I called my son" (Mt 2:15), Matthew follows the Hebrew "my son" *(běnî)* (that is, God's son), from the MT, over the Greek "his children" *(ta tekna autou)*, from the LXX. Thus Matthew connects "God's son" with the individual Son of God, Jesus, who will be taken to Egypt and then return to the Jewish homeland (cf. Mt 2:19-21). Hosea 11:1 clearly focuses on a *people* rather than an individual—specifically the people or children of *Israel*, whom God indeed brought out of Egypt during the days of Moses. Thus, we detect something of a tension between the communal and the individual in Matthew's thought.

Another tension, more problematic, soon comes into play with the verses in Hosea immediately following the sentence Matthew cites. The prophet laments Israel's tragic pattern of *disloyalty* and *disobedience* to God since first being delivered from Egypt (Hos 11:2-7), a pattern that will soon lead them *back to bondage in Egypt* under Assyrian rule (Egypt = Assyria in Hos 11:5). But all is not lost, as God promises to *restore his estranged people* yet again from Egyptian/Assyrian exile (Hos 11:11). Hosea 11 frankly makes one a little dizzy: in the space of a dozen verses, the prophet takes us on a rollercoaster ride with Israel: (1) brought out of Egyptian slavery through God's love (Hos 11:1); (2) forced back into Egyptian/Assyrian bondage because they have rejected God (Hos 11:5); yet still with the hope of (3) returning home from Egypt/Assyria through God's mercy (Hos 11:11). The dizziness all but knocks us out cold when we try to fit all this into *Matthew's* portrayal of the infant Jesus' migration *to Egypt* as a *place of refuge* from violent pursuit and then later being brought back safely *from Egypt* and settling in Galilee (Mt 2:21-22). And here's the real kicker: none of this stressful back-and forth itinerary owes one iota to Jesus' or his parents' faithlessness to God.

So what's a poor interpreter to do? By all means, don't flatten this complex intertextual collage into some mechanical, step-by-step procedure. Instead, by way of illustration, we might suggest a couple of angles amenable to the literary approaches outlined in this essay. First, the tension between the righteous, Spirit-guided individual son Jesus and the rebellious, God-forsaking collective "son" Israel finds some meaningful resolution in a representative typology of Jesus as embodying the people of God and reenacting, as it were, their exodus-exile history, but in a wholly faithful and "fulfilling" way that potentially restores Israel and "saves his people from their sins" (Mt 1:21).[38] Such a reading gains momentum beyond the brief Hosea citation with Jesus' *baptism*, where he reprises Israel's passage through the Jordan waters and "fulfills all righteousness" as God's Spirit-anointed "beloved son" (Mt 3:13-17), and the subsequent *temptation*, where he retraces, so to speak, Israel's forty-year slog through the wilderness (Mt 4:1-2), redeeming their repeated failures to obey and trust God with his staunch resistance of the tempter's schemes as the faithful, Spirit-led "Son of God" (Mt 4:1, 3-11).[39]

Second, the awkward placement, routinely noted by commentators, of "out of Egypt" in Matthew 2:15 just after young Jesus has *entered* Egypt, rather than at the "more logical point"[40] after Matthew 2:19-21, when he leaves Egypt, may not be so clumsy after all from a typological-intertextual and narrative-cotextual perspective. Though Egypt was known in biblical tradition as a place of *refuge* for Israelites escaping persecution in the Promised Land, bitter twists of tragedy and irony complicate this scenario.[41] For example, the patriarch Joseph finds protection, and eventually prominence, in Egypt, but only after he is sold into slavery there by his violent, jealous brothers and endures a period of unjust punishment (Gen 37–50). Something is terribly askew when Israelites must flee from *their own* oppressive rulers in *their own* sacred land to find safety *in Egypt*, which, in the dominant exodus tradition, echoed in Hosea and throughout the Old Testament, constitutes the principal site of Israel's brutal *bondage* (not refuge) that threatens the people's very existence.

So when Matthew first reports Jesus' family's evacuation to Egypt, alarm bells go off: things must be very bad again in the homeland; the

---

[38]Representative typology, in which an Old Testament figure standing for the people of God is applied to Jesus, is also evident with Isaiah's "Suffering Servant" (Mt 8:17) and Daniel's "Son of Man" (Mt 10:23); cf. France, *Gospel of Matthew*, pp. 80-81; Davies and Allison, *A Critical and Exegetical Commentary*, 1:263; Dan McCartney and Peter Enns, "Matthew and Hosea: A Response to John Sailhamer," *WTJ* 63 (2001): 103.

[39]Brown, *Birth of the Messiah*, 214-15; John Nolland, *The Gospel of Matthew: A Commentary on the Greek Text*, NIGTC (Grand Rapids: Eerdmans, 2005), p. 123.

[40]France, *Gospel of Matthew*, 79.

[41]Cf. George M. Soares-Prabhu, "Jesus in Egypt: A Reflection on Mt 2:13-15, 19-21 in the Light of the Old Testament," *EstBib* 50 (1992): 241: Biblical Egypt "is both a place of refuge in distress or danger . . . and a 'house of bondage.' . . . The word thus carries ambiguous associations."

tyrannical "king of the Jews" is on the rampage; we have to make a hasty flight to Egypt to survive; but are we just going from the frying pan to the fire? We know what happened in Egypt long ago during Moses' days. Are we safe anywhere in the empire? It sure would be nice in these desperate times to hear a word of hope—sooner rather than later. *And Matthew provides just that via Hosea:* no sooner does he mention the ominous departure to Egypt than he also signals the sure return "out of" there with the biblical hope for God's mighty deliverance, covenant love and patient guidance to reclaim the land of promise. It takes a few verses in Matthew to report the actual homecoming of Jesus' family, but we can wait, even through the unspeakable horror of the slaughtered innocents (Mt 2:16-18), clinging, if only by a thread, to the biblical hope of restoration.

Context. Having just considered the symbolic *spatial* context of Matthew 2:7-15 in conjunction with the Egypt-focused intertext of Hosea 11:1, we turn to concentrate on its *social* context, particularly concerning the identity and status of the famed magi in Matthew's narrative and cultural environments. At this point, it is methodologically significant that two established, frontline Matthean *literary-oriented* critics, Mark Allan Powell and Warren Carter, have pioneered fresh understandings of the magi's *social* roles within the ancient world as well as Matthew's story. Simply put, popular profiles of the magi (*magoi* in Greek) as *kings* and/or *wise men* fall apart under contextual analysis.[42]

Our starstruck seekers of the Jewish king are themselves never called "kings" in Matthew's text, and the *magoi* term—most literally rendered "magicians"—carries no royal status. In fact, typically they *serve* manipulative monarchical interests as sycophants and favor-granters, and when they fail to satisfy the despotic king, as often happens, they are quickly ridiculed, replaced and even exterminated. Witness the expendable *magoi* of Nebuchadnezzar, who barely escaped execution by the maniacal Babylonian king for their failure to interpret his disturbing dream (Dan 2:1-24). This case bolsters Powell's conclusion that court magicians were "victims of injustice, specifically at the hand of the king they serve," and "more oppressed *by* royal power than possessed *of* it."[43] Notice, too, that this biblical example features a *non-Israelite*, even *anti-Israelite*, king ill-served by

---

[42]Powell, *Chasing the Eastern Star*, pp. 131-96; Carter, *Matthew and the Margins*, pp. 73-89.
[43]Powell, *Chasing the Eastern Star*, pp. 142-43 (emphasis original).

ineffectual wizards.[44] The exercise of magical arts (sorcery, astrology, divination, necromancy etc.) was characteristic of the "abhorrent practices" of idolatrous nations, which Israel must avoid at all costs (Deut 18:9-14; cf. Is 47:12-15).[45] Hence magi appear doubly ostracized in the Bible—as reprobate Gentiles alienated from and antagonistic to Israel, and as "menial underlings"[46] exploited by their capricious royal masters.

The dealings of King Herod with the Eastern magi in Matthew fit this basic pattern, with the twists that Herod is the so-called *Jewish* king (but hardly serving Israel's interests), and the magi are *visiting* rather than local court servants. Far from rolling out the red carpet, Herod summons them "secretly" and promptly dispatches them on his self-serving mission (Mt 2:7-8); and when they fail to report back, as he had ordered, Herod explodes in a vicious rage à la Nebuchadnezzar (Mt 2:16). Herod and the magi occupy opposite poles of the social spectrum: the former representing the elite establishment; the latter, the subservient stranger. The magi *may* approximate Herod's *economic* status; but their offer of precious gifts to Jesus does *not necessarily* signal their wealth (cf. "gold" in Mt 10:9) and, in any case, scarcely impresses Herod. As Carter stresses, the social gap is stretched even wider by the magi's "liminal," "mobile," nomadic status versus Herod's entrenched Judean power base.[47] Far from being viewed as exotic dignitaries traveling from afar on a diplomatic mission, the magi appear more as quixotic, wandering star chasers—literally and figuratively—following an astrological sign in quest of a newborn celebrity ("star search").

The real *royal* juxtaposition in Matthew 2 is not between Herod and magi, but between Herod and *Jesus,* the true messianic regent of Israel. But here too a yawning spatial and social gap opens up: Jesus is identified six times in Matthew 2:7-15 as simply "the child [*pais*]," a weak, vulnerable, "helpless, dependent"[48] figure, who might easily be squashed by the pow-

---

[44]Other examples following the same cues include magicians of Pharaoh (Ex 8:18-19) and the mercenary diviner-sorcerer Balaam (Num 22–24).

[45]This pattern continues in the New Testament with the manipulative Samaritan *magos* Simon (Acts 8:9-24) and the Ephesian practitioners of worthless magical arts (Acts 19:18-19); another *magos* in Acts, variously known as Bar-Jesus and Elymas, was Jewish in origin but described as a "false prophet" and "son of the devil" (Acts 13:6-12).

[46]Powell, *Chasing the Eastern Star,* p. 145.

[47]Carter, *Matthew and the Margins,* pp. 73-74, 80-82.

[48]Dorothy Jean Weaver, "Power and Powerlessness: Matthew's Use of Irony in the Portrayal

erful tyrant Herod. This "child" is fixed firmly *outside* the Herodian hub
of power within the holy city. Jesus' context thus correlates more closely
with the "marginal magi"[49] than the hierarch Herod.

Open text. While socioliterary analysis complicates binary *royal* opposition between Herod and magi as bad Judean *king*/good Eastern *kings*, it
still retains a patent *moral* dichotomy between *good/bad characters*. And
who can argue with that? Feigning a desire to "pay Jesus homage," the dia-
bolical Herod only aims to eliminate a potential rival (Mt 2:8, 13, 16),
whereas the magi truly honor the Christ child with gifts worthy of a king
(Mt 2:11). As David Bauer states:

> Matthew draws clearly the lines of demarcation between the *magoi* (and
> Joseph) on one side and Herod (and "all Jerusalem" . . .) on the other. . . .
> [Jesus] necessarily evokes a response that separates persons into two
> categories: those who seek to kill him, and those who worship him.
> Matthew allows no middle ground between Herod and the *magoi*.[50]

But is the ground really so flatly and smoothly graded? Or does it begin, on closer analysis, to shift, destabilize and *open up* under our feet? At
this point we do well to reappraise the traditional "wise men" portrait of
the magi in contrast with the foolish, misguided Herod—or, more simply,
the *wise/fool* polarity common in Israel's wisdom tradition and, indeed, in
Matthew's Gospel (Mt 7:24-27; 10:16; 24:45; 25:1-10). The magi are never
dubbed "wise men" (*sophoi* or *phronimoi*); respected *sages* in the ancient
Near East were serious scholars of sacred wisdom texts and of the natural
world and were not dabblers in magic. Sages might study the stars and
other celestial phenomena (astronomy), but they would not follow the stars
(astrology), traipsing after some comet to an unknown destination. Thus
"magicians" in the biblical world were associated more with bungling court
fools than with respected counselors.[51]

Surely Matthew's magi break the mold: do they not show their consummate wisdom in following the star to Bethlehem and paying homage to

---

of Political Leaders," in *Treasures New and Old: Contributions to Matthean Studies*, ed. David
Bauer and Mark Allan Powell, SBLSymS 1 (Atlanta: Scholars, 1996), p. 185 (cf. pp. 184-87);
cf. Carter, *Matthew and the Margins*, pp. 80-81.

[49]Carter, *Matthew and the Margins*, p. 82.

[50]Bauer, "Kingship of Jesus," pp. 319-20.

[51]Powell, *Chasing the Eastern Star*, pp. 148-56.

God's true king? Well, yes they do, eventually, but along the way they hardly prove to be the sharpest tools in the box. Notice the following "gaffes" of the magi.[52] First, they follow the star as far as Jerusalem and start inquiring about the new king's birthplace in the power center where the current King Herod rules (Mt 2:1-2)! Then they become Herod's "secret" agents, clueless about his nefarious intentions. The magi get their Bethlehem destination from Herod; and only "when they heard the king, they set out" (Mt 2:9), resuming their "OnStar" trail to the special child's house. Finally, after the Bethlehem visit, the magi must be warned in a dream not to return to the devious Herod, implying that, without this divine intervention, that's exactly what they would have done. At the end of the day, our "wise guys" are hardly worthy of the name. They appear more like naive fools blindly following the shiny star here and the shady king there. Their hearts are in the right place with their humble worship of Jesus, but their minds are more than a little muddled. To be sure, by returning east "by another way" (Mt 2:12), they have the last laugh—out-tricking the devious Herod, making him play the fool (Mt 2:16). But the final result is anything but funny, as the outsmarted king erupts in unspeakable outrage, venting his frustration against myriad innocents (Mt 2:16). Foolishness has fatal consequences in Matthew 2—a foolishness in some sense *shared* by Herod and magi. Though distinct in their *intentions*, the magi function partly as Herod's *accomplices* in his terrorist plot. Character boundaries become more porous, more *open* than we might have noticed on a first reading or on a more pious, traditional reading. But let the reader beware! Let the reader not play the fool, but be "wise as a serpent" (Mt 10:16).

And let the reader not presume that I have tracked all the vast horizons opened up by our rich focal text. I have sketched a few constructive and deconstructive lines of interpretation seen through recent literary and postmodern lenses. But of course I have still seen fundamentally through *my eyes*—my male, middle-class, middle-aged, Western professorial, parental, churchly (etc.) eyes. Others will doubtless see things quite differently, and for that I can only be gratefully open to the fresh insights they will provide.[53]

---

[52]Cf. Spencer, *Dancing Girls*, pp. 37-39.
[53]E.g., see J. Enuwosa, "The Soteriological Significance of Matthew 2:15 in His Use of Hosea 11:1 from an African Perspective," *African Theological Journal* 24 (2001): 39-52; Aquiles

CONCLUSION

Though insisting that literary/postmodern approaches to biblical interpretation can happily coexist and even cooperate with historical studies, this essay has stressed their primary focus on synchronic connections in, around and in front of the text in contradistinction to diachronic developments behind the text. By way of review, we may replot this synchronic matrix of the literary/postmodern view in terms of *centrifugal motion*— tracking its various textual orientations concentrically, or inside out.

We begin by closely concentrating on the linguistic, stylistic, structural and thematic elements of the *final text* under investigation. From there, we widen out to connective *cotexts* within the larger narrative or book; then to suggestive *intertexts*, especially those ripe for fruitful "canonical conversation";[54] then to informative *contexts* in the surrounding rhetorical and cultural environments; and finally, to expansive horizons of different readers from diverse social locations and power positions, staking their distinctive claims to a dynamic *open text*. But no sooner do we fan out as far as we dare than we are drawn back in, with centripetal force, bringing our enhanced perspectives to bear on interpreting the focal text. And once in motion, the hermeneutical pulsing continues apace: popping back and forth, zooming in and out, cropping and recropping the picture, getting the full measure of forest and trees; and in the process we begin to find the text opening—and closing—in fresh and sometimes surprising ways.

But the proof of this, as with other hermeneutical processes, is in the product. Theory is well and good—but what is the exegetical payoff? Our literary/postmodern analysis of Matthew 2:7-15 especially (1) delineated part of the thick web of intertextual strands woven by the creative-redemptive God with and through chosen "sons" Israel and Jesus; and (2) deconstructed, with the aid of corrective contextual lenses, facile dichotomies between Herod and magi, Jew and Gentile, wise and foolish, in the interest of resisting premature and hypocritical judgments of the "other"— or in Matthean terms, dislodging the log in one's own eye in order to see

---

Ernesto Martínez, "Jesus, the Immigrant Child: A Diasporic Reading of Matthew 2:1-23," *Apuntes* 26 (2006): 84-114.

[54]Robert W. Wall, "Reading the New Testament in Canonical Context," in *Hearing the New Testament: Strategies for Interpretation*, ed. Joel B. Green, 2nd ed. (Grand Rapids: Eerdmans, 2010), pp. 384-86.

others justly and honestly, eye to eye (Mt 7:1-5). I make no claim, however, that these points can only be discovered through literary/postmodern methods, and I anticipate that scholars from other viewpoints (such as those in this volume!) will provide confirmation and critique.

3

The Philosophical/ Theological View

Merold Westphal

Philosophical hermeneutics" refers especially to the interpretations of interpretation given in the work of Hans-Georg Gadamer[1] and Paul Ricoeur.[2] The usual story is that they are the continuation of a history that runs through Friedrich Schleiermacher,[3] Wilhelm Dilthey[4] and Martin Heidegger.[5] But Immanuel Kant needs to be added to the list.[6]

There are three things philosophical hermeneutics is not. First, it is not just about interpreting the Bible. Schleiermacher noted three disciplines in which interpretation plays a major role: theology, law and classical philology (literary criticism). He sought to develop a theory that covered all

---

[1]See especially Hans-Georg Gadamer, *Truth and Method*, 2nd ed. rev., trans. Joel Weinsheimer and Donald G. Marshall (New York: Crossroad/Continuum, 1989/2004). These two versions of the 2nd edition have, unforgivably, different pagination and will be cited as *Truth and Method* x/y, where x = 1989 and y = 2004.

[2]See especially Paul Ricoeur, *Hermeneutics and the Human Sciences*, ed. and trans. John B. Thompson (New York: Cambridge University Press, 1981).

[3]See especially Friedrich Schleiermacher, *Hermeneutics and Criticism and Other Writings*, trans. and ed. Andrew Bowie; Cambridge Texts in the History of Thought (New York: Cambridge University Press, 1998).

[4]See especially Wilhelm Dilthey, "The Rise of Hermeneutics," in *Selected Works*, vol. 4, *Hermeneutics and the Study of History*, ed. Rudolf A. Makkreel and Frithjof Rodi (Princeton: Princeton University Press, 1996).

[5]See especially Martin Heidegger, *Being and Time*, trans. John Macquarrie and Edward Robinson (New York: Harper & Row, 1962).

[6]See especially Immanuel Kant, *Critique of Pure Reason*, trans. Norman Kemp Smith (New York: St. Martin's Press, 1961). For an overview of this prehistory, with special attention to Schleiermacher and Heidegger, see my *Overcoming Onto-theology* (New York: Fordham University Press, 2001), chaps. 8, 6 and 3, in that order.

three, abstracting from what might be distinctive to any one of them. Ricoeur calls this the "*deregionalization*" of hermeneutics.[7]

Second, philosophical hermeneutics is not restricted to interpreting texts. Taking that practice as its point of departure, it extends interpretation to the writing of history (Dilthey), to nonliterary works of art (Gadamer), to meaningful action (Ricoeur) and to the entire domain of human understanding (Heidegger). Ricoeur calls this the "*radicalization*, by which hermeneutics becomes not only *general* but *fundamental*."[8]

Finally, philosophical hermeneutics is not a method or strategy for interpreting. It is not a how-to discipline with rules or at least heuristics to follow. Dilthey had defined hermeneutics in just this way: "Such *rule-guided understanding of fixed and relatively permanent objectifications of life is what we call exegesis or interpretation. . . .* Hermeneutics is the theory of the rules of interpreting written monuments."[9]

But Gadamer undertakes a different task. "The hermeneutic phenomenon is basically not a problem of method at all."[10] It is concerned with a different kind of knowledge and truth from that of modern science. The task "is not to develop a procedure of understanding, but to clarify the conditions in which understanding takes place. But these conditions do not amount to a 'procedure' or method which the interpreter must of himself bring to bear on the text; rather they must be given."[11] Accordingly, "I did not intend to produce a manual for guiding understanding. . . . My real concern was and is philosophic: not what we do or what we ought to do, but what happens to us over and above our wanting and doing."[12] In other words, the question is: what is going on, often behind our backs, when we interpret texts and other phenomena?

THE HERMENEUTICAL CIRCLE

The most fundamental answer to the above question given by philosophical hermeneutics is this: we are working within a hermeneutical circle. The idea goes back to Schleiermacher. When we come to interpret texts

---

[7]Ricoeur, *Hermeneutics and the Human Sciences*, p. 44.
[8]Ibid.
[9]Dilthey, "Rise of Hermeneutics," pp. 237-38.
[10]Gadamer, *Truth and Method*, p. xx/xxi.
[11]Ibid., p. 295/295.
[12]Ibid., p./pp. xxviii/xxv-xxvi.

we presuppose and bring with us an idea of the whole that guides our reading of the parts. This anticipation may involve the genre of the work, the purpose of the author, the work's central theses and so forth. It functions, in Kantian language, as the a priori element in interpretation. It is the condition for the possibility of finding meaning in the text. Yet it is importantly unlike the Kantian a priori. Kant thinks the forms of sense and the categories of understanding are universal and necessary, ahistorically at work in human thought in all times and places. But within the hermeneutical circle the a priori elements, the presuppositions and anticipations, are not fixed and permanent. Rather, in light of the interpretations to which they give rise, they are revisable or replaceable.[13] The two elements of guiding presuppositions and guided interpretations mutually condition each other. This is the hermeneutic circle. We can think of it this way: the movement from twelve to six on a clock represents the shaping of the latter by the former, while the movement from six back to twelve represents the reshaping of the former by the latter.

For Schleiermacher, this hermeneutical circle is primarily a matter of whole and part both at the textual or grammatical level and at the psychological or biographical level. But the grammatical and the psychological dimensions of interpretation are also in a circular relation. Our understanding of the author is shaped by our reading of the text and vice versa. Neither is an independent variable; each is conditioned by the other. It's like two basketball players. The defender responds to the moves of the player with the ball and in so doing is a dependent variable; but the player with the ball is also a dependent variable who responds to the moves of the defender. For example, he may drive forward if the defender plays up close, or shoot if the defender backs off.

For Heidegger, Gadamer and Ricoeur, the hermeneutical circle is a matter of presuppositions in general and does not focus on the whole-part relation. The claim is that, in any domain where interpretation takes place, there is no such thing as presuppositionless thought. Since the latter ideal is typical of "modern" philosophy, philosophical hermeneutics is a postmodern tradition, especially as it extends to the domain of interpretation from texts, to the social or human sciences, and even to the natural

---

[13]Gadamer, *Truth and Method*, pp. 190/189, 267/269.

sciences.[14] Understanding is relative to the presuppositions of the interpreter. If the interpreter adopts a particular method or strategy, that method, so far from rendering thought presuppositionless, is a systematic presupposition about the best way to understand the matter in question.

Gadamer expresses this by writing, "And there is one prejudice of the Enlightenment ["modern" philosophy] that defines its essence: the fundamental prejudice of the Enlightenment is the prejudice against prejudice itself, which denies tradition its power."[15] Etymologically, "prejudice" is pre-judice, prejudgment, or presupposition. The attempt to rehabilitate prejudice is the acknowledgment that interpretation is never presuppositionless and that there are "legitimate prejudices"[16] that help us to understand what we are interpreting. The prejudice that the molecular structure of blood or muscle tissue is best studied with a microscope rather than the naked eye or a telescope is a legitimate prejudice; it helps us to see what we want to see. The task is to sort out the good presuppositions from the bad ones, not the impossible task of escaping them altogether.

> The overcoming of all prejudices, this global demand of the Enlightenment, will itself prove to be a prejudice. . . . If this is true, the idea of an absolute reason is not a possibility for historical humanity. Reason exists for us only in concrete, historical terms. . . . In fact history does not belong to us; we belong to it. . . . *This is why the prejudices [pre-judgments] of the individual, far more than his judgments, constitute the historical reality of his being.*[17]

The rehabilitation of prejudice restores to tradition its power because to a very large extent, prejudices (presuppositions, a priori anticipations) are carried and transmitted by traditions. Sometimes we choose to belong to a particular tradition. The methods of interpretation explained and illustrated in this volume represent such choices. Without denying this, Gadamer emphasizes the passive, involuntary ways in which we are shaped by traditions. For example, someone born and raised as an Anglican can

---

[14]On this latter point, see Westphal, *Overcoming Onto-theology*, pp. 118, 159, and idem, *Whose Community? Which Interpretation? Philosophical Hermeneutics for the Church* (Grand Rapids: Baker Academic, 2009), pp. 83-85.

[15]Gadamer, *Truth and Method*, p. 270/273.

[16]Ibid., p. 277/278.

[17]Ibid., pp. 276-77/277-78. The emphasis here is Gadamer's.

choose to convert to Catholicism, or vice versa. But those born and raised in any such religious tradition will already have been shaped by it in ways they did not choose and of which they are not fully aware. This applies to political, social and cultural traditions as well.[18]

Our inextricable embeddedness within history and its traditions means that our interpretations arise from particular locations. We are always somewhere (in semantic and cognitive space)[19] and never achieve what has been called "the view from nowhere." Just as in ordinary vision, where we are standing determines what we can see and what we cannot see of the object at which we are looking. This embeddedness means that understanding is necessarily plural, partial and perspectival.

This observation raises the important question of the objectivity of interpretation. We shall return to that question after we see another way in which it arises. For the moment, however, this observation will have to suffice. Perspectivism in epistemology is especially associated with Nietzsche, and this frightens some religious believers. Is it inherently atheistic? No, not at all. The passionately Christian writer Søren Kierkegaard is also a perspectivist. What this view commits one to is the essential finitude of human understanding. Unlike God, we cannot see the whole picture but only a finite subset of the facets of the real. Differently located subjects will have access to different facets and will have different blind spots; there will be an inevitable plurality of interpretations. Nietzsche says no one is God. Kierkegaard says someone is God, but not we. They are in full agreement on the fact crucial for perspectivism: we are not God and our understanding cannot be presuppositionless and absolute.

If, as Christians believe, we are fallen (even as believers) as well as finite, the problem will be exacerbated. Our vision will not just be limited; but it will be distorted as well. In wickedness we suppress the truth (Rom 1:18).[20] This is a reminder of Luther's formula, *simul justus et peccator* ("si-

---

[18]Gadamer's term for this is *wirkungsgeschichtliches Bewusstsein*. Our consciousness is not autonomous; it is historically effected, the working of history on and in us. This is why we belong to history (as subjects formed by historical processes) before it belongs to us (as the object of our investigation and interpretation).

[19]That is, we are always within some horizon of meaning and truth where certain meanings and certain truths are self-evident or axiomatic or at least privileged.

[20]That sin has wounded our intellects and is thus an epistemological category is the underlying presupposition of my treatment of Marx, Nietzsche and Freud in *Suspicion and Faith: The Religious Uses of Modern Atheism* (New York: Fordham University Press, 1998). In a secular vo-

multaneously righteous and a sinner"). Although we may be justified, we remain sinners. A Christian racist, for example, is operating within a hermeneutical circle whose a priori assumptions about minority persons reflect the fall and not just created finitude.

THE AUTHORITY OF THE AUTHOR

A highly contentious theme in philosophical hermeneutics concerns the degree to which the author determines the meaning of a text. Gadamer and Ricoeur deny to the author unilateral agency in fixing that meaning. This is another site at which the question of objectivity (universal validity) of interpretation will be raised. But first we must look at the debate.

For the "romantic" hermeneutics of Schleiermacher and Dilthey, the author fixes the meaning of the text because the author's inner experience simply is the meaning of the text. What makes this hermeneutics "romantic" is an expressivist theory of language.[21] The purpose of language is to give outer expression to the inner experience of the speaker or writer. The purpose of interpretation, consequently, is to reverse the movement, to uncover the inner experience by means of its outer expression. Thus, Dilthey writes, "We therefore call understanding that process by which we recognize, behind the signs given to our senses [inscriptions and utterances], that psychic reality of which they are the expression." Along with "psychic reality" Dilthey speaks of "psychic life" and "psychic facts" as the goal of interpretation. He says that process of interpretation is the "re-creation" of the author's inner experience, and speaks of "being able to feel the states of mind of others."[22] Early on in his writings, Ricoeur adopts this view when he speaks of interpreting as "sympathetic re-enactment in imagination," or as "a re-enactment in sympathetic imagination."[23]

This view is called "psychologism" in hermeneutics, and it is now widely rejected. In my opinion, the most eloquent repudiation of it comes from Nicholas Wolterstorff:

---

cabulary, they point to ways in which sin distorts our intellectual activities and, to this degree, they are to be taken seriously by believers.

[21]For a brief account of romantic expressivism as a theory of human nature, see Charles Taylor, *Hegel and Modern Society* (New York: Cambridge University Press, 1979), pp. 1-3.

[22]Dilthey, "The Rise of Hermeneutics," pp. 235-38.

[23]Paul Ricoeur, *The Symbolism of Evil*, trans. Emerson Buchanan (New York: Harper & Row, 1967), pp. 3, 19. Ricoeur will move away from this view as we'll shortly see.

The myth dies hard that to read a text for authorial discourse is to enter the dark world of the author's psyche. It's nothing of the sort. It is to read to discover what assertings, what promisings, what requestings, what commandings, are rightly to be ascribed to the author on the ground of her having set down the words that she did in the situation in which she set them down. Whatever the dark demons or bright angels of the author's inner self that led her to take up this stance in public, it is that stance itself that we hope by reading to recover, not the dark demons and bright angels.[24]

In other words, the goal of interpretation is not some private experience behind the text but the public speech acts of the author. What did the author say? Ricoeur puts it this way: "As the model of text-interpretation shows, understanding has nothing to do with an *immediate* grasping of a foreign psychic life or with an *emotional* identification with a mental intention."[25] We want to know "what the text is about . . . the kind of world opened up by the depth semantics of the text. Therefore what we want to understand is not something hidden behind the text, but something disclosed in front of it."[26]

The abandonment of psychologism does not, however, settle the question of authorial authority. Wolterstorff proposes a hermeneutics of authorial discourse in which the hermeneutical question is, "What speech act (assertion, promise, request, command, question, etc.) did the author perform by inscribing the text?" The answer to that question is the meaning of the text, the hermeneutical goal. Gadamer, however, would see this as still too close to romantic hermeneutics as it makes the author the unilateral source of a text's meaning. By contrast Gadamer writes,

Every age has to understand a transmitted text in its own way, for the text belongs to the whole tradition whose content interests the age and in which it seeks to understand itself. The real meaning of a text, as it speaks to the interpreter,[27] does not depend on the contingencies of the

---

[24]Nicholas Wolterstorff, *Divine Discourse: Philosophical Reflections on the Claim That God Speaks* (New York: Cambridge University Press, 1995), p. 93.

[25]Ricoeur, *Hermeneutics and the Human Sciences*, p. 220.

[26]Ibid., p. 218; cf. pp. 53, 93, 111, 141-42. Schleiermacher is ambiguous. He sometimes speaks the language of psychologism and sometimes sounds more like Wolterstorff and Ricoeur here. See my *Overcoming Onto-theology*, pp. 115-16. The phrase "intention of the author" is also ambiguous since it can refer to the author's inner psychic life or to what it was the author was trying to say about something, however ineptly.

[27]Gadamer emphasizes that texts address us, speak to us. See Gadamer, *Truth and Method*, pp.

author and his original audience. It certainly is not identical with them, for it is always co-determined *also* by the historical situation of the interpreter. . . . Not just occasionally but always, the meaning of a text goes beyond its author. That is why understanding is not *merely* a reproductive but always a productive activity *as well*. . . . It is enough to say that we understand in a *different* way, if *we understand at all.*[28]

Ricoeur agrees with Gadamer. He writes that

writing renders the text autonomous with respect to the intention of the author. What the text signifies no longer coincides with what the author meant. . . . The "world" of the *text* may explode the world of the *author*. . . . [The text] transcends its own psycho-sociological conditions of production and thereby opens itself to an unlimited series of readings, themselves situated in different socio-cultural conditions. . . . The text must be able, from the sociological as well as the psychological point of view, to "decontextualise" itself in such a way that it can be "recontextualised" in a new situation—as accomplished, precisely, by the act of reading.[29]

Viewing the Pauline corpus as a single text provides a helpful example of the world of a text exploding the world of the author. The Pauline corpus presents a world in which the institution of slavery is acceptable for Christians, but in a different context, that Pauline "text," especially Galatians 3:28, has helped to explode for most Christians the world in which slavery is acceptable. But how shall we understand Gadamer's claim that interpretation is at once *reproductive* by being faithful to what the author originally said to the original readership and *productive* by transgressing the bounds of that relation? Surprisingly (to some, at least), a helpful answer comes from Jacques Derrida. To interpret cannot consist in merely reproducing what the author said to the original, intended audience.

282/283, 373-74/366-67 and 395/396. See James Risser, *Hermeneutics and the Voice of the Other: Re-reading Gadamer's Philosophical Hermeneutics* (Albany: SUNY Press, 1997).

[28]Gadamer, *Truth and Method*, pp./p. 296-97/296; cf. p. xxxi/xxviii. Emphasis has been added to "also," "merely" and "as well." E. D. Hirsch Jr. is so eager to make the author sovereign that in quoting Gadamer he completely leaves out the "merely" and the "as well," making Gadamer say that interpretation is only productive and never reproductive. He then complains that for Gadamer the interpreter can ignore the text and attribute to it any meaning that may be desired. I expect more responsible reading from my undergraduates. See E. D. Hirsch Jr., *Validity in Interpretation* (New Haven: Yale University Press, 1973), p. 249.

[29]Ricoeur, *Hermeneutics and the Human Sciences*, p. 139; cf. pp. 91, 108, 203.

This moment of doubling commentary [the reproductive moment] should no doubt have its place in a critical reading. To recognize and respect all its classical exigencies is not easy and requires all the instruments of traditional criticism. Without this recognition and this respect, critical production [of an interpretation] would risk developing in any direction at all and authorize itself to say almost anything. But this indispensable guardrail has always only *protected*, it has never *opened*, a reading.[30]

Wolterstorff, surprisingly to some because of his desire to focus on authorial discourse, gives us a good example. Mom says at the dinner table, "Only two more days till Christmas." In a single utterance she performs two distinct speech acts. To the children she offers a word of comfort. To her husband she gives a word of exhortation—"Get off your duff and get your Christmas shopping done!" This doesn't take us beyond the relation between the author and the original addressees or the intended audience, since Mom was addressing both. It will not work to say there was a single speech act informing all hearers of the time left until Christmas; for neither speech act is reducible abstractly to an act of informing but is concretely either an act of comforting or of exhorting. Similarly Paul may be seen as giving words of comfort to those Galatians who have not strayed from the gospel he taught them, while directing words of warning to those who have.

But suppose Mom doesn't know that Dad is around. He is not an addressee of her speech act and not part of the intended audience. He is, unknown to her, in a nearby room where he overhears what she says. Now we have a situation that is analogous to the situation of historical distance between a writer and an audience unknown to the author. The hearer or reader who is outside the scope of the intended original audience is in a different context and legitimately construes the writing differently. Knowing what the original exchange was serves as a guardrail. Dad cannot interpret her words as a request for new diamond earrings. But he would badly be confusing himself with the children if he took her words to be words of comfort in his context.

Wolterstorff's hermeneutic is consistent with this example: "I cannot in

---

[30]Jacques Derrida, *Of Grammatology*, trans. Gayatri Chakravorty Spivak (Baltimore: Johns Hopkins University Press, 1976), p. 158.

general just assume that what God said to me in my situation, or to my group in our situation, by way of this text is exactly the same as what God said to other earlier readers and interpreters in their situations."[31] Accordingly in interpreting the Bible he calls for a double hermeneutic corresponding to two questions. The first hermeneutic asks, "What *did* the human author say to the original audience?" The second hermeneutic asks, "What *is* God *saying* to us here and now through these words of Scripture?"

The first hermeneutic serves as the Derridian guardrail. It places constraints on interpretation. One simply cannot interpret Galatians as an ode to human virtue. What Derrida calls doubling commentary, reproducing the original meaning as best we are able, is what theologians call exegesis. But on the model offered to us by Gadamer, Derrida and Wolterstorff (strange bedfellows to be sure), exegesis is not interpretation but only the preliminary, but indispensable, stage of interpretation. One must go on to the second hermeneutic and ask what God is saying to us now through the text whose original meaning we have tried to reproduce. This is the productive dimension of interpretation, grounded in but not identical with the reproductive dimension. There may well be methods that are useful for the first hermeneutics. Derrida calls them "the instruments of traditional criticism."[32] But it is far from clear that there can be a method for the second hermeneutics.

These analyses show why E. D. Hirsch is wrong to complain that unless the author is made the sole determiner of textual meaning the text is indeterminate and "anything goes."[33] What he fails to see is that a text is both determinate and indeterminate. It places limits on interpretation, to be sure, but it also remains open to different meanings in different contexts unanticipated by the author.

Ricoeur cites Gregory the Great as saying, "Scripture grows with its readers."[34] Ricoeur suggests that various methods of exegesis, by stopping

---

[31]Wolterstorff, *Divine Discourse*, p. 185. With reference to the statements of Mom to the children and to Dad, he writes, "What's not so obvious is that by way of a single locutionary act [utterance or inscription] one may say different things to different addressees" (p. 55).
[32]Derrida, *Of Grammatology*, p. 158.
[33]See Hirsch, *Validity in Interpretation*, especially chap. 1 and appendix 2.
[34]André LaCocque and Paul Ricoeur, *Thinking Biblically: Exegetical and Hermeneutical Studies*, trans. David Pellauer (Chicago: University of Chicago Press, 1998), p. xi.

in effect at the first hermeneutic, reduce the meaning of Scripture to what it was once upon a time. He objects that in the name of methodological rigor, rigor mortis has set in:

> Cut off from its ties to a living community, the text gets reduced to a cadaver handed over for autopsy. . . . It is almost as though one were to give the funeral eulogy of someone yet alive. The eulogy might be accurate and appropriate, but it is nonetheless "premature," as Mark Twain might have put it.[35]

The same principle applies to literary and legal interpretation. Although in the interpretation of Homer, or Shakespeare, or the United States Constitution, there is no appeal to a living speaker, God, as when we take the Bible to be the Word of God, the two questions remain: What did it mean then, in those circumstances? What does it mean now, in different circumstances?

Gadamer makes an important point here. We do not read culturally significant texts like these as artifacts in a museum. We want to be addressed by them, to be guided as the psalmist was guided, who wants to be led to human flourishing by the law of God. We want insight on who we are, how we ought to live, where the green pastures are and how we might find our way to them. Gadamer makes this point by insisting that application is an essential ingredient in interpretation.[36] This point means that the historical gap between ourselves and the original audience is not to be eliminated but bridged or, to use Wolterstorff's language, that the double hermeneutic will be necessary.

Ricoeur agrees. In saying that the goal of interpretation is not some inner psychic life hidden behind the text but the world that emerges out of and in front of the text, "what has to be understood is not the initial situation of discourse, but what points toward a *possible* world. Understanding has less than ever to do with the author and his situation. It wants to grasp the *proposed* worlds opened up by the references of the text."[37]

Especially in legal and theological contexts, "conservative" hermeneutics wants to reduce interpretation to what Wolterstorff calls "the first her-

---

[35]Ibid., p. xii.
[36]Gadamer, *Truth and Method*, pp. 307/306-341/336.
[37]Ricoeur, *Hermeneutics and the Human Sciences*, p. 218 (emphasis added).

meneutic" and what Derrida calls "doubling commentary." If we ask "Why?" The answer is clear: a desire for objectivity and a fear of relativity. If there isn't a single, fixed meaning to the text won't that mean that "anything goes," that the text becomes a "wax nose" to be shaped to order by any subjective preference?[38] Apart from the fact that this tends to reduce the text to a lifeless object, Ricoeur's "cadaver handed over for autopsy," an obvious problem with this move is that it presupposes that the first hermeneutic can neutralize the hermeneutical circle and itself be presuppositionless and thereby objective. The history of biblical interpretation renders this wish more than a little chimerical.

OBJECTIVITY OR RELATIVITY?

We have seen two contexts in which the relativity of interpretation emerges in philosophical hermeneutics. In looking at the hermeneutical circle, we have seen the relativity of interpretation to the reader's presuppositions and the traditions by which they have been formed. In looking at the question of authorial authority, we have seen the relativity of interpretation, in the second hermeneutic, to the reader's historical context. This latter location surely includes the locations generated by tradition-borne and individual presuppositions, but it suggests a richer and more concrete analysis of the "where" from which interpretation arises. It will include, for example, the problems and questions that press upon a particular community at a particular time, what we might call a community's agenda.

Since Dilthey sought to develop a hermeneutics for historical writing, he was especially aware of historical relativity, and it scared him. He asks, "But where are the means to overcome the anarchy of opinions that then threatens to befall us?"[39] When he wrote these words, he had already answered his own question. Interpretation must be "*scientific*" by being raised to the level of "objectivity" and "universal validity."[40] This suggests that

---

[38]See Wolterstorff, *Divine Disclosure*, chap. 13, for the wax nose metaphor.

[39]Wilhelm Dilthey, "Reminiscences on Historical Studies at the University of Berlin," in *Selected Works*, vol. 4, *Hermeneutics and the Study of History*, ed. Rudolf A. Makkreel and Frithjof Rodi (Princeton: Princeton University Press, 1996), p. 389. In the sociology of knowledge, this anxiety is called "the vertigo of relativity." See Peter L. Berger and Thomas Luckmann, *The Social Construction of Reality: A Treatise in the Sociology of Knowledge* (Garden City, N.Y.: Doubleday, 1966), p. 5, and idem, *A Rumor of Angels: Modern Society and the Rediscovery of the Supernatural* (Garden City, N.Y.: Doubleday, 1970), p. 32.

[40]Dilthey, "Rise of Hermeneutics," pp. 235-38.

differences of interpretation due to differences of context (subjectivity) should be eliminated so that everyone comes up with the same interpretation, relative to no particular context (universal validity). This is to be done by means of method, just as in the natural sciences.[41] As we have seen above, for Dilthey interpretation is to be guided by rules, and hermeneutics is the theory of those rules, the teacher of the method.

In the twentieth century, hermeneutical objectivism has been affirmed and argued by such as Emilio Betti, Jürgen Habermas and E. D. Hirsch Jr.[42] The desire by "conservative" legal scholars and theologians to reduce interpretation to exegesis is motivated by the desire for objectivity and uniform interpretation, assuming that somehow the reading of historically remote texts for their original meaning can be presuppositionless and context-neutral.

The desire for objectivity in the face of the "vertigo of relativity"[43] is not hard to understand. However, the opposite of "relative" is "absolute," and there is good biblical and theological reason to be suspicious of that desire. Only God is absolute. We simply are relative, both finite by virtue of creation and fallen by virtue of our sinful distortion of creation. Thus there is the very real danger that in desiring to free our knowledge from every relativity we are forgetting the difference between ourselves and God, saying, in effect:

> I will ascend to heaven;
> I will raise my throne above the stars of God. . . .
> I will make myself like the Most High. (Is 14:13-14 NRSV)

Philosophical hermeneutics is helpful here, offering a middle way between the claim to absolute understanding that may well be philosophically untenable and theologically unholy and the different-strokes-for-different-folks relativism that says, "Anything goes!"[44]

---

[41]But see n. 10 above.

[42]In addition to Hirsch, *Validity in Interpretation*, see the essays by Betti and Habermas, along with commentary on them, in Josef Bleicher, ed., *Contemporary Hermeneutics: Hermeneutics as Method, Philosophy and Critique* (London: Routledge and Kegan Paul, 1980).

[43]See n. 39.

[44]Those who flee to the former to escape the latter might well first pause to see if anyone actually holds to the latter view. Nietzsche, for example, does not. He is a radical perspectivist, but he does not think that Christianity and Platonism are just as good as his philosophy of the will to power.

Gadamer offers two models for interpretation that neither require "universal validity" nor entail "anything goes!" The first is performance, as when a pianist plays Beethoven's Appassionata Sonata or an actor plays Shakespeare's character King Lear. The pianist cannot play F-sharps where the score has D's; and the actor cannot say, "How sharper than a serpent's tooth it is to have a thankless wife!" rather than "thankless child." The score and the script are guardrails that give a determinacy to the text and place quite definite constraints on interpretation. Yet two interpretations of the sonata, say Artur Schnabel's and Alfred Brendel's, will be different from each other, and two interpretations of Lear, say Sir Laurence Olivier's and Kenneth Branagh's, will be different from each other. Yet all four are likely to be judged excellent, even world class. We expect different interpretations, and while we may prefer one to the other, we do not conclude that only one is right and all the others wrong in order to avoid the vertigo of relativity. This doesn't mean that it is impossible to get it wrong, only that there is not only one "right" interpretation.

We are familiar with this in relation to different translations of the Bible. The best texts we can produce of the original languages and the best lexicons we can produce of those languages provide a sturdy guardrail that constrains translation. Yet there will be a plurality of translations that will be judged both reliable and in certain respects exemplary. We may have a favorite, but we do not conclude that all the others are mistaken wherever they differ. We expect, and we often prize, the variety of readings provided by different translations. We compare them, hoping thereby to get closer to the original in a language we may not be able to read.

This brings us to Gadamer's second model, which is simply translation in general. What has just been said about translations of the Bible is true for translations of other kinds of texts as well. There surely are ways of getting it wrong, of violating the constraints of the guardrail, but just as there is no one and only right way to play Beethoven or Lear, so there is no one and only right translation of a classic text. For Gadamer every translation is an interpretation, and every interpretation is a translation, even if it stays within a single language.

The conclusion of philosophical hermeneutics is that we need not flee the relativity of interpretation and the plurality it entails, partly because it is an inescapable product of the human condition and partly because it can be enriching. We do not have to deny the existence of weeds to say, "Let many flowers bloom."

BIBLICAL INTERPRETATION

It will long since have been evident that there can be no such thing as an interpretation of Matthew 2:7-15 or any other biblical passage in the light of philosophical hermeneutics. It is not a method, a strategy, a procedure, much less a set of rules that tells us how to go about interpreting the Bible. I could offer some thoughts of my own about the passage, but they would not be expressions or examples of philosophical hermeneutics. What we can say from the perspective of philosophical hermeneutics could include the following:

First, we should expect a variety of interpretations, in both the first and second hermeneutics, since interpreters will be differently located.

Second, in any particular interpretation, we will often be able to identify the methodological and theological locations, in other words, the presuppositions, at work. Sometimes, however, an interpreter's location will be at a confluence of a variety of methodological and theological traditions, and no single one will stand out.

Third, regarding Matthew's allusion to Hosea 11:1 (but also to many similar passages), philosophical hermeneutics gives no guidance as to whether Matthew finds a straightforward prediction in Hosea, or a type that is duplicated and deepened in Jesus, or a text calling for allegorical embellishment.

Fourth, we can ask whether interpretations we run across, including those in this volume, practice the double hermeneutic called for by our strange bedfellows, Gadamer, Derrida and Wolterstorff.

I want to apply this last question especially to sermon preparation, for it is in sermons that most of us are exposed to interpretations of the Bible other than our own (which may be largely dependent on other sermons we have heard). Using this double hermeneutic in sermon preparation requires that the sermon have a tight and visible connection with the text. Too often sermons remind one of the diner who complained to the cook that there wasn't much in the chicken soup to justify its name. The cook was surprised, since, as he said, "The chicken walked through the soup twice—with galoshes on." Too many sermons have walked through the text twice—with galoshes on. The results are likely to be (1) a report of the interesting events in the life of the pastor during the previous week, (2) a motivational speech with occasional biblical allusions, (3) a rant on some pet peeve or pet project of the pastor's with little or no relation to the text dishonestly announced as the basis for the sermon, or (4) a repetition of some very general Christian truths which, in the absence of any detectable relation to the text, tend to become platitudes, providing neither comfort nor challenge.

I have been calling the first hermeneutic "exegesis," though I mean by this more than linguistic and conceptual analysis. I mean the entire task that Gadamer calls reproductive and that Derrida calls doubling commentary. It seeks to answer the questions, "What did the text mean then? What was the author trying to say to the immediately intended readership, and how would they have understood the speech acts inscribed in the text?"

We can call the second hermeneutic "application." Here the question is no longer what Isaiah or Matthew or Paul were trying to say to their contemporaries, but what God is saying to us now through the words they wrote.

There are three things to notice here. First, "application" is a misleading name if we take it to mean the transition from theory to practice. The movement is rather from then to now. Pauline epistles often have a first "half" of heavy "theology," followed by a second "half" of "ethical" exhortations and guidance. The hermeneutical task in *both* cases is to hear what God is saying to us now, in different contexts, through what human authors said to their readerships then.

Second, this second hermeneutic presupposes that God continues to speak to the people of God through the words of Scripture, but it does not presuppose any particular theory of the inspiration of the Bible. It only presupposes that however the Holy Spirit was involved in the production of the biblical text he continues to be involved as teacher and interpreter to those who read it today.[45]

Third, although philosophical hermeneutics generally abstracts from differences between scriptural, literary and legal texts, we are here dealing

---

[45]See Wolterstorff, *Divine Disclosure*, chap. 3.

with a distinctive of the biblical text. For literary and legal texts, the second hermeneutic does not ask what Homer or Shakespeare or the Founding Fathers are saying to us today. These authors are long dead. We ask what the *texts* they wrote have to say to us today. However, when we say that the Bible is the Word of God we refer not only to God's role in producing the text such that God is the ultimate author of it; but we also say that God is alive and speaking to us today. Given who this author is, listening for that word is of utmost existential importance.

To take this double task seriously in sermon preparation is not easy. It calls for thorough preparation in terms of theological education and ongoing reading and for the hard work of struggling with each text as Jacob struggled at Peniel with the man of whom he later said, "I have seen God face to face" (Gen 32:30 NRSV). Good preaching requires serious and sustained wrestling.

It becomes easier, much too easy, in fact, if the task is reduced to either the first or the second hermeneutic. We saw Ricoeur earlier complain that when interpretation is reduced to what is here called "exegesis," the text is reduced to a museum artifact, a once-upon-a-time, lifeless curiosity. When this bad habit spills over into preaching, the result is to collapse the historical distance between ourselves, on the one hand, and the world of the author and the original addressees, on the other. The congregation is asked to pretend that they are nomads, or exiles, or dwellers in Corinth under the Roman Empire. There is something unreal about this, and the pretense cannot be maintained; or, to the degree that it is, the new world of the believer turns out to be less a new creation in Christ but the old, historical world of long ago. There is an aura of unreality about the Christian life. For example, we are not confronted with whether or not to eat food offered to idols, but we are confronted with whether or not to eat foods that are harmful to ourselves and our children.

N. T. Wright worries about the opposite simplification of the task: "the fact that exegetes have often been more concerned to apply the text to their own times than to understand it within its own."[46] When this bad habit spills over into preaching, the congregation is returned to its real home in the world(s) of the present. However, where the applications have not been

---

[46]N. T. Wright, *Paul: In Fresh Perspective* (Minneapolis: Fortress, 2005), p. 61.

faithful to the reproductive task (doubling commentary), the productive application to contemporary life is less likely to be the word of God than the preferences of the pastor, some political party, or some cultural constructions. If, in the previous case, the text is honored by being rendered lifeless, in this case the text is honored by being ignored.

Some preachers are embarrassed to preach from an elevated pulpit. Their motives are better than their understanding. The elevation of the pulpit signifies not the elevation of the clergy over the laity but the supremacy of Scripture over the whole congregation, clergy and lay. Preachers should explain this clearly to their congregations. Then, they should do the hard work to be as worthy as possible of their calling, to be the human voice through whom once again, week after week, God addresses the people of God through the words of Scripture. No doubt prayer is an important part of this scary responsibility, but if philosophical hermeneutics is on the right track, it also involves the hard work of the double hermeneutic.

CONCLUSION

Philosophical hermeneutics takes us, philosophically speaking, from the modern to the postmodern world. For two reasons that is not as scary as it might sound to some. In the first place, philosophical modernity has not been especially friendly to biblical faith. What is sometimes referred to as the Age of Reason or the Enlightenment project is all too often a promise of a certainty, an objectivity and an autonomy that are at once undeliverable and unbiblical insofar as they are denials of our creaturely finitude and our fallenness. Although some of the thinkers frequently associated with postmodernism are in effect or explicitly atheists, there is nothing inherently secular about the challenge they pose to philosophical modernity. It is often the case that biblical reasons for parting company with modernity are as compelling as secular reasons, or more so.

Like bad politics, the enchantments of modernity appeal to both our fears and our arrogance. We would like to have the guarantees it purports to provide that our interpretations are the right ones and "theirs," whoever "they" may be, are simply wrong. We are afraid to really admit to ourselves that faith is not sight, and that our insights and interpretations are at best partial and perspectival and at worst perverse. In this fear we may lapse into the arrogance that assumes that we, perhaps with the help of some method, can see the world and the biblical text definitively, as if we were God. The good news, of course, is that God is God and we are not. Philosophical hermeneutics can be read as a nontheological reminder of this important theological truth. Then theology can remain a matter of Word and Spirit and not of Word and Method.

4

The Redemptive-Historical View

Richard B. Gaffin Jr.

The terms *redemptive history* and *salvation history* have a fairly broad currency.[1] My own use will emerge as I sketch the basic elements, as I understand them, of a redemptive-historical (or biblical-theological) approach to interpreting the Bible and then discuss the selected passage in Matthew 2.

IDENTIFYING A REDEMPTIVE-HISTORICAL APPROACH

The German terms *Heilsgeschichte* and *heilsgeschichtlich* ("salvation history" and "salvation-historical") appeared for the first time about the middle of the nineteenth century.[2] The approach taken in this chapter, however, does not stem, at least in any direct or substantial way, from the developments that gave rise to this term and its English equivalents above. Rather, its roots are earlier, in developments present in the Reformation and in post-Reformation Protestant, especially Reformed, theology. More specifically, it builds directly on the work of Geerhardus Vos (1862-1949), first occupant of the then newly created chair of biblical theology at Princeton Theological Seminary from 1893 until his retirement in 1932.[3]

---

[1]Robert W. Yarborough, "Paul and Salvation History," in *Justification and Variegated Nomism*, vol. 2, *The Paradoxes of Paul*, ed. D. A. Carson et al. (Grand Rapids: Baker, 2004), pp. 297-322, 339-42. His focus on Paul has a broader sweep and also notes how various salvation-historical views have been and continue to be contested or rejected, often emphatically.

[2]A. Josef Grieg, "A Critical Note on the Origin of the Term Heilsgeschichte," *ExpTim* 87 (1976): 118-19, cited in Yarbrough, "Paul and Salvation History," p. 310.

[3]Richard Gaffin, "Vos, Geerhardus," in *Dictionary of Major Biblical Interpreters*, ed. Donald K. McKim (Downers Grove, Ill.: InterVarsity Press, 2007), p. 1016. Some material from this article (pp. 1016-19) is incorporated in this chapter. See also my introduction to Geerhardus

Writing in 1916, Vos observed of Reformed theology that

> it has from the beginning shown itself possessed of a true historic sense
> in the apprehension of the progressive character of the deliverance of
> truth. Its doctrine of the covenants on its historical side represents the
> first attempt at constructing a history of revelation and may be justly
> considered the precursor of what is at present called biblical theology.[4]

Vos saw essential continuity between his own work in biblical theology or,
using what he deemed a more suitable designation, "History of Special
Revelation,"[5] and this earlier appreciation of the historical character of
revelation present in Reformation and post-Reformation orthodoxy. His
work is an effort to provide an alternative to the dominant view of biblical
theology that had begun emerging a century earlier with the late Enlightenment (e.g., Johann Philipp Gabler). This view is wedded to the historical-critical method with its controlling commitment to the rational autonomy of the interpreter and its correlative rejection of Protestant
orthodoxy's understanding of the Bible's canonicity and inspiration/divine
authorship (e.g., the seminal and highly influential work of Johann Sa-
lomo Semler).[6]

At the same time, Vos recognized the need for more adequate attention
to the historical aspect of revelation than was present in earlier Protestant
orthodoxy. That perception is reflected in two statements that bracket his
life's work, the first from his 1894 Princeton inaugural address and the
second written in retirement: "It is certainly not without significance that
God has embodied the contents of revelation, not in a dogmatic system,
but in a book of history, the parallel to which in dramatic interest and
simple eloquence is nowhere to be found"; and, "The Bible is not a dogmatic handbook but a historical book full of dramatic interest."[7] Along
with the positive point expressed, the "nots" in these statements point to

---

Vos, *Redemptive History and Biblical Interpretation: The Shorter Writings of Geerhardus Vos,* ed.
Richard B. Gaffin Jr. (Phillipsburg, N.J.: P & R, 2001), pp. ix-xxiii.

[4]Vos, *Redemptive History and Biblical Interpretation,* p. 232.

[5]Geerhardus Vos, *Biblical Theology: Old and New Testaments* (Grand Rapids: Eerdmans, 1948),
preface, p. 23. Vos rarely uses the expression "redemptive-historical" (or "redemptive history").
Still, it aptly describes his hermeneutical approach.

[6]For further information on Gabler and Semler, see William Baird, *History of New Testament
Research,* vol. 1, *From Deism to Tübingen* (Minneapolis: Fortress, 1992), pp. 117-26, 183-93.

[7]Vos, *Redemptive History and Biblical Interpretation,* p. 23; idem, *Biblical Theology,* p. 26; "The
circle of revelation is not a school, but a 'covenant'" (Vos, *Biblical Theology,* p. 17).

Vos's concern to redress perceived traces of an intellectualistic or unduly notional understanding of revelation within Protestant evangelicalism more broadly and his own tradition of confessional Reformed orthodoxy in particular, a tradition to which he remained fully and cordially committed. The hermeneutical stance elaborated in this chapter is in this tradition.[8]

BASIC ELEMENTS OF A REDEMPTIVE-HISTORICAL OR REVELATION-HISTORICAL APPROACH

1. *Distinct from but always within the context of his self-revelation in creation and history (or "general revelation"), God's special revelation has two basic modes: deed revelation and word revelation.* These modes may also be distinguished as redemptive deed and revelatory word, or redemption and (verbal) revelation.[9] Though the point cannot be developed here, apart from general revelation and a biblical understanding of creation and general revelation, redemptive special revelation is basically unintelligible.

2. *Redemption/revelation is historical.* It has its truth and validity as it occurs in history, as multiple historical events that together constitute an organically unfolding whole, a completed history.[10] This history begins when into God's original creation, which he saw was "very good" (Gen 1:31), human sin subsequently enters with its curse-incurring and death-dealing consequences (Gen 3). In its organic and progressive[11]

---

[8]The opening chapter of his *Biblical Theology* ("Introduction: The Nature and Method of Biblical Theology," pp. 11-27) is still among the best introductory statements of a redemptive-historical approach; cf. "The Idea of Biblical Theology as a Science and as a Theological Discipline," in Vos, *Redemptive History and Biblical Interpretation*, pp. 3-24.

[9]As these interchangeable expressions show, "redemption" and "revelation" overlap in their senses. The distinction between verbal and nonverbal is irreducible, but God's nonverbal acts are always revelatory and his verbal activity is redemptive, that is, in the interest of his realizing his redemptive purposes.

[10]"Redemption" ("salvation") here and throughout refers to its completed, once-for-all accomplishment *(historia salutis)*, in distinction from its ongoing application, its individual and corporate appropriation *(ordo salutis)*.

[11]"Progressive" is not the most apt word here, particularly if taken in the sense of smoothly evolving advancement or steady and untroubled improvement. This description hardly characterizes Israel's history. Marked by constantly recurring decline and apostasy and eventual exile, it is apparently the opposite of redemptive history, *Unheilsgeschichte*. Yet "progressive" is properly retained in view of the inexorable forward movement of this history, in all of its twists and turns, toward its intended goal, Christ.

unfolding, it incorporates the history of Israel, his covenant nation, until it culminates in Christ. The history of (verbal) revelation may be
viewed as a stream within and conforming to the contours of the history
of redemption, in its uneven movement marked by epochal junctures
(e.g., exodus, Davidic monarchy, exile).

3. *Jesus Christ in his person and work, centered in his death and resurrection
   (e.g. 1 Cor 15:3-4), is the culmination of the history of redemption (revelation).* As its final goal, realized "in the fullness of time" (Gal 4:4), Christ
   is also, either explicitly or implicitly, its ubiquitous focus throughout,
   from beginning to end. He does not simply end that history. As the
   Triune God's final and supreme redemptive self-revelation, he is history's consummation, nothing less than its eschatological omega point,
   by which redemption restores creation from the ravages of sin and perfects it.

4. *The subject matter of revelation is redemption.* Revelation—excluding
   prefall, preredemptive revelation in Eden[12]—is the interpretation of redemption, as revelation either attests or explains, describes or elaborates. There is no hard and fast line between these two revelatory functions; both are always selective and so interpretive. In this sense (verbal)
   revelation is derivative, relative to God's nonverbal redemptive and revelatory acts. Verbal revelation is always focused on or oriented toward
   God's activity in history as Creator and Redeemer.

   This generalization only holds with an important qualification. As
   verbal revelation documents and explains God's activity in history, so it
   also points beyond history to his antecedent self-existence (aseity) in its
   ultimate incomprehensibility and the ultimate impenetrability of his
   all-controlling pretemporal purpose ("before the foundation of the
   world," e.g., Eph 1:4). As the one who dwells with the contrite and the
   humble, he is, as such, the one who lives in a high and holy place and
   inhabits eternity (Is 57:15), whose thoughts and ways, ultimately, are as

---

[12]This exclusion hardly means that special revelation prior to the fall has little or no significance
for the history of redemption. In fact, as special revelation is unintelligible apart from general
revelation, so redemptive revelation is inexplicable apart from God's purposes in view for the
creation, especially for his image-bearing creatures, from the beginning. The consummation
forfeited in Adam has been realized in Christ (e.g., Rom 5:12-19; 1 Cor 15:21-22, 44-49).
"The eschatological is an older strand in revelation than the soteric" (Vos, *Biblical Theology*, p.
157). Redemption restores and perfects creation.

high above ours as the heavens are above the earth (Is 55:9). God is not exhausted in his redemptive/revelatory activity, nor is his person actualized in that activity. As Creator and Redeemer he is more than Creator and Redeemer, infinitely and incomprehensibly more.

With that essential qualification kept in view, however, invariably God's speech is related to his actions, his word to his work. Given the fall, redemptive deed is the raison d'être for the revelatory word. "Revelation is so interwoven with redemption that, unless allowed to consider the latter, it would be suspended in air."[13]

5. *Scripture is itself revelation, not somehow less than revelation.* The Bible may be fairly characterized as a record of the actual history of redemption (revelation), as a witness to revelation. As such its own origin, including each of the constituent documents as well as the whole, is an integral part of this history, of which it is the permanent record and witness. In this sense, the redemptive-historical approach in view here is a canonical approach. Our only revelatory access to the history of redemption is the biblical canon.[14] The limits set by the canon provide the boundary to what we can know by revelation about the history of redemption.[15]

6. *To focus the preceding points hermeneutically: As revelation is the interpretation of redemption, so the interpretation of Scripture is always derivative, the interpretation of interpretation.* Biblical interpretation is not autonomous assessment of a distanced textual datum but receptive appropriation of the God-authored preinterpretation of redemptive history consummated in Christ, preinterpretation that includes the revelation of his will for loving service to him and others.

---

[13]Vos, *Biblical Theology*, p. 15.

[14]For a redemptive-historical approach to issues of canon, see esp. Herman N. Ridderbos, *Redemptive History and the New Testament Scriptures* (revised trans. Richard B. Gaffin Jr. (Phillipsburg, N.J.: P & R, 1988), pp. vii-x, 1-47; cf. my "The New Testament as Canon," in *Inerrancy and Hermeneutic: A Tradition, a Challenge, a Debate*, ed. Harvie M. Conn (Grand Rapids: Baker, 1988), pp. 165-83.

[15]In this regard, John H. Sailhamer's basic criticisms of Vos seem misplaced (*Introduction to Old Testament Theology: A Canonical Approach* [Grand Rapids: Zondervan, 1995], pp. 67-70, 111-12; cf. pp. 153, 185, 215). Vos's interest is not a reconstructed history that goes beyond the Bible, but the history that is the subject matter of the biblical text, however factored, considered within the context of the canon as a whole and what "by good and necessary consequence may be deduced from Scripture" (*Westminster Confession of Faith*, 1.6).

Any valid interpretive approach ought presumably to be appropriate to the text and its subject matter. On that assumption—self-evident, it would seem, even in our hermeneutically turbulent and contentious times— Hebrews 1:1-2 provides a particularly instructive biblical instance of and thus warrant for the redemptive-historical approach just sketched. Along with a couple of other closely correlative references to God's speaking in Hebrews 2:2-3 and Hebrews 3:5-6,[16] this declaration both substantiates and facilitates elaboration of the points made above about a redemptive-historical approach.

> God, having formerly spoken at many times and in various ways to our fathers by the prophets, has in these last days spoken to us through the Son.[17]

This declaration covers, umbrella-like, all, or at least much, of what the writer goes on to say in the rest of the document. As such, it also provides a sweeping, overarching perspective on God's speech or revelation, a controlling perspective arguably shared, more or less explicitly, by the other New Testament writings. Several interrelated factors may be noted about this assertion, reducible to the definitive nuclear assertion "God has spoken."

First, revelation is in view as a historical phenomenon. Further, revelation has taken place as an ongoing history, a history that unfolds in two basic stages. The contrast between the old and new covenants prominent later, especially in Hebrews 8–10, is fairly seen as implicit or anticipated in the twofold division of Hebrews 1:1-2 as well as in Hebrews 2:2-3 and Hebrews 3:5-6. The writer's revelation-historical outlook is as such a covenant-historical outlook.

Second, God's Son is the consummate and integrating focus of this history. The history of revelation is both complete and a unity. God's having spoken "in the Son" is his "last-days" speaking. Any thought that this speech might be surpassed or superseded is plainly foreign, not only here but everywhere else in the New Testament as well. God's Son-speech has nothing less than eschatological finality.

---

[16]Likewise with *theos* as the explicit or implied subject of forms of *laleō*.
[17]Scripture translations are my own unless otherwise noted.

The history completed by the Son is also unified in him. Overall christocentric unity is particularly clear in Hebrews 3:5-6. Here instead of the prophets (Heb 1:1) or angels (Heb 2:2), Moses stands for the whole of the old covenant, for the law (Heb 2:2) as well as the prophets.[18] As such, in his servant capacity "in all God's house,"[19] he is the key witness to "the things that would be spoken,"[20] that is, to those things spoken by God in Christ, to God's future last-days speech in the Son.[21] All told, the old functions as a witness that looks toward and anticipates the new. Explicitly, more clearly than in the other two passages, God's revelation in his Son terminates the covenant-historical house-building process, as he is its completion. He is the *telos* (cf. Rom 10:4), the goal that gives unity and coherence to the history of revelation, old covenant as well as new, in its entirety.

This focus on Christ, as comprehensive and completing as it is unifying, shows clearly that the history of postfall revelation, considered in terms of its subject matter, is in fact the history of *redemption*. God's speech "in the Son" is "salvation . . . spoken through the Lord" (Heb 2:3), with both its realized and still future (Heb 9:28) aspects. He embodies, climactically and uniquely, both word (verbal) revelation and deed revelation (cf. Jn 1:1) with the former interpreting the latter.

Third, this Christ-centered history, complete and unified in its basic two-stage unfolding, is marked by diversity. The diversity of old-covenant revelation is accented by the adverbs *polymerōs* and *polytropōs* and by their position in the Greek text as the opening words in Hebrews 1:1. If, as seems likely, a distinction is to be made between them (they occur nowhere else in the New Testament), the first has in view different parts or instances (different times and places), the second, different modes and genres.[22]

Whether or not directly within the purview of the text, this emphasis on diversity accommodates and even sponsors the kinds of concerns that

---

[18]"Moses" (Heb 2:2, 5) as well as "prophets" (Heb 1:1) and perhaps "angels" (Heb 2:2) are each plausibly taken as synecdochic for the whole of the old-covenant period, both before and after Moses.

[19]Note, *all* he does is in God's *one, single* covenant-house building project in history.

[20]The implied speaker of the substantive future passive participle *tōn lalēthēsomenōn* is God.

[21]Cf. Jn 5:46, "If you believed Moses, you would believe me, for he wrote about me" (NIV).

[22]"At many times and in many ways" (ESV), "at many times and in various ways" (NIV).

have increasingly occupied biblical interpretation in the modern period, but with a basic proviso. For the author of Hebrews, literary interests and historical interests are never competitive or even independent of or indifferent to each other. Genre factors, no doubt semantically significant, and essential theological considerations do not override or supplant but subserve more basic redemptive-historical concerns as those concerns always involve reliable reference to actual historical occurrence.

The diversity of God's speaking is a function of its taking place "through the prophets." With an eye to the preposition "through" *(en)* we may speak advisedly of the prophets as instruments. The way the author of Hebrews views the activity of Old Testament authors is instructive in this regard. In Hebrews 4:7, the quotation from Psalm 95 (Ps 94 LXX) is what God (the implied subject from Heb 4:3-5) is saying "through David," while in Hebrews 3:7 the same quoted material is, without qualification, what "the Holy Spirit says." The Holy Spirit utilizes David such that what David says in the psalm is primarily and more ultimately what the Holy Spirit says. Similarly in Hebrews 9:8 both the actual Day of Atonement ritual and the account of it in Exodus and Leviticus seen together (word focused on deed) are what "the Holy Spirit indicates." In Hebrews 10:15, the promise of the new covenant in Jeremiah 31 is what the Holy Spirit "bears witness to" and "says."[23]

A redemptive-historical orientation requires giving careful attention to this instrumental role of the human authors of the biblical documents, but that is not due to captivation with the "humanity" of Scripture or at the expense of downplaying its primary divine authorship. A concern with revelation as a historical process should inevitably draw one to the varied human instrumentality that is an integral factor in giving shape to that process. The distinguishing characteristics and peculiarities of each of the human authors and what they have written are essential to revelation as historically differentiated. But divine and human authorship, the unity and diversity of Scripture, are not in tension. Attention to the writings of the various authors in all their respective individuality and particularity serves to disclose in its rich diversity the organic unity and coherence of the Bible as revelation. Nothing in Hebrews suggests that diversity in-

---

[23]Accordingly, Hebrews supports something like the classical distinction between God as the primary author of Scripture and the human authors as secondary.

volves conflict or disunity. Every indication is to the contrary. Hebrews 9–10 particularly works out the unity of the old-new relationship in terms of the organic tie between type and its antitype, shadow and the reality shadowed.

A couple of final observations may serve to round out this presentation of the redemptive-historical method.

First, a primary concern of this method is fidelity to the fundamental hermeneutical proposition given with the Reformation's *sola Scriptura,* the well-known "Scripture interprets Scripture."[24] The sense of this self-interpretation, which focuses the general interpretive principle that a text is to be interpreted in the light of its context, is that the diverse teaching of Scripture, as God's written Word, is a concordant unity. Any one part is located within an expanding horizon of God-given contexts that, with whatever imponderables involved, serve to clarify. Biblical revelation is self-elucidating because in all its parts it is a unified whole.

This overall unity, considered in terms of its subject matter, is redemptive-historical. Biblical revelation faithfully records the actual history of special revelation. That history, in turn, is unified as the ongoing interpretation of redemptive history, which, centered on Christ, unfolds organically, like a maturing organism. Exegesis controlled by this redemptive-historical, eschatological framework, established by Scripture itself, will not only be prone to reach more thoroughly biblical conclusions but will also tend to begin with the right questions. Not only for Paul and Hebrews but also for the other biblical writers the principle holds, "The historical was first, then the theological"[25]—and, we may add, with the theological, the literary.

Second, redemptive-historical interpretation is marked by a sense of *continuity* between the interpreter today and the New Testament writers. While essential categorical differences—inspired and uninspired, canonical and noncanonical—need to be properly maintained and safeguarded, at the same time both the New Testament writers and their interpreters share a common concern in their subject matter, the history

---

[24]The concept is already clear in Luther, e.g., Martin Luther, "The Bondage of the Will," in *Martin Luther's Works,* vol. 33, *Career of the Reformer* III, ed. J. J. Pelikan, H. C. Oswald and H. T. Lehmann (Philadelphia: Fortress, 1972), pp. 25-26. My thanks to Carl R. Trueman for this reference.

[25]Geerhardus Vos, *The Pauline Eschatology* (Grand Rapids: Baker, 1979), p. 41.

of redemption, and they share that concern from within basically the same redemptive-historical, eschatological context, bracketed by Christ's resurrection and his return. The church today, like the Thessalonian church, is made up of those who have "turned to God from idols to serve the living and true God, and to wait for his Son from heaven, whom he raised from the dead, Jesus who delivers us from the wrath to come" (1 Thess 1:9-10 ESV). An indispensable aspect of this "waiting service" of the church is the interpretation of the New Testament, along with the Old, as the redemptive-historically focused, Christ-centered revelation sufficient for the life and needs of the church in every generation as long as this interim continues. If one grants that theology ought to be essentially exegetical, based on interpretation of Scripture, then along with due consideration of differences also involved (apostolic and postapostolic), awareness of this redemptive-historical continuity, compounded in terms of context as well as content, tends to ensure a more rigorously biblical focus and more biblical boundaries to the entire theological enterprise.

MATTHEW 2:7-15

Since the most-discussed issue facing interpretation of Matthew 2:7-15 is the use of Hosea 11:1 in Matthew 2:15, before we look at this passage, some general though necessarily brief comment about the New Testament use of the Old is in order.[26]

The New Testament use of the Old. The use of the Old Testament in the New has two basic aspects: (1) the specific and varied ways in which the New Testament quotes, appeals to and otherwise utilizes the Old, and (2) general statements about the Old, whether as a whole or in part. Each aspect informs the other and both need to be explored. To ignore or otherwise obscure either will likely result in a distorted understanding of the place and function of the Old Testament in the New.

From a redemptive- or revelation-historical and canonical perspective, hermeneutical priority belongs to New Testament statements, especially overall generalizations, about the Old. These statements with their impli-

---

[26]The comments that follow adapt some material from my "'For Our Sakes Also': Christ in the Old Testament in the New Testament," in *The Hope Fulfilled: Essays in Honor of Dr. O. Palmer Robertson,* ed. Robert L. Penny (Phillipsburg, N.J.: P & R, 2008), pp. 61-81.

cations provide a controlling framework for understanding numerous instances of quotation like Matthew 2:15, as well as other uses of the Old throughout the New. Two such general statements, particularly instructive, are Luke 24:44-47 and 1 Peter 1:10-12.

Luke 24:44-49 lacks a specific time marker and so is best taken as showing what was typical or characteristic between the resurrection (Lk 24:1-43) and the ascension (Lk 24:50-53). Luke 24:44-47 shows it to be a period marked largely by instruction (cf. Acts 1:3), a forty-day intersession, as we might picture it, in which Jesus gave a crash course in Old Testament hermeneutics and theology from a postresurrection perspective.

Two things about this teaching are clear. First, its substance (Lk 24:44-45), pre- ("while I was still with you") as well as postresurrection, was the necessary fulfillment of everything written about him "in the Law of Moses and the Prophets and the Psalms." The scope of this prepositional phrase (cf. "in all the Scriptures," Lk 24:27) is best taken as all-inclusive and comprehensive, not partial. It covers the Jewish Scriptures in their entirety, not just certain strands within each of the three major sections of the canon.

The summary nature of the passage just noted favors this conclusion. It is highly implausible that throughout this period Jesus only discussed certain parts of the Old Testament and kept the rest a closed book. More decisive is Luke 24:45: "Then he opened their minds to understand the Scriptures" (ESV; cf. Lk 24:32). The content of the teaching was not "these Scriptures" in distinction from others, not a specific set of Scriptures or a particular aspect of the Old Testament but simply "the Scriptures," a conventional designation within contemporary Judaism and the New Testament for the Old Testament as a whole. Nothing in the Old Testament, Jesus taught, is not "about me." In its entirety the Old Testament is essentially forward-looking and, in that sense, prophetic. Further, the focus of that fundamentally prophetic outlook is Christ.

Second, if Luke 24:44-45 circumscribes the Old Testament's outlook, then Luke 24:46-47 specifies its center: "written" there are the Messiah's suffering, his resurrection and, syntactically coordinate, world-wide preaching of the gospel or, with an eye to the effective outcome of that proclamation, the church. "Everything about me" written in the Law, Prophets and Psalms (Lk 24:44) has its central focus in Christ's death, his resurrection and the consequent worldwide, church-building preaching of the gospel.

Since no one Old Testament passage mentions together the Messiah's death, his resurrection and the church, either verbatim or as a paraphrase, "it is written" is best read here in a looser, more general sense. Christ is foreseen in the Old Testament as a whole in the sense that his death and resurrection are its integrating focus. The various parts and diverse teaching of the Old Testament have their coherence and unity in him. He is "the consent of all the parts, the scope of the whole," to borrow the language of the *Westminster Confession of Faith* (1.5).

In 1 Peter 1:10-12, the general concern of the Old Testament prophets with the grace that would come to New Testament believers has an even more direct bearing on Matthew 2:15. We can see this in three ways.

First, given that "this salvation," predicated on Christ's resurrection, is in view in its present-future comprehensiveness (1 Pet 1:3-9) and considering as well the compound Greek verbs in 1 Peter 1:10 (they "searched intently and with the greatest care," NIV), the prophets' preoccupation was both comprehensive and intensive, as absorbing as it was complete.

Especially pertinent is the indication of the prophets' comprehension of what they wrote. With all that was undoubtedly limited and shadowy about their understanding, these verses express an essential and pervasive continuity between their limited understanding and the divine intention of what they wrote. They also indicate the organic flow from the prophets' seedlike grasp of what they wrote to the final and fully flowered revelation of the New Testament.

A specific instance is the Evangelist's comment in John 12:41 (cf. Jn 12:38-40): "Isaiah said this because he saw Jesus' glory and spoke about him" (NIV). Not only did Isaiah speak (or write) but also, in speaking, he himself saw or understood. In fact, with an eye to the syntax of John 12:41, he spoke "because he saw"; he said it because he saw it.

Further, in ministering as each did in his own time and place, the prophets understood, by revelation (1 Pet 1:12), that ultimately they were not serving themselves and their contemporaries but New Testament believers. This passage, in other words, affirms continuity between the ministries of the prophets, including the Scriptures they wrote, and the post-Pentecostal, Spirit-empowered proclamation of the gospel.

Second, what the various prophets say is unified and integrated, for ultimately the one Spirit, as "the Spirit of Christ,"[27] was indicating and predicting through each of them. Because of this overarching activity of the Spirit, "the consent of all the parts, the scope of the whole" is present and discoverable in Old Testament prophecy as a whole. The prophets' multiauthored diversity constitutes an organically unfolding and divinely determined didactic unity.

Third, at the center of the comprehensive and integrated body of Old Testament prophecy is "the sufferings of Christ and the glories to follow." Its overall focus is messianic humiliation and exaltation, the same centering outlook on prophecy as a whole present in Luke 24 for the Old Testament as a whole.

The global and unifying outlook of Luke 24 and 1 Peter 1 as well as Hebrews 3 (Moses, standing for the entire old covenant, as witness to Christ; Heb 3:5-6), fairly taken as representing the remaining New Testament writers, hardly squares with the view that the Old Testament comprises unrelated or discordant trajectories of meaning. Instead, a unidirectional path or set of multiple paths leads to Christ, however obscure and difficult at points the way may be to follow. In any event, multivalent, even contradictory, trajectories will appear to be the case when the Old Testament documents are read "on their own terms" in the sense of bracketing out fulfillment in Christ and the interpretive bearing of the New Testament. For new-covenant readers submissive to both the Old and New Testaments as the Word of God, such a disjunctive reading of the Old Testament is illegitimate, as well as redemptive-historically (and canonically) anachronistic. To seek to interpret the various Old Testament documents for themselves and apart from the vantage point of the New exposes one ultimately to misinterpreting them. The Old Testament is to be read in the light of the New not only because Jesus and the New Testament writers read it this way, but also because Jesus and the New Testament writers are clear about the continuity in intention and meaning that exists between themselves and the various Old Testament authors and what those authors wrote in their own time and place.

---

[27]As the subject of the verb in its clause, this expression is best taken to refer to the unified activity of the preincarnate Christ along with the Holy Spirit under the old covenant (cf. 1 Cor 10:4), adumbrating their conjoint post-Pentecost activity, based on the cross and resurrection (e.g., Acts 16:7; Rom 8:9-10; 1 Cor 15:45; 2 Cor 3:17; Eph 3:16-17).

Hosea 11:1 and Matthew 2:15. The fulfillment of Scripture is a central theme in all four Gospels, as each is concerned in its own way with showing that Jesus as God's Son is Israel's promised Messiah. That motif is particularly in evidence in Matthew, with more than double the number of Old Testament quotations of any of the other Gospels.[28] Fulfillment is an especially prominent theme in the infancy narrative (Mt 1:18–2:23), which contains five of the ten (or eleven) "formula quotations" distinctive to Matthew.[29] Without being insistent here on one particular way of subdividing this narrative, the passage does lend itself to being considered in five sections, each marked by one of the quotations: Matthew 1:18-25, 2:1-6, 2:7-15, 2:16-18, 2:19-23. In the four units in Matthew 2, the quotation provides the conclusion. In Matthew 2:7-15, the quotation of Hosea 11:1 in Matthew 2:15 is pivotal. It not only concludes the account of the divine measures taken in the face of Herod's murderous duplicity but also sets the direction for the narration to the end of the chapter.[30]

A good number of past and current commentators and other interpreters, probably a majority presently, recognizes here an instance of some form of typology, a way of handling Old Testament texts present elsewhere in Matthew and throughout the rest of the New Testament (notably Hebrews).[31] The validity of this typological use, however, has long been a matter of considerable debate. On that question, the redemptive-historical and canonical view of this chapter holds that Matthew's use is true to the sense of Hosea 11:1, in terms of its both divine and human authorship.

---

[28]Craig L. Blomberg, *Matthew*, NAC 22 (Nashville: Broadman, 1992), p. 30.

[29]On Matthew's use of these quotations, see R. T. France, *The Gospel of Matthew*, NICNT (Grand Rapids: Eerdmans, 2007), pp. 10-14; Donald A. Hagner, *Matthew 1–13*, WBC 33A (Dallas: Word, 1993), pp. liv-lvii.

[30]On the historical reliability of the narrative in chapter 2, assumed here, see R. T. France, "Scripture, Tradition and History in the Infancy Narratives of Matthew," in *Gospel Perspective: Studies of History and Tradition in the Four Gospels*, ed. R. T. France and David Wenham (Sheffield: JSOT Press, 1981), 2:239-66, esp. 260-61; on the historicity of Mt 2:13-23, see Hagner, *Matthew*, p. 35.

[31]With Goppelt, "Only historical facts—persons, actions, events, and institutions—are material for typological interpretation," and "only if they are considered to be divinely ordained representations or types of future realities that will be greater and even more complete" (Leonhard Goppelt, *Typos: The Typological Interpretation of the Old Testament in the New*, trans. Donald H. Madvig [Grand Rapids: Eerdmans, 1982], pp. 17-18); cf. France, *Matthew*, p. 11: "OT people, events, or institutions which may serve as models for understanding the continuity of God's purpose as now supremely focused in the coming of Christ."

Some supporting reflections can be facilitated by reference to a couple of other treatments of this passage. A brief consideration of Calvin's view will show that the difficulties often perceived in this text and other New Testament uses of the Old have clear "premodern" roots and do not stem basically from our post-Enlightenment situatedness or "modern" expectations shaped by historical-critical or full-blown grammatical-historical methods.

Calvin discusses Matthew's use of Hosea in both his *Harmony of the Evangelists* (1555) and his Hosea commentary (1557), interestingly at greater length in the latter.[32] Matthew makes more than "only a comparison"[33] but draws "this analogy,"[34] where the exodus is one among Old Testament events and persons that are "types of Christ."[35] By arguing that this analogy involves Matthew doing "nothing inconsistent,"[36] Calvin distances himself from the view of some[37]

> that the intention of the prophet was different from what is here stated, and have supposed the meaning to be, that the Jews act foolishly in opposing and endeavoring to oppress the Son of God, because the Father hath called him out of Egypt. In this way, they grievously pervert the words of the prophet, the design of which is, to establish a charge of ingratitude against the Jews.[38]

He adds, "Beyond all question, the passage ought not to be restricted to the person of Christ: and yet it is not tortured by Matthew, but skillfully applied to the matter in hand."[39] While Matthew "accommodates this passage" to Christ,

> they who have not been well versed in Scripture have confidently applied to Christ this place [Hos 11:1]; yet the context is opposed to this. Hence it has happened, that scoffers have attempted to disturb the

---

[32]John Calvin, *Commentary on a Harmony of the Evangelists, Matthew, Mark, and Luke,* trans. William Pringle (Grand Rapids: Baker, 1996), 1:156-58; John Calvin, *Commentaries on the Twelve Minor Prophets,* vol. 1, *Hosea,* trans. John Owen (Grand Rapids: Baker, 1979), pp. 386-88.

[33]Calvin, *Hosea,* p. 387.

[34]Calvin, *Matthew,* p. 157.

[35]Calvin, *Hosea,* p. 388.

[36]Ibid., p. 388.

[37]He does not identify them.

[38]Calvin, *Matthew,* p. 156.

[39]Ibid., p. 157.

whole religion of Christ, as though the Evangelist had misapplied the declaration of the Prophet.[40]

Whether Matthew's typological understanding, as Calvin views it, is consistent with Hosea or has misapplied him may be addressed in light of a fairly recent interchange on this issue.[41] John Sailhamer is insistent that "Matthew did not resort to typology"[42] but instead cites the literal sense of Hosea as intended by its human author, based, in turn, on the literal sense of the Pentateuch. In response, Dan McCartney and Peter Enns emphatically reject this view. They hold that Matthew, following current Second Temple interpretive methods, adopts a christological or typological reading of Hosea. However, they are at best unclear how the literal sense intended by Hosea (the human author) is compatible with Matthew's reading.[43]

The view consonant with the redemptive-historical approach of this chapter lies between these two. On the one hand, Sailhamer overstates Hosea's own grasp of the messianic future in view in what he wrote and is wrong in rejecting Matthew's use as an instance of typology. (Much of the exegesis of Hosea he offers in fact serves a typological reading.) On the other hand, a typological reading of the Old Testament, like Matthew's, is only as sound as it is continuous and concordant with the sense intended by the human author.[44]

---

[40]Calvin, *Hosea*, pp. 386-87.

[41]John H. Sailhamer, "Hosea 11:1 and Matthew 2:15," *WTJ* 63 (2001): 87-96; Dan McCartney and Peter Enns, "Matthew and Hosea: A Response to John Sailhamer," *WTJ* 63 (2001): 97-105. Enns has subsequently expressed his view in *Inspiration and Incarnation: Evangelicals and the Problem of the Old Testament* (Grand Rapids: Baker Academic, 2005), pp. 132-34, 153, and in his contribution to *Three Views of the New Testament Use of the Old Testament,* ed. Kenneth Berding and Jonathan Lunde (Grand Rapids: Zondervan, 2007), pp. 198-202, 206, 208, 210; cf. pp. 161, 163-64.

[42]Sailhamer, "Hosea 11:1 and Matthew 2:15," p. 96.

[43]Subsequently, Enns is clear, even emphatic, about the discontinuity he sees between the human authorial meaning of Hosea and Matthew. As something of a bottom line to his view, he states: "And so Hosea's words, which in their original historical context (the intention of the human author, Hosea) did not speak of Jesus of Nazareth, now do" (*Inspiration and Incarnation,* p. 153), a statement repeated in *Three Views of the New Testament Use of the Old Testament,* p. 202, without the parenthesis but, as far as I can see, still saying the same thing (see n. 45 below).

[44]McCartney and Enns stress the importance of distinguishing between method and goal in the New Testament use of the Old ("Matthew and Hosea," pp. 99-100), certainly a valid distinction. But the goal (finding Christ in the Old Testament) hardly justifies using just any means. A method that ignores or is at odds with the meaning intended by the human author,

This is true for at least three reasons. First, as we have seen, 1 Peter 1:10-11 says so. Or, to take another, Matthean example, when Jesus, speaking of himself and his ministry, says, "Truly, I say to you, many prophets and righteous people longed to see what you see, and did not see it, and to hear what you hear, and did not hear it" (Mt 13:17 ESV; cf. Lk 10:24), are we to conclude that he meant to exclude Hosea?[45]

Second, and with an importance I cannot begin to address adequately here, if there is not continuity or basic agreement in intention between God as the primary author and the human authors of the Old Testament in what they wrote, then the Bible, as a whole and in its parts, textually considered, is basically incoherent and any meaningful notion of its divine authorship excluded.

Third, and related to the preceding point, if this basic congruence is lacking, then it is also difficult to see how the unity of biblical religion— salvation by old-covenant faith in God's promises in continuity with new-covenant faith based on their fulfillment in Christ—can be maintained— as Hebrews 11:1–12:2, for one, does.

How then should we understand the particular instance of Hosea 11:1 in Matthew 2:15? In answer, the following sketch, necessarily brief, builds on more extensive discussions of others.[46] Craig Keener writes, "When Matthew quotes Hosea, he knows Hosea's context."[47] To this key consideration, which there is no good reason to question, we may add, "When Hosea wrote Hosea, he knew Hosea's context." It is thoroughly gratuitous to hold that Matthew takes out of context and gives a future reference to a statement Hosea makes about the past and no less groundless to hold that

---

regardless of accepted Second Temple hermeneutical conventions, has to be judged invalid.

[45]At issue here, if it needs to be said, is *not* that, in the light of the fulfillment in Christ, the New Testament writers (and many readers) undoubtedly have a deeper, fuller and richer understanding of the Old Testament authors they cite than do those authors (and their contemporary and subsequent readers) had. Enns, however, envisioning Matthew going back in time and telling Hosea about Jesus and his death and resurrection, maintains, "I am not sure if Hosea would have known what to make of it" (*Inspiration and Incarnation*, p. 153; *Three Views of the New Testament Use of the Old Testament*, p. 201). A thoroughgoing disjunction or lack of any continuity in understanding between the two seems to be the point of this scenario.

[46]See esp. John Murray, "The Unity of the Old and New Testaments," in *Collected Writings of John Murray* (Edinburgh: Banner of Truth, 1976), 1:25-26; G. K. Beale, "Did Jesus and the Apostles Teach the Right Doctrine from the Wrong Texts?" *Themelios* 32, no. 1 (October 2006): 21-23.

[47]Craig S. Keener, *Matthew*, IVPNTC 1 (Downers Grove, Ill.: InterVarsity Press, 1997), p. 70.

Hosea made that statement with no thought of the future.[48]

There are multiple references to Egypt in Hosea.[49] Together these constitute an unmistakable pattern with central theological, that is, redemptive-historical, significance. A number of these references, like Hosea 11:1, have the exodus in view as a past event (Hos 2:15; 12:9, 13; 13:4), while others speak of an impending return to Egypt (Hos 7:16; 8:13; 9:3, 6). Further, these references do not merely point to an isolated occurrence in distant antiquity, however memorable, but to what throughout the Old Testament is the preeminent event of salvation, the nation-constituting event of deliverance, which has contemporary significance.[50] In Hosea this enduring relevance is clearest in Hosea 13:4, "But I am the LORD your God from the land of Egypt; you know no God but me, and besides me there is no savior" (ESV). The exodus is the archetypal evidence that the Lord God is the savior of his people.

At the same time the future references just noted link Egypt with Assyria as a place of exile (Hos 9:3; 10:6; 11:5, 11), an association compounded by Israel/Ephraim's currently ongoing disobedient political maneuvering with both Assyria and Egypt (Hos 5:13; 7:11; 8:9; 12:1). These associations along with the other references to Egypt point to what some fairly see as Hosea's Egypt typology. One of its functions, plain enough in the context of the document as a whole, is to highlight that Assyrian exile—Israel's punishment for persisting apostasy and hardened rebellion—amounts to a reversal of the exodus. Impending exile in Egypt-Assyria will be like having to go back to the ancient Egyptian "house of slaves" (Ex 20:2).

---

[48]Dale C. Allison Jr., *The New Moses: A Matthean Typology* (Minneapolis: Fortress, 1993), pp. 140-41: "It is one thing to assert that Matthew's hermeneutical methods were far from ours, quite another to imply that he could not comprehend the plain sense of a Hebrew sentence. Surely, it is reasonable, at least, initially to assume that he knew what Hosea intended to say." This comes close to saying that along with his typological approach (however one assesses it), Matthew also possessed incipient grammatical-historical sensibilities.

[49]The following reflections hold for the canonical form of Hosea, seen here as having a single author, the eighth-century-B.C. preexilic prophet identified in Hosea 1:1, perhaps with a few subsequent additions (e.g., some of the references to Judah); see, e.g., Raymond B. Dillard and Tremper Longman III, *An Introduction to the Old Testament* (Grand Rapids: Zondervan, 1994), pp. 354-55.

[50]See, e.g., the survey of Rikki E. Watts, "Exodus," in *New Dictionary of Biblical Theology*, ed. T. Desmond Alexander and Brian S. Rosner (Downers Grove, Ill.: InterVarsity Press, 2000), pp. 478-84.

The subunit comprising Hosea 11:1-11 opens by recalling Israel's primeval exodus-redemption as "my [God's] son" (cf. Ex 4:22). The verses immediately following (Hos 11:2-4), "the design of which," as Calvin says, "is to establish a charge of ingratitude against the Jews,"[51] lead to the grim prospect of exile as the consequence of this persisting disregard of God's gracious "call" and constant care (Hos 11:5-7). Yet that dark reality will not be God's final dealings with his unrepentant son (Hos 11:8-11). "In wrath [he will] remember mercy" (Hab 3:2; cf. Is 60:2). Israel will return from exile in Egypt-Assyria (Hos 11:11). The exile-reversal of the exodus will itself be reversed. This climactic promise of future exodus-deliverance fills Israel's horizon with prophetic hope in the face of the presently unresolved consequences of its sinful rebellion.

By quoting Hosea 11:1, Matthew taps directly into the whole of Hosea 11:1-11, which is marked by its realized-future Egypt typology with related allusions and associations within the overall context of Hosea. Significantly, as frequently noted, instead of the Septuagint with "his children" (plural), he cites (or correctly translates) the Hebrew with the singular, "my son." This singular, collective here for Israel as God's chosen son-nation is linked to references elsewhere to a royal individual, to a chosen son set apart from the rest of the nation yet in solidarity with it (e.g., Ps 2:2, 6-7, 12; 80:15, 17; 89:26-27).[52]

The intrinsic, integral tie between these two senses is plain in prophetic literature from the same preexilic period as Hosea (or from the same section of the canon), namely, the prominence of references to the servant of the Lord in Isaiah. Collectively, Israel, called out as the Lord's firstborn son (Ex 4:22), is to be his servant. However, what Israel has failed to be, the one who is set apart as the Lord's anointed servant will be in its stead (e.g., Is 42:1-4; 49:1-13). This messianic servant, as sin-bearer (Is 52:13–53:12), will do for the servant-nation what they cannot do for themselves because they are a nation of sinners, and the outcome will be salvation for sinners not only in Israel but also in all nations (e.g., Is 49:6). From a revelation-historical and canonical perspective the prophetic outlooks of

---

[51]Calvin, *Matthew*, p. 156.

[52]Plausibly in the background here, for either Hosea or Matthew or both, are Balaam's otherwise identical dual oracular utterances, one plural, one singular, to God "bringing [Jacob] out of Egypt" ("them," Num 23:22; "him," Num 24:8); cf. Hagner, *Matthew*, p. 37; France, *Matthew*, p. 80 n. 17.

Isaiah and Hosea inform each other. The promised exodus-salvation of the sinful son-servant nation in view in Hosea 11:11, for which return from Assyrian exile was and could be only a pointer, will be accomplished by the messianic servant-son.

Matthew's use of Hosea, far from being a grammatical-historically indefensible or inexplicable textual grab, lays hold of the single Old Testament passage, including the intention of its human author, that perhaps better than any other serves what Matthew chooses to highlight about Jesus of Nazareth. Hosea's typology of slavery/exile-exodus, both realized and future, has been fulfilled in Christ. Jesus in his person and activity fulfills Israel's prophetic, forward-looking history by recapitulating its central thread through his identity as God's Messiah-Son and his messianic task "to fulfill all righteousness" confirmed by his submission to John's water baptism, a sign of his solidarity with the repentant as their sin-bearer (Mt 3:13-17). Jesus goes to Egypt, the primeval place of God's people's enslavement and perennial sign of the need for deliverance caused by human sin, so that he may be called out from there to an exodus ordeal of wilderness testing, leading to salvation for sinners, not only in Israel but also in all nations. The immediate duress of the desert events of Matthew 4:1-11 sets the tone for the subsequent course of Jesus' entire ministry. The testing of his messianic faithfulness that culminates in his death and resurrection secures eschatological deliverance from sin and its consequences.[53]

One need not flatten out the differences between the Old and New Testaments nor lose sight of clearer and fuller understanding after the cross and resurrection in order to recognize in the text of Hosea an incipient and seminal grasp, however otherwise shadowy and inchoate, of the messianic plant whose eventual full flowering in Christ Matthew documents and explicates. What Jesus said of Abraham is also true of Hosea in his time and place—commensurate with and certainly not at odds with grammatical-historical reflections—he "rejoiced to see My day, and he saw it and was glad" (Jn 8:56 NASB).

---

[53]"The beginning of the Decalogue ('I am the LORD, your God, who has led you out of Egypt, the house of slavery') comes to stand on a firm foundation when God the Father led our King Jesus out of Egypt" (Jakob van Bruggen, *Matteüs: Het evangelie voor Israël* [Kampen: Kok, 1994], p. 54).

CONCLUSION

Comments in two areas may serve to provide a closing perspective on the hermeneutical outlook of this essay.

First, while the language and explicit concept of "salvation history" is relatively recent, the significance of the redemptive-historical view sketched in this chapter is not its novelty or distance from all earlier forms of exegesis. The factor of continuity needs to be appreciated. A credible case can be made that already in the second century, the confrontation with Gnosticism indelibly impressed upon the church the controlling biblical insight of a redemptive-historical approach: salvation resides ultimately not in who God is or even in what he has said but in what he has *done* in history, once for all, in Christ. Virtually from its beginning on and more or less consistently, especially beginning with the Reformation, the approach of the church to the Bible has been incipiently redemptive-historical or biblical-theological.

Second, on the much-debated issue of the relationship between biblical theology (biblical interpretation) and systematic theology (dogmatics), the redemptive-historical approach of this chapter entails a noncompetitive, mutually dependent relationship in which biblical theology is the indispensable servant of systematic theology. The former serves the latter on the understanding that systematic theology aims for a presentation of the overall teaching of the Bible as God's Word under appropriate topics. To that end, redemptive-historical interpretation is indispensable because sound exegesis is the lifeblood of systematic theology, and it is essential for sound exegesis to pay careful attention to the redemptive-historical subject matter of Scripture and to the revelation-historical context of the various biblical documents.[54]

This reciprocal relationship may be aptly compared to literary analysis of a great epic drama. Biblical theology is concerned with the redemptive-historical plot as it unfolds scene by scene. With an eye to that entire plot, systematic theology considers the roles of the primary actors, God and humanity. It notes in particular the constants that mark their characters

---

[54]At any one point in actual practice the relationship between biblical theology and systematic theology is of course reciprocal. As systematic theology builds on biblical theology, so biblical theology inevitably is influenced, at least implicitly, by some operating form of systematic theology and assessment of the Bible as a whole.

and the dynamics of their ongoing activities and interactions. A focus on this reciprocal relationship within a redemptive-historical approach minimizes the tendency, often present in systematic theology, toward unwarranted speculation and "dehistoricizing" in its formulations, and yet maintains the importance of systematic theology for biblical interpretation.

5

The Canonical View

Robert W. Wall

Unlike other interpretive models, which are typically defined by a distinctive set of methodological interests, the variety of canonical approaches is guided by a common commitment to a theological conception of the Bible's final (or "canonical") shape and to those Bible practices performed by a community of faithful readers. By using the term *canon* (a "straight rod" used for measuring) the church envisions the Bible as essential for building an accurate and consistent faith. Its instruction regulates theological understanding for accuracy and consistency in forming the one, holy, catholic and apostolic church.

In America, the principal proponent of this approach is the late Brevard Childs, whose extraordinary body of work explored the exegetical importance of Scripture's "canonical context" as the most essential place in which the church reads and uses biblical texts to cultivate its covenant relationship with the living God.[1] According to Childs, the canonical status of Scripture points to "the received, collected and interpreted material of the church and thus establishes the theological context in which the tradition continues to function authoritatively for today."[2]

---

[1]For a fine example of an interpreter using a wide range of critical methods regulated by an overarching interest in the elevated theological and hermeneutical importance granted to the final literary shape of Scripture (in this case the Pauline letter collection), see Childs's final published work, *The Church's Guide for Reading Paul: The Canonical Shaping of the Pauline Corpus* (Grand Rapids: Eerdmans, 2008). For a helpful summary of Childs's canonical approach to biblical interpretation, see Christopher R. Seitz, *The Character of Christian Scripture* (Grand Rapids: Baker Academic, 2011), pp. 27-91.

[2]Brevard Childs, *Biblical Theology of the Old and New Testaments: Theological Reflection on the Christian Bible* (Minneapolis: Fortress, 1993), p. 71.

Further, this approach places importance on Scripture's sacred nature: not only is Scripture's referent a holy God, but its purpose is also to form the theological understanding and moral discipline of a holy people.[3] Put this way, the exegetical strategies of a canonical approach are text-centered (i.e., more linguistic than historical) and its intended applications are church-related (i.e., more incarnational than intellectual).

While the formation of this biblical canon is studied as an historical phenomenon—"canonization from below"—it should hardly be viewed as an arbitrary process that produced an ancient artifact without relevance for today. Rather, the choices made in forming the biblical canon may also be understood as a community's discernment led by the Holy Spirit—"canonization from above"—for its spiritual benefit and with timeless purview.[4] Put more simply, the Bible is conceived as a particular and portable place, built over considerable time by the church under the direction of God's Spirit; and biblical interpretation is that worshipful activity of entering into a sacred place to gather with other readers across history and cultural settings to hear a pertinent word from God. The practices of interpretation are necessarily restrained not only by rigorous linguistic analysis that illumines what the text plainly says but also by a confession of faith that apprehends what it reveals about God's way of ordering the world. Thus, the endgame of biblical interpretation will ultimately reflect God's purposes for Christ's disciples.

ORIENTING CONCERNS AND RELATED PRACTICES

The following orienting concerns and related interpretive practices engender the core beliefs about the nature of Scripture outlined above.

Scripture is approached as a **human** *text.* The canonical approach is characterized by a firm recognition of the human agency and historical

---

[3]The "canon criticism" of James A. Sanders also emphasizes the sacred nature of Scripture in light of its relationship to the ecclesial community. While Childs concentrates on the final literary shape of the biblical text as Scripture, Sanders is more interested in the entire canonical process. Particular meanings are thereby relativized as the interpreter tracks how the faith community's readings of a sacred text change with its passage from its point of composition to its point of canonization. Cf. J. A. Sanders, *Canon and Community* (Philadelphia: Fortress, 1984).

[4]One often finds this same "below-above" rubric used when distinguishing between the scholarly quest of the historical Jesus (i.e., "from below") and the church's Spirit-led confession of the risen Christ of faith (i.e., "from above").

nature of biblical texts. Like the apostolicity of Paul's gospel, the apostolicity of Scripture should be regarded as a "treasure in earthen vessels" (2 Cor 4:7 NASB). All the factors that shaped the earliest literary history of individual biblical compositions at their diverse points of ancient origins—language, date and location, religious experience, spiritual crisis or social struggle—should also inform the exegete's understanding of what the text actually says, even if written and first read/heard for reasons that differ from why it is subsequently received by a later generation of readers/hearers as Scripture. The aim of faithful exegesis is not to hunt down "the" normative meaning of a text based on what the author intended or first readers apprehended; rather, the aim is to address a text's lack of clarity as a major cause of its misuse or nonuse among its present interpreters. The goal of critical exegesis is to build a consensus within a community of readers, agreeing what a text plainly says ideally in anticipation of its various performances as a sacred text.[5]

Exegesis that clarifies what a text plainly says should also aim at restoring to full volume the voice of every biblical witness. The endgame of this critical work is the recovery of the whole sense or "tenor" of Scripture, which is vocalized as a chorus of its various witnesses to God's word. To presume the simultaneity between every part of the whole, without then adequately discerning the plain sense of each, not only shortchanges the diversity of the whole but also undermines the integral nature of Scripture. This distorts its full witness to God.[6] If the penultimate aim of hard-nosed exegesis is to expose the theological pluriformity of Scripture, its ultimate purpose is "to put the text back together in a way that makes it available in the present and in its (biblical) entirety—not merely in the past and in the form of historically contextualized fragments."[7] In this sense, then, exege-

---

[5]Although we disagree about the ends of exegesis, John Barton's *The Nature of Biblical Criticism* (Louisville: Westminster John Knox, 2007) is to my mind the best available discussion of this crucial point. According to Barton, the goal of exegesis is to determine the "plain sense" of a biblical text based upon a careful reader's responsible analysis of its language; see especially pp. 101-16.

[6]The work of Mikhail Bakhtin has been especially helpful in reimagining how the theological diversity of Scripture's multiple witnesses requires a clear definition of each and creative reflection on how it interacts and continues to influence every other witness. Most critics cite Bakhtin's discussion of the nature of "polyphony" in *Problems of Dostoevsky's Poetics*, ed. and trans. Caryl Emerson, Theory and History of Literature 8 (Minneapolis: University of Minnesota Press, 1984).

[7]Jon D. Levenson, *The Hebrew Bible, the Old Testament, and Historical Criticism: Jews and Chris-*

sis of the literal or plain sense of Scripture is foundational for scriptural interpretation, but has value only in relationship to a more holistic end.[8]

The linguistic priority of the exegetical task does expose the inherent elasticity of words and their grammatical relationships. Further changes in the perception of a text's meaning may result from new evidence and different exegetical strategies and from interpreters shaped by diverse social and theological locations. Our experience with biblical texts in particular, layered into the history of their interpretation, cautions the exegete not to absolutize a particular textual meaning. Building a critical consensus regarding what a text plainly says is never static and requires the careful and current thinking of an entire community gathered to work toward this common end. This text is canonical for a particular religious community. Thus, the community's teachers should use exegesis to gain greater clarity of the Bible's plain sense for a practical end: in order to know more precisely what to believe and how to behave as God's people.

Scripture is approached as a **sacred** *text.* Beyond their reception by their original audiences, these canonical texts have remained in use over a sustained period of time and within a diversity of congregations to perform a range of religious functions (e.g., catechetical, missionary, preaching, liturgical). Facing the challenges of an ever-expanding religious movement, the texts that survived were those that best adapted to these changes. Put in theological terms, the church recognized the Spirit's inspiration of an emerging collection of writings, not only by the theological perspicuity of its content but also by its practical performances within a congregation in forming disciples of the risen Lord. While historical narratives frequently emphasize the church's external threats (e.g., Roman culture, Gnostic religions) as the impetus for the creation of its biblical canon, its formation (and the church's ecumenical creeds) may be understood in ecclesial and pneumatological terms as well.

For this reason, canonical interpreters speak purposefully of the Bible as *holy* Scripture, a sanctified book that serves holy ends. This orienting concern stipulates that the Bible's primary residence is the church rather than the academy. Whether practiced in the mainline or evangelical academy, modern biblical criticism is typically preoccupied with reconstructing

---

tians in Biblical Studies (Louisville: Westminster John Knox, 1993), p. 79.

[8]Esp. Childs, *Biblical Theology of the Old and New Testaments*, pp. 719-27.

the historical circumstances or literary conventions of antiquity used by particular authors in producing biblical compositions for their ancient audiences. However, the real task of Scripture is the formation of Christian disciples for today's world, which modern criticism often ignores or subverts. The canonical approach employs all the tools of modern criticism, but the aim of their skillful use is to make believers wise for understanding salvation and mature for every good work (see 2 Tim 3:15-17).

Three important practices of the canonical approach follow from this perspective: the exegesis of Scripture, the effects of Scripture and the spiritual authority of the interpreter. First, exegesis mines the raw materials of a biblical text for teachers to use when forming their congregation's understanding and application of God's Word. This interpretive practice is constrained from beginning to end by the so-called rule of faith. Irenaeus's use of the rule is instructive for biblical interpretation. In response to rival movements, the fathers of the church summarized and ordered the core beliefs received from the apostolic witness of Jesus into a working grammar of faith. This grammar of faith not only supplied the interpretive key for recognizing sacred texts but then guided their use for theological understanding—in Tertullian's apt phrase, a *gubernaculum interpretationis,* or "governor for interpretation."[9]

From antiquity the application of this common rule in regulating a theological use of Scripture was hardly restrictive. Rather, it allows an interpreter to extend the text's plain sense to include other theological or ethical senses—that more closely approximate the fullness of truth contained therein. Moreover, the different expressions of this same grammar, shaped by different creeds, cultures and crises, ordered the faith traditions of the West and East in a theological variety that extends further Scripture's revelation of God's way of ordering the world.

Second, the social history of the actual "effects" of Scripture when "received" within these diverse faith communities as a sacrament of the Word is an important witness to its full meaning. According to this history of reception, the biblical text functions canonically whenever faithful and competent interpreters pick it up again and again to hear a word from God to comfort the afflicted or afflict the comfortable.[10] Anyone who has read

---

[9]Tertullian *De praescriptione haereticorum* 9.1.
[10]I admit to the bifurcation of this history during the modern period, when the effects of the

different commentaries is aware of the diversity of meanings the biblical text can convey to different readers. Yet this history of reception within the church is hardly arbitrary and evinces a concern that the content and consequence of a text's interpretation coheres to the church's apostolic rule of faith. Theological stability and life-giving adaptability are indispensible characteristics of any faithful interpretation of a sacred text.[11]

Thus, third, a canonical approach has a corresponding interest in the spiritual authority of the interpreter who is able to guide a congregation toward God's Word. Modern criticism is preoccupied with an assessment of the Bible's continuing authority including its relevance, its accuracy, its authenticity and so forth. Stephen Fowl contends that the costly "battle for the Bible" is less about biblical interpretation and more about the disconnection of interpretative practices from the interpreter's "readerly virtues" formed within a communion of saints worshiping together.[12] Truth seeking and truth telling, forgiveness and repentance, patience and prophetic boldness are all formed by the practices of a worshiping community and essential to interpretation that seeks God's way of ordering the world.

Scripture is approached as a **single** *text.* The canonical approach proceeds from recognition of Scripture's simultaneity. Recognizing that the single biblical canon was formed under the direction of one God for the edification of one church creates a new context in which the texts of di-

---

academy's interpretation of a biblical text has diverged, sometimes sharply, from the church's appropriation of the same text, most especially in the Protestant West. Differing practices and aims, rooted in differing epistemologies, well explain this great divorce that only recently has become a topic of considered importance for scholars of the church. Whether or not reconciliation is possible, neither the scholarly nor the ecclesial reception of the text should trump the other, but interpreters should consider each in turn with modesty in its own setting before then engaging them in a mutually informing and self-correcting conversation. In my experience, both histories of reception, when taken together and if properly aimed at learning what the canonical text actually says, have the power to awaken the minds of its faithful readers.

[11]While admitting the importance of the Protestant "Scripture principle" in recovering the Bible's canonical status, it also has problematized the relationship between Scripture and the church. That is, Scripture does all the heavy lifting in forming a Christian understanding of God; it has become the rule of faith rather than an analogy of it. The earliest and programmatic examples of the apostolic rule of faith are not summaries of Scripture's master narrative (since it says nothing of Israel), nor is Scripture *the* rule (see Jason Vickers, *Invocation and Assent: The Making and the Remaking of Trinitarian Theology* [Grand Rapids: Eerdmans, 2008], pp. 69-101). Scripture is rather analogical of the rule, as is the canon of ecumenical creeds that was formulated during the same historical moment in which the canon of sacred texts was produced.

[12]Stephen E. Fowl, *Theological Interpretation of Scripture* (Eugene, Ore.: Cascade, 2009), pp. 54-70.

verse witnesses are read together, one text illuminating the fuller meaning of another. In addition to the antecedent canonical texts alluded to or quoted by biblical writers, the linguistic and thematic connections between texts within the Christian biblical canon create "intracanonical conversations" that illumine the theological understanding of faithful readers. This unity should not be misunderstood as the rejection of modern criticism's finding of diversity among biblical witnesses but as an addition to it.

For example, while Jesus retained the same "stable" beliefs about God, to whom Israel's Scripture bore witness, he found new implications and different applications for his disciples that challenged traditional interpretations (cf. Mt 5:17-20). Indeed, the existential necessity and eschatological urgency of God's Word, mediated by this textual *traditum*, is formative of theological understanding, yet constantly requires every faithful reader to seek out from the old, old gospel story those new meanings *(traditio)* that are "adaptable to the life" of today's believers who continue to submit to Scripture's instruction, rightly rendered, as a word from the Lord God Almighty.[13]

Scripture is approached as a* shaped *text. The canonization process involved a gathering of collections of individual writings, which were formed into coherent units in a purposeful way. Careful study of the canonical process indicates that each collection was designed to perform certain roles within Scripture, typically in relationship to other collections. This process concluded only when the community recognized the collection's scope and shape were complete. The church formed the Bible by observing the good effects of using particular texts to teach and train, reprove and correct ever-changing Christian congregations, especially in combination with other canonical texts. One could describe this appreciation by the church as "the aesthetic principle" of the canonical process.

Nicholas Wolterstorff advances a philosophical conception of aesthetic excellence that connects the ultimate importance of a work of art to its enrichment of the public good. If the purpose of an art form is geared toward self-interest rather than to inspiring its audiences to do good or to

---

[13]For a fuller discussion of this interpretive practice, see Robert W. Wall, "Intra-Biblical Interpretation," in *Dictionary of Biblical Criticism and Interpretation*, ed. Stanley E. Porter (London: Routledge, 2007), pp. 167-69.

live more virtuously, then the aesthetic of its form is of lesser quality.[14] This conception of aesthetic excellence provides a typology that may help explain why the church valorizes a particular shape and size of biblical canon over other possible templates.

Thus, describing the church's recognition of Scripture's shape as the "aesthetic principle" of the canonical process informs two senses that guide this approach to biblical interpretation.[15] The first sense concerns the full scope of theological content delineated by the biblical canon in its final form. When the believer speaks of the biblical canon as a sanctified "place" into which we come to hear God's word, one can also speak of a sanctified "placement" in which collections are arranged (and perhaps individual writings within them) to articulate God's word in the way that it can be heard best. For example, the church recognized the canonical gospel about Jesus Christ at some point during the second century, when it was edited and shaped into its final fourfold form in the Gospels. While other memories of what Jesus did and said could have been added to it, nothing else is needed (so Jn 20:30-31).

The second sense regards the canonical function of the Bible's final form. An interest in Scripture's final form values not only the range of its witnesses to God's word and work but also the range of its practical uses across a global church.[16] For example, Eusebius observed that certain

---

[14]Nicholas Wolterstorff, *Art in Action: Towards a Christian Aesthetic* (Grand Rapids: Eerdmans, 1980).

[15]See Robert W. Wall, "The Function of the Pastoral Letters within the Pauline Canon of the New Testament: A Canonical Approach," in *The Pauline Canon*, ed. Stanley E. Porter, PAST 1 (Leiden: Brill, 2004), pp. 27-44.

[16]The Spirit's communicative intention in directing the community's decisions that produced a single biblical canon of a particular shape and size may be understood by rough analogy of Paul's discussion of spiritual gifts in 1 Corinthians 12 (cf. Rom 12:3-8). According to this biblical analogy, the Spirit's operation within the community is observed by its apportionment of diverse spiritual gifts to individual members of the same community. Rather than dividing the community, these different gifts intend to serve its "common good" (1 Cor 12:7; cf. Rom 12:5) according to the will of one God (1 Cor 12:11) in order to produce a single body of mutually edifying but *not* interchangeable parts (1 Cor 12:20; cf. Rom 12:4). Every individual *charism* is related to every other *charism* within a single body so that they work together—Paul uses the metaphor of body parts—to produce, each in turn, a salutary result for the common good of the entire congregation. Likewise, diverse individual texts are appointed by the Spirit to work together with other texts within a single body for the spiritual benefit of all. The use of individual sacred texts for self-interested ends, similar to that of individual spiritual gifts (cf. 1 Cor 12:17-21), is not only contrary to the Spirit's purpose but also subversive of the good functioning of the single body of texts.

books, although apostolic in content (e.g., *Shepherd* of Hermas), were not deemed canonical in practice because their limited use was inadequate in forming the faith of the catholic (or universal) church.

While the community's capacity to recognize excellence derives from discerning the will of the abiding Spirit, what they sense by the actual use of these sacred texts is that the Bible works best as a complete whole—the literary shape of an edited book or the final redaction of a collection of books or the placement of that collection within a single biblical canon. The community recognized that a dynamic and fluid canonical process had come to its end with a restricted range of sacred texts. For this reason, the traditional rubrics of "old" and "new" testament are apropos of a completed canon, since the community envisages no third testament beyond the twofold canon and the meaning of texts within this canon is thereby fixed and interrelated.

One of the exegetical practices that follows from this attention to aesthetics is elevating the theological or hermeneutical importance of the phenomenon of collection-building in the formation of the biblical canon. For example, a canonical approach to the corpus of Catholic Epistles would consider the theological and functional coherence of the entire collection and thus learn to read each epistle in turn as one bit of the integral whole. Such a strategy goes against the grain of modern criticism, which typically treats each epistle in isolation from the others or in alternative groups according to date, region or apostolic tradition.[17] Or, again, quite independent of modern criticism's exclusion of the "Pastoral Epistles" from the Pauline canon on the basis of their disputed authorship, a canonical approach would not only receive them as integral parts of the Pauline corpus based upon the church's decision to do so but also read them as an indispensable guide to a faithful reading of the entire Pauline corpus.[18]

Further, while reading biblical texts according to a chronology of their compositional history has value, the canonical approach, with its emphasis on the aesthetics of Scripture, values the theological (and perhaps practical) significance of the arrangement of canonical units within

---

[17]Robert W. Wall, "Unifying Theology of the Catholic Epistles: A Canonical Approach," in *The Catholic Epistles and the Tradition*, ed. Jacques Schlosser, BETL 176 (Leuven: Peeters, 2004), pp. 43-47.

[18]Childs, *The Church's Guide for Reading Paul*, pp. 65-78.

the biblical canon and the sequence of individual writings within a particular collection. In other words, the interpreter approaches the Bible assuming the priority of what comes first when one picks up the Bible to read it. The first collections or first books are read first because to do so is the most effective articulation of the textual word. For example, the Old Testament is read before the New Testament in order to follow more effectively its narrative plotline or thematic developments. In a similar manner, the opening sentence of Acts assumes the prior reading of Jesus' story narrated in "the first book." A canonical reading of Acts reads this "first book" not primarily as Luke's Gospel but as the fourfold Gospel of Jesus.[19]

This approach also appreciates the importance of textual seams created as a result of the canonical process. For example, the placement of Matthew as the first narration of Jesus' life in the fourfold Gospel may be viewed as strategic since it opens by introducing Jesus in a way that links his story of fulfillment with the prophetic promise of Israel's future restoration. Likewise, the placement of John as the final narration of the canonical Gospel may also be viewed as strategic since its concluding episode connects the future of the risen Lord's apostles and God's Spirit in a way that aims the reader at Acts as the continuation of the gospel story. Even the final snapshot of Acts, which finds Paul under house arrest in downtown Rome but still proclaiming the victory of God, nicely frames the introduction to the Pauline canon of Romans 1. Such an evaluation sees worth in these literary seams, whether or not it was ever the author's intention to make such connections.

Finally, a variety of interpretive cues are added to the final form of the biblical canon to guide its faithful use. Book titles and even attributions of authorship may be at odds with historical constructions, but they remain useful as markers that help readers "locate" a sacred text for theological understanding. Scripture was put into its final canonical shape by the addition of nonauthorial properties, such as book titles, that facilitate its con-

---

[19]While I have no objection to the historical conclusion that the Evangelist had in mind Theophilus's prior reading of the third Gospel, the intentions of the canonical process are different and override the author's intent. The result is a fresh reading of the opening line of Acts. See Robert W. Wall, "A Canonical Approach to the Unity of Acts and Luke's Gospel," in *Rethinking the Reception and Unity of Luke and Acts*, ed. Andrew F. Gregory and C. Kavin Rowe (Columbia: University of South Carolina Press, 2010), pp. 172-91.

tinuing *revelatory* purpose as God's Word.

Scripture is approached as the **church's** *text.* Based upon these other concerns, it is not surprising that the canonical approach recognizes the importance of congregational worship in forming the believer's capacity for faithful interpretation. Not only do various Bible practices find their home in a congregational setting and their purpose in aiming believers at God, but also it is in the company of the saints that the spiritual authority of the biblical interpreter is honed and confirmed. Along with the intellectual equipment required to work with biblical texts skillfully, the virtues necessary to read sacred texts after the mind of Christ are also formed within the body of Christ. The congregation encourages the self-awareness and maturity of one who can avoid sinful tendencies in interpreting biblical texts.

If the Bible's legal address is the church, the interpreter's principal concern should be to facilitate Bible practices within a congregation of believers. The terms of Scripture's authority (e.g., divine inspiration, special revelation, sacrament of the word) are defined in functional rather than in dogmatic terms. Teaching that either lacks relevance or comprehensibility for the believer's contemporary situation may cause them to question the authority of Scripture. If such a situation persists, believers may seek other resources found outside of the church's canonical heritage and even secular in cast, which can lead to serious distortions of the apostolic faith. In this situation, sound interpretation demonstrates the Bible's authority for a particular congregation of readers by first clarifying what the text actually says (text-centered exegesis) and then by seeking the particular textual meaning that addresses the current theological confusion or moral dilemma in productive ways.

Of course, the legitimacy of any biblical interpretation as truly Christian is not determined by its practical importance for a single readership but by general agreement with the church's rule of faith, whose subject matter has been disclosed through the incarnate Word of God, Jesus Christ; witnessed to by his apostles; and preserved by the Holy Spirit in the canonical heritage of the one, holy, catholic and apostolic church. Thus the limits of a properly interpreted text are not determined by an interpreter's critical orthodoxy but by whether an interpretation's content and consequence agrees with the church's rule of faith.

THREE PROBES INTO THE CANONICAL CONTEXT
OF MATTHEW 2:7-15

Although canonical interpretation first reads for the plain sense of the text, this section will focus on three ways that a canonical approach can provide unique insight into the passage, while keeping the plain sense of the text in mind.

Probe 1: Reading Matthew first. Little is known about the origins and date of Matthew's Gospel. It is an anonymous narrative composed without an address or clear statement of purpose. What seems clear from the sparse evidence available to us is that the ancient church had come to recognize this Gospel as one of four integral "Gospels of the apostles" at least by the time Irenaeus wrote *Against Heresies* (ca. A.D. 175).[20] Every canon list includes this same fourfold Gospel; and manuscript evidence from the mid-second century places these four Gospels together in single codices for wide use.[21] A canonical approach is interested in the literary shape of this fourfold Gospel. Since each Gospel was originally composed for particular communities, one might assume each also circulated independently prior to their canonization as a collection; this assumption, however, is based on little hard evidence. As Brevard Childs puts it, "The major formal sign of canonical shaping of the collection is the juxtaposition of the four books with titles which introduce the books as witnesses to the one gospel."[22]

The interpretive problem of reading Matthew is to do so in light of the Gospel's own distinctive understanding of Jesus yet within the bounds of Scripture's fourfold Gospel canon. The difficulty of doing so has occasioned various reductionisms. The most ancient is illustrated by Tatian's *Diatessaron*, which reconstitutes the gospel narrative by eliminating redundant or contradictory elements among the four canonical Gospels. Accordingly, our passage from Matthew is harmonized with Luke's radically different telling of this same event by combining details of each to form

---

[20]See Martin Hengel, *The Four Gospels and the One Gospel of Jesus Christ* (Philadelphia: Trinity Press International, 2000), pp. 34-115, although his reconstruction of the evidence is contested.

[21]Cf. Graham N. Stanton, "The Early Reception of Matthew's Gospel: New Evidence from Papyri?" in *The Gospel of Matthew in Current Study*, ed. David E. Aune (Grand Rapids: Eerdmans, 2001), pp. 42-61.

[22]Brevard Childs, *The New Testament as Canon: An Introduction* (Minneapolis: Fortress, 1984), p. 155.

another (noncanonical) story of Jesus' infancy. Harmony comes at the expense of Matthew's distinctive (and canonical) telling of the episode.

The reductionism of modern criticism moves in the opposite direction, emphasizing the differences between the Gospels due to different historical backgrounds, literary genre, Gospel traditions and so forth. The result is Matthew's seeming detachment from or even opposition to the other Gospels. In our passage, Matthew's story of Jesus' escape into Egypt from Herod's infanticide, found in no other Gospel, reflects the Evangelist's distinctive portrayal of Jesus in response to his audience's concerns.

The "Synoptic Problem" represents an illustration of this modern approach. This "problem" is the invention of critics whose reading of Matthew follows from its family resemblance to Mark and to a lesser extent Luke. These three books form the so-called Synoptic Gospels because they look ("optic") alike ("syn-") and are set apart from the Fourth Gospel, which is different in almost every aspect. Most scholars today defend the "priority of Mark," arguing that the second Gospel is actually the first written and was then used in writing Matthew and Luke.[23] Virtually every modern introduction to the Gospels, adverse to the canonical shape of the fourfold Gospel, begins its survey with Mark, often relocating the study of John to a separate unit. The effect of this modern sequence of the canonical Gospels, led by Mark's chronological priority, is to identify the reading of Matthew's infancy narrative as an add-on to Mark. Matthew's additions are typically understood as a literary fiction that intends to stage the Evangelist's distinctive portrait of Jesus in a way that Mark does not.[24]

This same Synoptic Problem extends to the relationship between Matthew and Luke, both of which edit Mark by adding different stories of the Messiah's birth. The effort to explain their different redactions of Mark has had the effect of creating even more distance between them and makes

---

[23]The evidence is nicely set out by Robert Stein, "Synoptic Problem," in *IVP Dictionary of the New Testament*, ed. Daniel G. Reid (Downers Grove, Ill.: InterVarsity Press, 2004), pp. 1053-62.

[24]The groundbreaking collection that introduced and illustrates this point most clearly is Günther Bornkamm, Gerhard Barth and Heinz Joachim Held, *Tradition and Interpretation in Matthew*, NTL (Philadelphia: Westminster, 1963). In introducing his contribution to the miracle stories of Matthew ("Matthew As Interpreter of the Miracle Stories"), Held asks this programmatic question, "How are we to account for the fact that Matthew does not simply hand on the tradition as he receives it (from Mark) but retells it?" (p. 165). What follows in his influential essay is a construction of Matthew as an innovative interpreter of miracle stories received from Mark to secure his belief in the risen Jesus' ongoing authority.

it ever more difficult to relate them together as integral parts of an inter-penetrating fourfold whole.

By contrast the formation and final form of the fourfold Gospel canon cues Matthew's rather than Mark's priority; that is, if Markan priority is defended by a history of its composition, Matthean priority is defended by a history of its canonization. Édouard Massaux's expansive work in recon-structing the earliest history of Matthew's Gospel prior to Irenaeus makes it clear that it was "by far the most popular gospel in the second century, having more parallels in second century writings than do Mark, Luke or John."[25] This preference extends into the third century and is reflected in the seminal work of Cyprian, who quotes Matthew more than any other biblical book.[26] By comparison, Augustine referred to Mark as Matthew's "epitomizer"—a kind of *"Reader's Digest"* version of Matthew's normative rendering of Jesus.[27] It is quite possible that the importance of Matthew's story of Jesus within earliest Christianity is due to its close proximity to Israel's Scripture (LXX), which remained through the first half of the sec-ond century the church's book. In any case, Stanton and Massaux sketch the earliest history of Matthew, which evinces its priority for Christian worship and instruction at the very moment when oral traditions about Jesus were written down and edited, then collected and fixed into a four-fold Gospel canon.[28] Sharply put, Matthew was placed first because it was

---

[25]Lee Martin McDonald, *The Biblical Canon: Its Origin, Transmission, and Authority* (Peabody, Mass.: Hendrickson, 2007), p. 255. McDonald cites Édouard Massaux, *The Influence of the Gospel of Saint Matthew on Christian Literature Before Saint Irenaeus*, ed. Arthur J. Bellinzoni, trans. Norman J. Bavel and Suzanne Hecht, 5 vols., NGS 5 (Macon, Ga.: Mercer University Press, 1990); but note Helmut Koester's criticism of Massaux's methodology, which considers only literary correspondence between written texts but not the possibility of shared oral tradi-tions, in "Written Gospels or Oral Tradition?" *JBL* 113 (1994): 293-97. Dating the history of a text's reception "before Irenaeus" is especially crucial since it is he who originates the formal idea of a Christian biblical canon. Harry Y. Gamble says about Irenaeus that his discussion and use of certain Christian writings (e.g., Acts) indicates a "relative novelty" when elevating them to the same level as the "gospels of the prophets" that suggests he is the first to do so. See Gamble, "The New Testament Canon: Recent Research and the Status Qaestionis," in *The Canon Debate*, ed. Lee Martin McDonald and James A. Sanders (Peabody, Mass.: Hen-drickon, 2002), p. 277.

[26]McDonald, *The Biblical Canon*, p. 255.

[27]C. Clifton Black, *Mark: Images of an Apostolic Interpreter* (Columbia: University of South Caro-lina Press, 1994), pp. 127-35.

[28]This is so even in the East where John's gospel was practiced more than Matthew; this datum is reflected in some of its canon lists that place John before Matthew. But certainly regarding those three Gospels that "look alike," Matthew's priority is consistently instantiated in lists, writings and worship practices that mark out the entire canonical process into the fifth century when the

used most in fashioning the church's understanding and worship of the
risen one and also due to his continuity with Israel's biblical story: Messiah
Jesus instantiates a faithful God's fulfillment of promises made to the covenant community.

The canonical effect of Matthew's placement within the fourfold Gospel also envisages a reading strategy. Simply put, Matthew is the Bible's
introduction of Jesus; readers first meet him there. Matthew performs the
role of a narrative frontispiece that frames a reading of the other three
Gospels.[29] When the Gospel's own sequence is followed, it is not as a rewritten Mark but as a rewritten story of a faithful Israel with its antecedent
in the Old Testament story of Israel.[30] If Mark is picked up next and read
as an "epitomized" Matthew, fresh impressions of Mark's Jesus are now
possible. For example, precisely because Mark's story does not begin with
an infancy episode or ancestral trope, the primacy of Jesus' messianic mission is emphasized. Rather than reading Matthew 1–2 as adding an episode to Mark's narrative, Matthew's narrative introduces the infant Jesus
in a way that elaborates central claims about him that the New Testament
reader then assumes when reading the other three canonical Gospels.[31]

The canonical approach to Matthew also notes that its title provides an
incisive clue about its role within Scripture. Not only did the church supply
the singular "Gospel" to title the collection of four as an integral whole, but
also the individual narratives are titled "according to . . ." in order to locate
each among "the Gospels of the apostles." The purpose is not to attribute

---

final redaction of the New Testament canon was recognized by the church's episcopacy.

[29]Curiously, in treating the fourfold Gospel as a collection, Childs reverts to historical criticism's verdict of Markan priority to detect the discrete theological contribution of Matthew
to the canonical witness to Jesus based upon changes made from the Markan original (see his
Biblical Theology of the Old and New Testaments, pp. 262-76). From a canonical perspective,
whether based upon the final literary form of the fourfold Gospel (at least in the West) or
upon the church's reception of Matthew before Mark, Matthew has priority and Mark should
be read in light of Matthew's narrative, not the reverse (see below for the implications of this
approach when treating the Gospel's infancy narrative).

[30]Brevard Childs, *The New Testament as Canon: An Introduction* (Philadelphia: Fortress, 1985),
pp. 69-71. Cf. Ulrich Luz, *Matthew 1–7: A Continental Commentary*, trans. Wilhelm Linss
(Minneapolis: Fortress, 1989), pp. 127-63.

[31]There may be still other impressions made on the reader of Mark if she assumes the prior reading of Matthew's Gospel. The material Mark seems to elaborate in comparison with Matthew,
for instance, seems to fill in gaps that Matthew leaves out. Further, the quick-paced action of
Mark's telling of the story may be read as buttressing Matthew's more didactic emphasis on Jesus' teaching ministry. Indeed, it is his interpretation of Scripture that provokes unrest within
Israel according to Matthew but his messianic actions that provoke similar unrest in Mark.

authorship to a particular Evangelist but to legitimize its narrative as apostolic and therefore authorized for use among those Christian congregations whose faith belongs to the one, holy, catholic and apostolic church.

Probe 2: Reading Matthew 2:7-15 with other Scripture. A second probe of the canonical approach regards allusions and quotations of parallel texts within the single biblical canon, which will add texture to our Matthean text. The relationship between Matthew and other biblical texts is not only based on linguistic agreements but also on common themes or typologies.[32] If a reader of Matthew has followed Scripture's own canon logic, she will approach the narrative with the Old Testament story of Israel in mind. She will read our passage and hear loud echoes of antecedent stories that replay the plotline of the biblical drama of Israel's primal history. Jesus is a type of Moses whose infancy tells of another exodus, kingship and exile. The repetition of *anachōreō* (Mt 2:12-14) to indicate that Jesus' departure from Israel for Egypt was a flight from Herod's terror echoes its use in Exodus 2:15 of Moses' flight from Pharaoh's threat and toward his encounter with God, who calls him to lead Israel out of Egypt to the Promised Land. Indeed, the exodus is the principal *typos* echoed to shape this passage. Thus the announcement that Jesus had come to save his people from their sins (Mt 1:21) serves as a type of deliverance from slavery—from sin, not Roman occupation.[33] Of course the most prominent cotext is Hosea 11:1, "Out of Egypt I have called my son" (NIV), which is quoted in Matthew 2:15 to concentrate Matthew's account of Jesus' beginnings as a new beginning for Israel similar to the exodus/ Mount Sinai. Matthew's use of the MT's preference for *ben* ("son") over the LXX's *ta tekna* ("children") extends the exodus motif to Israel's king (so Num 24:8): the conflict between Herod and Jesus is between two kings and which of the two is God's royal son (or David's son; cf. Mt 1:1; 2 Sam 7) and rightful heir to Israel's throne.[34]

---

[32]Cf. Childs, *New Testament as Canon*, pp. 161-65. Richard Bauckham's substantial argument that eyewitness memories lie behind the Gospels (*Jesus and the Eyewitnesses: The Gospels as Eyewitness Testimony* [Grand Rapids: Eerdmans, 2006]) may well extend to the infancy narratives, thought by many to be literary fictions that serve a rhetorical or theological but not an historical purpose. If so, perhaps Mary is the source of Luke's tradition and Joseph of Matthew's given their pivotal characterization in each story.

[33]All modern commentaries note this phenomenon but develop its interpretive importance differently.

[34]John Nolland argues that the Hosea quotation does not confirm an implicit claim for Jesus'

The fulfillment formula that introduces the Hosea quotation in Matthew 2:15 provides a Scriptural witness to a particular historical event—in this case, Herod's threat and the holy family's flight to Egypt. In doing so, the quoted cotext cues up a prophetic context that includes the entire Old Testament script, pointing to Israel's future reconciliation with God. In fact, the subsequent adumbration of the "out of Egypt" catchphrase in Hosea (Hos 11:1; 12:9, 13; 13:4) recalls Israel's previous encounters with God, most especially in the exodus event, that lead inevitably to the climactic conclusion that Israel "has known no God but me and there is no savior besides me" (Hos 13:4, author's translation). Set within this prophetic setting, Matthew's story of Jesus' infancy is testimony to God's fulfillment of a biblical promise made to Israel: Emmanuel is Israel's only hope. Since the magi's worship of Jesus (Mt 2:11) is suggestive of the Gospel's advance beyond Israel into "all the nations" (Mt 28:19-20), Jesus' exile into Egypt (Mt 2:13-14), when interpreted by Hosea (Hos 2:15), implies that Jesus is a type of Israel sent out to enlighten and save the nations.

Based upon this intertext, the historical events are recounted in Matthew 1–2 to testify to a faithful God's intention to save and restore Israel. The reader of the Hosean cotext will also learn, however, that obdurate Israel's response to God is typically one of unbelief; this impression will also prepare the reader for a reading of the Gospel. Finally, then, the fulfillment formula reminds the reader that what is central to Hosea is also central to the Gospel. Hosea's rehearsal of Israel's encounter with God, itself a synthesis of the Old Testament testimony, continues in the story of Emmanuel, whose offer of God's salvation is rejected once again by Gomer-Israel.

Canonical exegetes also render our text in Matthew within the bounds of a fourfold Gospel. They will observe that this Gospel includes two infancy narratives, one in Matthew and one in Luke, and that the independence of the two is demonstrated by an array of source and redaction-critical studies. They know to resist harmonistic or historicist reductions of the two, while recognizing the common traditions they do share that

divine sonship made earlier in Mt 1, especially by the Emmanuel prophecy; rather, this quotation introduces this crucial theme into the Gospel, which is developed more fully in Mt 3–4. See John Nolland, *The Gospel of Matthew: A Commentary on the Greek Text*, NIGTC (Grand Rapids: Eerdmans, 2005), p. 123.

help sketch a unified narrative of Jesus' beginnings: the Messiah's name is given as "Jesus," whose messianic vocation is predicted by an angel; and his family's residence is in "Nazareth," which explains some of the political and religious conflict that follows.

When read after Matthew, however, Luke's infancy narrative elaborates the distinctive elements of the first. In some sense, the manner of Jesus' introduction to the reader by the magi and star, by Herod's infanticide, by the holy family's escape to Egypt and return to Israel instantiates "hidden and revealed elements" that frame a reading of Luke.[35] The character of the intertextual relationship between Luke and Matthew is not linguistically adduced, since Luke's "hidden and revealed elements" are independent of Matthew's; rather, the nature of this intratext is typological and elaborative. For example, the arrival of Palestinian shepherds intensifies the universal scope of God's salvation in his Messiah, which includes the marginal ones of Israel and adds weight to the angel's initial prophecy that Matthew's Jesus will "save his people from their sins" (Mt 1:21). Although Luke's narrative locates Jesus firmly within Israel's redemptive history, its canticles clearly move the reader beyond Scripture's promise of a restored Israel (so Mt 1) to emphasize salvation's international reach, which includes all the nations (so Lk 2:29-32). The shift from Matthew's "righteous" Joseph (Mt 1:19) to Luke's "servant" Mary (Lk 1:38, 48) as the pivotal character in the birth drama rounds out the profile of the Messiah's holy family, which is exemplary of faithful (or remnant) Israel. Powerfully imagined by the two infancy narratives, the importance of the holy family lends authority to the fourfold Gospel, especially by the mid-second century, when the fourfold Gospel was first recognized as canonical within the church.[36]

Probe 3: Reading Matthew 2:7-15 by the rule of faith. Irenaeus's programmatic statement of the apostolic rule of faith begins with the elemen-

---

[35]Childs, *New Testament as Canon*, p. 162.

[36]I would argue the harmony of the infancy narratives in the *Protevangelium of James* (midsecond century), although mostly dependent on Luke's version to venerate Mary, also includes snapshots of Matthew's faithful Joseph in veneration of the entire holy family. Although the intention of doing so is unclear, one may reasonably suspect this is a practice of the canonizing community—that in some sense the holiness of Jesus rubs off on his entire family. For this reason, for example, the collection of Catholic Epistles is formed with James at its head and Jude as its other bookend. Bracketing the entire collection with letters attributed to the Lord's brothers, James and Jude, sounds a sacred note that underwrites the collection's canonicity when read as an integral whole.

tal confession that there is "one God, the Father Almighty, maker of
heaven, and earth, and the sea, and all things that are in them" (*Adversus
haereses* 3.4.1-2, author's translation). In a church whose theology is typically ordered by its core beliefs about salvation, it is God's work in and
with creation that tracks and interprets God's redemptive action in the
world. The exodus narrative that helps shape our passage is replete with
creational images (e.g., Ex 15).[37] Not only does God use nonhuman creatures to plague Egypt and force its release of captive Israel, but also the
narrator boldly claims that the prolongation of these horrific acts is to
confirm "my name" throughout all creation, especially to the pagan Egyp-
tians. In fact, the justice of such an act even upon the enemy of the elect
people can only be understood by the prior claim that "the earth is God's
earth" (Ex 9:29; 19:5, author's translation).

The exodus typology that shapes the narrative of the holy family's great
escape cues the creational images found in the exodus narrative. This
highly textured reading of the set text helps to illumine its analogical relationship to the rule's confession of the church's Creator God. In particular,
the odd presence of the star, which guides the guileless Gentiles to the
world's ruler, is a theological prompt in this regard. There is no indication
in the text that God sent the star to guide the Magi; the star simply "appeared" (Mt 2:7) and was "observed" by the Magi (Mt 2:10). In fact, the
narrative is severely gapped and provides no details about the manner by
which the Magi observed the star's location or why they respond in joy and
worship Jesus (rather than the star; cf. Deut 4:19) upon seeing it. What is
the reader to make of this textual element?

While there may be intertextual allusions to draw on in this regard (e.g.,
Rev 22:16), the best course is to read the meaning of the star by our confession that God is the "maker of heaven and earth, and of all things visible and
invisible" (Nicene Creed). The rule prompts us to assume that this is the
Creator's (rather than an astrologist's) star, which is providentially guiding
Gentiles to the place of creation's Lord. While criticism's concern is to re-
construct the background of the Magi's interest in the star or even to test its
historicity, I think such an interest is misplaced if it is motivated by apolo-
getics more than by theological illumination. The plain sense of the text is

---

[37]See Terence E. Fretheim, *Exodus*, IBC 2 (Louisville: Westminster John Knox, 1991), pp. 12-
  14.

that the star is a celestial compass that serves as a heavenly agent of natural revelation for those who do not have Scripture. What the text suggests, of course, is that the triune Maker of heavenly creatures, such as stars, can use them all to achieve God's redemptive purpose for all things made.

CONCLUSION

The canonical approach is ordered by theological rather than hermeneutical commitments. Rather than offering a distinctive interpretive strategy, its practices are of a piece with the church's core beliefs about Scripture and the relationship of its canonization to the inspiring and sanctifying work of the Holy Spirit. A corresponding emphasis on the formation and final form of a canon of sacred texts does, however, underwrite a shift of interest from a biblical text's point of composition to its point of canonization, from how an authored text may have been understood by its first readers/hearers in light of their particular needs to how the church of every age continues to practice and parade this same text in ways that target holy ends: to make faithful readers wise for salvation and mature for every good work (2 Tim 3:15-17).

While a rigorous appraisal of the text's plain sense, the result of careful exegetical analysis, is the first step of any faithful interpretation, the applications of a sacred text are best protected from abusive, self-promoting interpreters by wrapping it in its various contexts (historical, linguistic, literary, rhetorical, compositional and canonical) in a way that coheres critically to the grammar of theological agreements articulated by the apostolic rule of faith. Moreover, reading texts with a fellowship of believers that cultivates spiritual virtues necessary for faithful reading and hearing of God's Word, such as love for God and neighbor, truth-seeking, humility, patience and forgiveness, is critical for using Scripture in a way that targets holy ends.

Finally, the marks of the Christian church—one, holy, catholic and apostolic—are analogous of the marks of its biblical canon. Accordingly, the practices of faithful interpretation must pay attention to the interpenetrating relationships of one text to other canonical texts (one), to the effect an interpretation has on its recipients (holy), to the global scope of its influence in a diversity of social settings (catholic), and to the trustworthiness of its witness to God's truth (apostolic).

PART TWO

RESPONSES

6

The Historical-Critical/ Grammatical Response

Craig L. Blomberg

As I suspected when I saw the lineup of contributors and viewpoints for this book, I found much more to agree with than to disagree with in these chapters. As I noted in my position essay, I do not wish to argue for a historical-critical/grammatical approach to the exclusion of all other approaches but for the historical-critical/grammatical approach as the necessary foundation for these other approaches. Various comments each of the other four contributions makes suggest that they either agree or should agree with this assertion, if they are consistent with what they have written. I can happily support much of what each additional perspective contributes on top of this foundation, although there are a few places where I must demur. I will make specific remarks addressing these elements for each of the other four essays, one at a time, and then conclude with a few general observations pertaining to the entire collection of methods.

THE LITERARY/POSTMODERN VIEW

Scott Spencer begins his essay by rightly acknowledging the diversity of perspectives that comes under his purview. His particular use of literary and postmodern methods places him on the conservative end of the spectrum of scholars who would identify their approach with these adjectives. While focusing on "text and reader" in the "author-text-reader" triad, Spencer nevertheless insists that they "hardly nullify" the presence of the author as "an intelligent, careful and purposeful writer." Spencer's version of literary criticism "offers a sample 'index' of likely objectives the author had in mind," based on that author's narrative (i.e., textual) strategies, which "provides a set of controls for assessing the multiplicity of reader responses." Thus Spencer comes close to providing a full-orbed hermeneutic that outlines what all readers of texts should seek. However, like me, he then concentrates on that portion of the complete package that he agreed to write on. Yet even in his application of the literary/postmodern approach, Spencer focuses more on texts than on readers, that is, more on classic literary criticism than on postmodern criticism.

Spencer identifies five key foci of his approach—all of which tellingly have "text" (rather than "reader") as part of their description—final text, cotext, intertext, context and open text. Spencer's concern for the *final text* of a Gospel corresponds to what I sketch out under redaction criticism. However, in Spencer's approach the interpreter reaches this *final text* more by means of what has been called reading vertically (down through an entire scroll from top to bottom, as it were, looking for recurring themes, key stylistic devices and other synchronic features) than by reading horizontally (across the columns of a synopsis, looking for differences among parallels).[1] Spencer's reading also asks additional questions that historical critics frequently have not asked—about characterization, plot development, the effects of hearing a text read aloud and the like. All of these for Spencer remain grounded in the historical context of that final text. He does not, for example, propose a genre for a given text that as far as we know did not exist in its historical setting, as some scholars do, for example, when they identify certain biblical narratives as akin to modern historical fiction.[2]

Spencer's description of *cotext* corresponds roughly with "the structure of phrases, clauses, sentences, paragraphs and increasingly larger units of thought up to the level of an entire book," which I place under grammatical methods.

Spencer's *intertext* considers the significance of Old Testament quotations, allusions and echoes, which inevitably involves historical and diachronic concerns. This is especially true for our assigned example of Mat-

---

[1]Gordon D. Fee and Douglas Stuart, *How to Read the Bible for All Its Worth*, 3rd ed. (Grand Rapids: Zondervan, 2003), pp. 135-40.
[2]Cf., e.g., throughout Richard I. Pervo, *Acts*, Hermeneia (Minneapolis: Fortress, 2008).

thew 2:7-15. Antecedent Scripture is always crucial material for interpreting any biblical text. Intertextual study can also helpfully appeal to any nonbiblical texts that a biblical writer is likely to have known and even to texts he would not have known but that contain information he is likely to have known or agreed with. Intertextual studies become problematic, however, when they utilize later historical, theological or literary developments that differ in significant ways from what was known to an earlier writer and thus interpret that writer in some anachronistic fashion. Thus when Spencer writes that relationships between texts function dialogically, "mutually addressing and responding to each other," I must dissent, at least if he intends his statement to be a general principle for interpretation. I *may* use a text from a medieval European empire that describes social dynamics between classes to illuminate a gap in my knowledge of the sociology of the Gospels *if, and only if,* I have reason to believe that it speaks paradigmatically for most empires organized the way Rome was in the early first century. However, I may *not* interpret that Jesus was able to walk on water by standing up in a camouflaged, motorized hovercraft simply because I have recently been reading about such inventions in my favorite boating magazine![3]

Spencer's term *context* most closely approximates what I call historical criticism, including sociological analysis. It is thus the element out of Spencer's five that most overlaps with my concerns and that I can most quickly adopt.

Spencer's term *open text* is characterized by the example of how readers interact with a preached text during and after a sermon and this corresponds most closely to legitimate application, which I heartily endorse, but which is not part of the historical-critical/grammatical method per se. This is also the element of Spencer's hermeneutic with the greatest number of potential pitfalls. We must certainly avoid an objectivism or naive realism that thinks we can interpret comprehensively or flawlessly, precisely because as Christians we affirm that we are both finite and fallen creatures. However, we must also avoid a postmodernism that rejects the possibility of all metanarratives or absolute truths, even from God's perspective. Mediating between the two is a critical realism that allows us to

---

[3]Parts of Stephen D. Moore, *Mark and Luke in Poststructuralist Perspective* (New Haven: Yale University Press, 1992), are almost this bizarre.

increasingly and successively approximate the original meaning of a text
through all the legitimate tools of study that this book surveys, without
ever claiming exhaustive or inerrant interpretation.[4] Thus we welcome to
the conversation the voices of previously stifled readers to the extent, but
only to the extent, that they help us to recover parts of a text's original
meaning or its contemporary significance that we may have missed because we were blinded to it by our social and personal locations, presuppositions or prejudices. As P. D. Juhl suggests, significance for individuals
and individual situations, as well as entire interpretive communities, may
vary almost infinitely, but original meaning must be fixed, at least in
principle,[5] or there is no way to assess the merits of any given application
or claim of significance other than creativity or internal coherence (recall
above, p. 41).

Thus, when we turn to Matthew, keeping historical concerns at the
forefront of our study, we should reject both Dube's and Carter's extreme
and contradictory views, which Spencer cites, that Matthew is "an insidious patriarchal and imperialist manifesto," and that it is primarily inclusive, egalitarian and anti-imperial, respectively. Understanding the other
main options on these matters *in Matthew's world* enables us to recognize
that, on the one hand, Matthew retains certain dimensions of patriarchy
and imperialism—one could scarcely imagine anyone in his world not doing so—but, on the other hand, that what stands out against the prevailing
options is his inclusiveness. He is not fully egalitarian concerning gender
roles or the organization of Jesus' community of followers, but he takes
more steps in this direction than most others in his day. Matthew is not
directly anti-imperial, but he describes a community that significantly
lived out the vision of his portrayal of Jesus and God's reign in a way that
would be an implicit threat to any empire.[6]

With respect to Matthew 2, I can accept almost all of Spencer's observations as possibilities (although some are better grounded in the text or in
appropriate historical, cultural and sociological dynamics of the day than
others) so long as he does not exclude other explanations for the phenom-

---

[4]Ben F. Meyer, *Reality and Illusion in New Testament Scholarship: A Primer in Critical Realist Hermeneutics* (Wilmington, Del.: Glazier, 1995).
[5]P. D. Juhl, *Interpretation* (Princeton: Princeton University Press, 1980), esp. pp. 199-200.
[6]Stuart L. Love, *Jesus and Marginal Women: The Gospel of Matthew in Social-Scientific Perspective* (London: James Clarke, 2009).

ena as well. A literary seam, for example, may be intentionally designed by an Evangelist, or it may be the sign of weaving two sources together, or it may be both at the same time. Each instance must be examined on its own merits. Observations about the contrasts and tensions between various characters in Matthew's narrative have been made by other commentators, who were not thinking they were performing either literary or postmodern criticism but were providing a careful historical-critical (including sociological)/grammatical reading of the text.[7] The only truly deconstructive piece of Spencer's analysis is his demonstration that any thoroughgoing attempt to characterize the *magoi* as wise men undermines itself. Yet this illustration of postmodernism itself fails *as exegesis of Matthew* once we recognize, as Spencer himself points out, that the text makes no claim that the *magoi* were wise men. What is deconstructed is the popular Christian notion of them as "wise men." No instability in the text itself emerges here.

THE PHILOSOPHICAL/THEOLOGICAL VIEW

Merold Westphal's chapter turned out to be least like what I was expecting, based on its title, out of all the other four in this book. In the five-views format, I anticipated the lauding of both biblical and systematic theology's impact on biblical hermeneutics. Since the redemptive-historical view deals with biblical theology as opposed to systematic theology, I expected Westphal's contribution to focus on the merits of systematic theology, replete with all its appropriate philosophical underpinnings. Instead, Westphal leads us into thoughtful and helpful reflection on the philosophical questions underlying interpretation. He returns to the original distinction in German philosophy between hermeneutics and exegesis, frequently blurred in contemporary scholarship. Strictly speaking, *hermeneutics* discusses questions of knowledge, validity in interpretation, distinctions between meaning and significance, the possibility of objectivity, and much more, but not the actual strategies or methods for telling us what a text means or implies. The tools for the latter form the discipline of *exegesis*. In other words, given this distinction, Westphal is the only contributor to this book to write exclusively on hermeneutics. The other four of us, in fact, make some hermeneutical comments but focus primarily on

---

[7]E.g., my "The Liberation of Illegitimacy: Women and Rulers in Matthew 1-2," *Biblical Theology Bulletin* 21 (1991): 145-50.

varying exegetical tools. Thus, consistent with these definitions, when Westphal comes to Matthew 2, he has nothing to tell us about what it meant for Matthew or his readers or for any other readers throughout history, including today. Such an analysis of Matthew would depart from hermeneutical theory and impinge on the discipline of exegesis.

The hermeneutical circle may be the most important and lasting legacy of the discussions Westphal surveys, especially when it is redefined as the hermeneutical spiral.[8] This is precisely what critical realism endorses, as I noted above in discussing Spencer's chapter. When we allow the text to change some of our views as we interact with it and if we do so in light of good *exegesis* (or good hermeneutics in the looser sense that the rest of us in this volume are discussing), then we actually can advance in our understanding of an author's intentions for a particular audience as disclosed in a written text. Yet precisely because of our finitude and fallenness, which Westphal rightly stresses, and which perhaps is the one feature that makes his contribution not merely philosophical but also theological, we will never arrive at pure, objective meaning. The spiral never reduces to a single dot.

Much confusion has resulted when discussions in philosophical hermeneutics about authorial intent have been transferred to the realm of biblical interpretation. Nineteenth-century romanticism did indeed seek to recover internal mental processes of authors, yielding psychological interpretations of what those authors were doing as they wrote. Some applications of this approach did cross over into biblical interpretation, but they have not lasted nearly as long or had as dominating an influence as they did in European literary criticism of modern texts. At the popular level, Christians have always been fascinated with the psychology of biblical characters (not authors), often without realizing how little biblical data they actually have to work with in this endeavor. A small discipline of psychological biblical criticism exists today, even at the scholarly level, but it shows little sign of growing into a significant force in the guild.[9] Most of what writers like E. D. Hirsch Jr. have meant in insisting on interpretation according to authorial intent refers to those dimensions of a writer's designs that are

---

[8]Grant R. Osborne, *The Hermeneutical Spiral*, 2nd ed. (Downers Grove, Ill.: InterVarsity Press, 2006).

[9]D. Andrew Kille, *Psychological Biblical Criticism* (Minneapolis: Fortress, 2001).

disclosed in the actual text he or she produced, especially when one can locate the text in its original historical context and analyze the sociocultural settings and contexts in which it was composed. Westphal is right that Hirsch's *Validity in Interpretation* contains seemingly contradictory statements in places, but many of these are clarified in his later *Aims of Interpretation*.[10] In this latter work, Hirsch's perspectives do not seem to be far from Westphal's at all.

At the same time, Westphal joins a distinguished cadre of interdisciplinary scholars who have applied speech-act theory to the interpretation of texts, especially biblical texts, to indicate what *is* recoverable of authorial intent.[11] It is not some access to the psyche of a departed person from a different time and culture, but what that author intended to accomplish by means of a text and its constituent elements. Here speech-act theory overlaps with form criticism, to the extent that the function of a certain kind of speech or literary form is in view. Thus Westphal could have applied speech-act theory to Matthew 2:7-15, highlighting and unpacking the functions of guidance (Mt 2:9), joy-production (Mt 2:10), worship and gift-giving (Mt 2:11), warning (Mt 2:12), commands (Mt 2:13), obedience (Mt 2:14), and the fulfillment of prophecy (Mt 2:15).

Some of these performative utterances are obviously nontransferrable to other contexts. Matthew was not likely envisioning that others who heard or read his text would take it as God's command to move *their* families to Egypt (though misguided players of "Bible roulette" over the ages may have done so!). Matthew certainly could have hoped that others would be inspired to rejoice over what God brought to the earth through Christ and to worship him and give him their very best service. On a higher rung of the ladder of abstraction,[12] all God's people must pay attention to God's guidance, warnings and commands elsewhere in Scripture that do apply to them more generally, perhaps being open to the possibility that God's direction might come in the form of a dream. There is a growing body of increasingly sophisticated hermeneutical literature reflecting on legitimate and illegitimate forms of application (significance, implications, connec-

---

[10]E. D. Hirsch Jr., *Aims of Interpretation* (Chicago: University of Chicago Press, 1976).
[11]See esp. Kevin J. Vanhoozer, *Is There a Meaning in This Text?* (Grand Rapids: Zondervan, 1998).
[12]Craig L. Blomberg with Jennifer F. Markley, *Handbook of New Testament Exegesis* (Grand Rapids: Baker Academic, 2010), pp. 66, 251-57.

tions to modern life, the fusion of horizons, etc.) that could be profitably mined at this juncture.[13]

THE REDEMPTIVE-HISTORICAL VIEW

Richard Gaffin's contribution is the one with which I find myself most in agreement. While biblical theology today often highlights the distinctive themes of each biblical book, corpus or testament, or traces the appearance and development of one or more important themes throughout part or all of Scripture, it has historically also meant looking for the unity in Scripture's revelation of God's mighty acts in history, from creation to consummation. Sometimes key terms or themes are presented as the "center" of a given corpus, testament or even the whole Bible. Sometimes the unity is described in a series of propositional statements or in a concise narrative summary of the overall plot of the Bible's story line.[14] Sometimes a particular theological framework is consciously or unconsciously utilized in this process; in evangelical circles the opposite approaches of covenant theology and dispensationalism have been perhaps the most influential and best known. Gaffin, reflecting his Calvinist tradition, clearly comes down on the side of covenant theology. However, different strands of evangelical, Protestant or Christian theology could illustrate the same concerns Gaffin represents, even if to varying degrees.

What is crucial to discuss about Gaffin's chapter is the use of his method with Matthew 2:7-15. Gaffin's analysis restricts the application of the redemptive-historical hermeneutic to the quotation of Hosea 11:1 in Matthew 2:15. This need not be the case. Gaffin could have pointed out continuities, for example, between the instructions to Old Testament Joseph by means of dreams and to New Testament Joseph by those same means. Or he could have discussed the Moses typology present in the attempts to kill the Christ child, just as a ruthless Pharaoh prefigured King Herod in trying, equally unsuccessfully, to kill the baby who would grow up to inaugurate God's earlier covenant with Israel.

---

[13]William W. Klein, Craig L. Blomberg and Robert L. Hubbard Jr., *Introduction to Biblical Interpretation*, rev. ed. (Nashville: Thomas Nelson, 2004), pp. 477-504, and the literature there cited.

[14]See my "The Unity and Diversity of Scripture," in *New Dictionary of Biblical Theology*, ed. T. Desmond Alexander and Brian S. Rosner (Leicester, U.K.: Inter-Varsity Press, 2000), pp. 64-72, and the literature there cited.

Gaffin, however, focuses solely on Matthew's use of typology in quoting Hosea 11:1. Agreeing with one group of specialists, whom he cites (against another group, whom he does not note),[15] Gaffin insists that the original biblical writer (in this case Hosea) must have understood, however seminally and imperfectly, the meaning that the later biblical writer (in this case Matthew) asserts based on that earlier text. Gaffin also maintains that it is legitimate to use the later text to interpret the earlier one, a view we will comment on again when we come to Robert Wall's essay on canonical hermeneutics.

The problem with maintaining both of these points simultaneously is that they remain in considerable tension with each other. If part of accepting the entire canon of Scripture as inspired and authoritative means that we can use the New Testament to interpret the Old (or, more generally, later Scripture to interpret earlier texts), then there is no need to insist that the first author had the later writer's meaning in mind. Because the later text is "God-breathed" (2 Tim 3:16), that alone makes its interpretation correct and profitable, irrespective of the earlier text's intention. In other words, only if our best efforts at determining what the earlier author meant do *not* yield what the later writer claims he meant do we confront a conundrum. Conversely, if we determine that there *are* hints in the larger literary context of, in this case, Hosea that justify Matthew's use, then we have no need to insist that we must use Matthew to interpret Hosea. We may rather affirm that Matthew has interpreted Hosea fairly along lines that readers might have been expected to conclude from the book of Hosea itself.

Gaffin's more fundamental problem here, however, lies with his overly narrow understanding of typology. Jews were accustomed to mining Scripture for divinely disclosed patterns of God's revelation of himself and redemption of his people, which were repeated on later occasions. In the case of Matthew's use of Hosea, a first-century Jew who already believed in Jesus as Messiah would have found it striking to observe that just as Hosea reminded his audience that God had brought his son, Israel, out of Egypt at the time of the Mosaic covenant's establishment, so also God was orchestrating events so that Jesus, his greater Son, would come out of Egypt

---

[15]R. T. France actually belongs in the camp opposite of Gaffin, despite Gaffin's using him for support. See France, *Matthew: An Introduction and Commentary* (Grand Rapids: Eerdmans, 1985), p. 40.

at the time of the inauguration of God's new covenant with his people. Neither Moses nor Hosea need have suspected in the slightest that one day the Messiah would come out of Egypt in order for this kind of typology to have had a profound and even apologetically significant impact on Matthew's audiences.[16] Surely God's hand was disclosed in the later event simply because of its striking similarity to the former one. The term "fulfill" in both Greek and Hebrew can mean to "fill full"—that is, to invest with fuller meaning—just as easily as it can mean that a prophesied event has now occurred.[17]

Nothing in 1 Peter 1, Luke 24 or Hebrews 3 teaches otherwise. First Peter 1:10-12 gives no indication of how much was revealed to the prophets who intently sought to gain additional information concerning the contents of their prophetic utterances. First Peter 1:12 says they realized they were speaking of a later time and not only their own, but the extent of their understanding is left entirely unspecified. In Luke 24:44 Jesus explicitly declares, "Everything must be fulfilled that is written about me in the Law of Moses, the Prophets and the Psalms," *not* that everything written in these three parts of the Hebrew Scriptures was about Jesus! Hebrews 3:5 declares that "'Moses was faithful as a servant in all God's house,' bearing witness to what would be spoken by God in the future." However, this text says nothing about how much of Moses' witness is about God's future speech, nor about how much of God's future speech Moses witnessed to, nor even about the nature of that witness whenever it did occur. Some New Testament texts, it is true, *do* declare that an Old Testament author understood christological significance in what he was promulgating, but no biblical text ever implies that all or even most of them did. Again, we must examine each passage one by one rather than make sweeping generalizations.[18]

THE CANONICAL VIEW

Robert Wall has done more than any other individual scholar to appropri-

---

[16]Tracy L. Howard, "The Use of Hosea 11:1 in Matthew 2:15: An Alternative Solution," *BSac* 143 (1986): 314-28, speaks of "analogical correspondence."

[17]R. Schippers, "πληρόω," in *New International Dictionary of New Testament Theology*, ed. Colin Brown (Grand Rapids: Zondervan, 1975–1978), 1:733-41.

[18]See esp. G. K. Beale and D. A. Carson, eds., *Commentary on the New Testament Use of the Old Testament* (Grand Rapids: Baker Academic, 2007).

ate canonical criticism for evangelicalism and to adapt it to a form consistent with historic Christian tenets, and for this we owe him a profound debt of gratitude. Wall repeatedly and rightly stresses that the canonical view begins with and is built on foundations of historical-critical/grammatical exegesis, exactly as I have stressed. There is no question that historical and grammatical study agrees with canonical criticism that the Scriptures are completely human texts. Unfortunately, historical and grammatical study has often stopped there. Christians, however, as Wall properly points out, must approach Scripture as a sacred text that is fully divine as well as fully human. The history of interpretation (or "history of effects" so that art, music, literature, etc. inspired by the text is taken into account along with formal commentary) is important in order to see what insights we may have missed that others have gleaned, even as we weed out fanciful interpretations that we cannot accept. The rule of faith is an important safeguard for interpreters, though it must never be used as a straightjacket, lest no one ever discover new truth from the Scriptures or lest we assume that classic, creedal formulations of the faith are as inerrant as the Scriptures themselves. The whole process of application, not only for individuals but also for gathered communities of Christians, remains equally important. These observations also make it appropriate to agree quickly with Wall that Scripture must be approached as the church's text.

There are only two topics in his essay where Wall may need to exercise more care, lest he mislead: Scripture as a single text and as a shaped text. In his discussion of Scripture as a single text, Wall, like Gaffin, allows for the idea that the meaning of later texts can actually inform our understanding of the meaning of earlier texts. Because of this, Wall runs the risk of confusing original meaning with later significance (recall above, pp. 141-42). Later biblical uses of earlier materials can all be explained through a variety of hermeneutical observations without resorting to the claim that a canonical writer may actually give new meaning to an earlier text that could not otherwise be justified on historical-critical/grammatical grounds of some kind.

Further, additional problems occur as Wall speaks of Scripture as a shaped text. It is indisputable that collecting the books of the Bible into a single canon has created juxtapositions that tempt us to interpret one document in light of another in ways we might well not have done if each biblical book had remained an individual scroll. However, simply because I might observe, for example, that the fourfold Gospel collection has inserted John in between the volumes of Luke's two-part work does not justify my interpreting the end of Luke's Gospel in light of John's prologue or vice versa. Wall's essay fails to distinguish between (1) parts of the Scripture that the church recognized as already mutually illuminating and therefore chose to juxtapose, at least in part for that very reason, and (2) juxtapositions of parts of Scripture for reasons unrelated to their mutual illumination, which therefore distract from and possibly contradict the meanings of the juxtaposed works.

Thus the normative authority of the Gospel of Matthew is located in the final form of Matthew, not in either Matthew's redaction of Mark (rightly Wall) or in Matthew's later function as the first in the fourfold Gospel canon in the New Testament (against Wall). All of Wall's insights with respect to Matthew 2:7-15 based on Old Testament texts and themes are legitimate, not because they represent distinctively canonical readings, but because they appeal to *antecedent* Scripture that Matthew almost certainly knew.[19] Thus they form a central portion of the historical background to Matthew's Gospel.

When Wall uses Luke's infancy narrative to interpret Matthew's, however, he juxtaposes texts that first-century readers, as far as we know, would never have juxtaposed. It is no doubt true that over the centuries many readers of the completed Bible in its canonical form may have interpreted Matthew's infancy narrative in light of Luke's (or vice versa), because of reading the two accounts one shortly after the other. However, that history of interpretation does not make the practice a good one. For example, Luke's first beatitude ("blessed are you who are poor"—Lk 6:20) has regularly been interpreted in light of Matthew's ("blessed are the poor in spirit"—Mt 5:3) and in so doing Luke's recurring emphasis on God's concern for the materially impoverished has almost been completely obscured.[20] It is at this point where the canonical method must be tempered with literary criticism's concern for the final form of an individual book of the Bible and with the redemptive-historical movement's emphasis on the chronological development of doctrine.

---

[19]Walter C. Kaiser Jr., *Toward an Exegetical Theology* (Grand Rapids: Baker, 1981), pp. 134-40.
[20]See Frederick D. Bruner, *Matthew, A Commentary: The Christbook*, 2nd ed. (Grand Rapids: Eerdmans, 2004), p. 159.

CONCLUSIONS

The historical-critical/grammatical method seeks the *original* meaning of biblical authors as they wrote texts to specific audiences. All the other methods envision something else going on as well that takes later writers, texts and/or readers into account! I fully appreciate the potential sterility of biblical analysis that does not ask questions about literary style, speech-acts, how one book relates to later ones, the canonical shape of the entire Christian Scriptures, subsequent reader reception and proper application to believers' lives, individually and in community. All of those issues are important. However, none of these questions can be addressed properly unless the foundation of historical-critical/grammatical analysis of each text's constituent elements is laid down first and remains of primary importance. Of course, no one ever comes to the study of Scripture this simply or methodically. Almost everyone has a sense of various wholes before they scrutinize the parts, and few readers come to any part of the Bible without some preformed sense of what the Bible is about that colors their reading of the text. Hence, we need the hermeneutical spiral to continually test our previous understandings against the details of Scripture itself.

Diversity of interpretations is important because all of us are finite and fallen, and we miss things and misconstrue things. Yet reveling in diversity simply for diversity's sake, or using diversity as an occasion to celebrate an interpreter's creativity, is not a Christian virtue. Nevertheless, orthodox interpretations, however faithful they are to apostolic tradition or later creedal formulations, if they do not express what a given text under consideration is actually teaching, must also be rejected. The right doctrine from the wrong texts continues to plague our pulpits around the world every Sunday in far too many places. The historical-critical/grammatical method, when properly used, not to exclude other methods but as the foundation for those other methods, provides many of the necessary checks and balances to keep interpreters from going off track in either of these two directions.

7

The Literary/
Postmodern Response

F. Scott Spencer

I wish to thank my colleagues for such clear and challenging presentations of their respective hermeneutical positions. I will respond in an order proceeding from tighter exegetical-textual approaches to broader theological-theoretical viewpoints. I slot my literary/postmodern view toward the middle of this spectrum.

THE HISTORICAL-CRITICAL/GRAMMATICAL VIEW

Craig Blomberg makes a strong case for the "logical priority" and "necessary foundation" of establishing the most "original" text and expounding its formative historical context and grammatical construction. All hermeneutical moves must start with some ground rules about *what* we are interpreting. On the historical side, Blomberg provides a nicely balanced and nuanced discussion of "authorial intent" as "shorthand" (rather than straightjacket) for exploring "the most likely meaning" of a text in its native milieu—"not seeking [the author's] irrecoverable mental processes" and not always attaining certainty about original meaning. However, by respecting the author's contribution and situation, "one can at least rule out many unlikely possibilities" (p. 30 n. 9).

Moreover, Blomberg helpfully reminds us of the ancient *oral culture* in which the biblical texts first developed, a phenomenon that my heavily "literate" literary/postmodern approach tends to neglect and needs to take more seriously in light of recent scholarship. Dependence on orally transmitted material confronts us with critical issues of history and interpretation, remembrance and revision. The pattern of carefully memorizing oral traditions in antiquity provided "fixed points" for checking a speaker's—or author's—account amid the inevitable fluidity of storytelling for various purposes and audiences. While stressing the historical reliability of ancient historical narratives, like the New Testament Gospels, Blomberg by no means denies their interpretive dimensions or "ideological spin." The Gospels are not bland transcripts or chronicles of events, practices alien to ancient historiography. Such congressional-record-like documents are "largely a modern invention," Blomberg astutely observes (p. 33). My literary/postmodern view revs up the ideological spin cycle to include the variable viewpoints readers bring to the interpretive enterprise; but it remains vital, in my judgment, for readers not simply to exploit biblical texts for their own aims but to engage these ideologically (theologically) motivated accounts in rigorous, respectful dialogue.

While I concur about the foundational nature of "lower-critical" exegetical work, I am less sanguine about the *priority* of "higher" moves of source, form and redaction criticism over (or before) narrative or final-text analyses. I do not doubt, as Luke's prologue indicates, that the Gospel writers incorporated and edited oral and written sources in composing their narratives, but I am not confident about standard procedures of identifying sources and separating tradition from redaction, especially given the careful, "orderly" (Lk 1:1, 3) design of the final product (not to mention the lack of footnotes and bibliography!). Even where gaps and seams appear, a narrative-oriented approach *first* probes what these breaks might signify *within the story* rather than what lies behind it, as I did with the Herod and magi material in Matthew 2—suggesting, for example, the breakdown or unraveling of the Herod *character* in the narrative instead of discrete underlying sources about Herod.

This does not mean that my view has no interest in the historical Herod or magi or the geopolitical contours of first-century Judea, Galilee and Egypt shaping the milieu in which Matthew's narrative is embedded. Such assumed information influences (informs our understanding of) the story's composition and reception. As a *historical* narrative, Matthew's Gospel offers a stylized portrait of the *real* Jesus and Herod, not fictionalized personas. Hence, while I grant that there have been some extreme practitioners of literary/postmodern criticism, I reject Blomberg's assess-

ment of the literary thrust of this approach, in contradistinction to his
own, as "*ahistorical* . . . seeking *merely* to understand the literary elements
of plot, theme . . . and the like" and aiming to "stop with the narrative
world internal to a document that focuses *only* on implied authors . . . and
implied readers" (p. 39; emphasis added).[1] And, as my essay demonstrates,
I too resist, as Blomberg puts it, "those forms of postmodernism that so
revel in diversity in the interpretation of texts that they reject the constraints of limiting meaning" (p. 39). Further, I think humor plays a key
role in Matthew's account. As a result the birth story has a sharp, satirical
edge addressing deadly serious business that a literary/postmodern view
helps us to appreciate.[2] In any case, Matthew is not just playing around,
and I am not just "seek[ing] an interpretation that is fun to read" (p. 41).

Blomberg thus drives the wedge too deeply between our hermeneutical
perspectives. Nevertheless, there are differences. For example, in interpreting Matthew 2, I am happy to know everything I can about first-
century Egypt, including Blomberg's point that a large Diaspora Jewish
community resided there. However, here I would argue that Blomberg's
inference from this historical datum misses the point of Matthew's story.
Rather than reading Matthew as suggesting the congenial notion that
"undoubtedly Joseph and Mary headed to a community with a settlement
of their own kinfolk" (p. 44), from the beginning Matthew's birth narrative stages the hopeful coming of Jesus Messiah against the painful and
disruptive backdrop of *exile* (see Mt 1:17). Accordingly the flight to Egypt
in Matthew's story represents a precarious *dislocation from kinfolk*, reminis-
cent of Israel's hard history up to their present vulnerable status under
harsh Roman-Herodian rule.

On the vital matter of the New Testament's use of the Old Testament,
my view aligns with Blomberg's in "not read[ing] New Testament meanings back into Old Testament texts" (p. 40) and in appreciating Matthew's
citation of Hosea 11:1 to forge a typological/representative link between

---

[1] I stress the compatibility of narrative criticism with historical analyses in F. Scott Spencer,
"Acts and Modern Literary Approaches," in *The Book of Acts in Its First Century Setting*, vol.
1, *The Book of Acts in Its Literary Setting*, ed. Bruce W. Winter and Andrew D. Clarke (Grand
Rapids: Eerdmans, 1993), pp. 381-414.
[2] I discuss Matthew's critical use of humor in "Those Riotous—Yet Righteous—Foremothers of
Jesus: Exploring Matthew's Comic Genealogy," in *Dancing Girls, "Loose" Ladies and Women of
"the Cloth": The Women in Jesus' Life* (New York: Continuum, 2004), pp. 24-46.

Jesus and the people of Israel as "God's son." Moreover, Blomberg beautifully captures Matthew's "fulfillment" perspective in terms of the Hosea text in particular and the Old Testament in general being "'filled full' in Jesus' life" (p. 44). My only quibble here is with Blomberg's granting a necessary "consistency" between Hosea's aims and the "fuller meaning" Matthew derives beyond Hosea's "historical intention." He cites Carson for support: "Had [Hosea] been able to see Matthew's use of 11:1, he would not have disapproved, even if messianic nuances were not in his mind when he wrote that verse" (p. 31 n. 14). That may be true, but how can we possibly know what Hosea might have approved or disapproved of eight centuries later? Like most of the prophets, he was a strange bird. It is hard enough to decide what he meant in his own context! Here my literary/postmodern view pushes harder to maintain strangeness and distance between Hosea and Matthew, to let each text stand on its own and enter into full-throated, tension-fraught dialogue with the other.

THE CANONICAL VIEW

The issues of hearing and heeding Matthew's intertextual dialogue with Hosea and other biblical literature are at the heart of Robert Wall's canonical approach. My response to Wall's engagement with this "canonical conversation" will follow the three "probes" he makes in his stimulating analysis of our focal text. As I indicate in the conclusion of my position essay, I take a rather pragmatic line on hermeneutics, judging the "proof" of any theory or strategy by its "product" or "payoff" in illuminating the text. Wall's study is especially strong in demonstrating the fruitfulness of his approach to understanding Matthew 2:7-15.

Probe 1: Reading Matthew first. While it is not his main meaning, by "first," I think Wall would support a narrative-critical emphasis on giving primary attention to Matthew's entire, distinctive story as the principal context for interpreting any particular Matthean text. Wall's push toward "holistic" and "final-form" canonical readings encompasses careful consideration of overarching plots and patterns within biblical books; and his symphonic-choral perspective, "aim[ed] at restoring to full volume the voice of every biblical witness" (p. 113) in concert with other canonical strains, appreciates Matthew's unique contribution to the biblical message. Wall seeks to balance scriptural "unity" and "diversity"/

"pluriformity," though with a decided tilt toward the former under the "rule of faith" rubric (pp. 113-14; see probe 3 below).

Wall's chief interest in reading Matthew "first" concerns the *priority* of this Gospel in its canonical placement at the head of the fourfold Gospel collection and, indeed, the entire New Testament. Such prime location was no publishing accident, but rather the early church's ratification of Matthew as "by far the most popular gospel" (p. 124, quoting Lee Mc-Donald) across the wide swath of Christian communities (the "catholic" church). Further, far from being a mere historical curiosity, Matthew's canonical position assumes major hermeneutical significance in Wall's view. This first Gospel and New Testament book begs to be read "as a rewritten story of a faithful Israel with its antecedent in the Old Testament story of Israel" and as "a narrative frontispiece that frames a reading of the other three Gospels" (p. 125). As such, historical criticism's dominant stress on *Markan* priority goes out the window: instead of rewriting Mark, Matthew has a pivotal canonical function, picking up the thread of Israel's Old Testament narrative and setting the stage for Mark and the rest of the New Testament.

Hence canonical interpretation is preeminently *intertextual* rather than source-, form- or redaction-critical. It thus fits well the intertextual, dialogic framework of my literary/postmodern view, but with a more limited focus. Whereas I stress a more back-and-forth, give-and-take, open-forum "canonical conversation" (a phrase I owe to Wall!) among biblical witnesses, Wall's essay in this volume advocates a more linear, orderly hearing/reading process. Matthew, for example, introduces and informs Mark, Luke and John, who in turn take up the story. While together they constitute a harmonic (not monotone) Gospel quartet, Matthew retains the lead part. Or to shift the image, all the Gospel parties may have their say around the table, but Matthew chairs the meeting—which suggests that Mark, Luke and John are not quite given their "full voice" or opportunity to shape the discussion. However, the proof is again in the product, and Wall's next probe demonstrates more precisely how he brings our focal text into conversation with the Old Testament and Gospels.

Probe 2: Reading Matthew 2:7-15 with other Scripture. In treating Matthew's use of Hosea 11:1, Wall concentrates less on "linguistic agreements" (and deviations) than on "common themes or typologies" Hosea "cues up" for Matthew within the wider "canon logic" of Israel's over-arching Old Testament story (p. 127). Of signal importance here is Ho-sea's recurrent "'out of Egypt' catchphrase" (Hos 11:1; 12:9, 13; 13:4), evoking the whole complex of redemptive events surrounding the *exodus,* including the horror of infanticide, the special protection of Israel's fu-ture leader (Moses), and the clash of good (Yahweh) and evil (Pharaoh) kingly power. Such narrative typology comports well with Matthew's infancy story of Jesus—the consummate, Moses-style Savior—and with my literary analysis, though I paid more attention to the conflict dynam-ics in the immediate cotexts of both Hosea 11:1-11 and Matthew 2:13-23. Moreover, while I am happy to endorse Wall's theological emphasis on Jesus' effecting salvation "from sin" via the exodus typology and Mat-thew 1:21, I do not see why he opposes this to political liberation in stressing "a type of deliverance from slavery—from sin, *not Roman occu-pation*" (p. 126, emphasis added). To be sure, Jesus does not lead an armed revolution against Rome, but the exodus connection with its obvi-ous Pharaoh-Herod link nonetheless packs a strong, one-two punch of theological *and* political salvation *and* liberation.[3]

As for correlating Matthew 2:7-15 with the fourfold Gospel, Wall fo-cuses on the conversation with Luke's infancy narrative. While this is a common, natural juxtaposition of nativity stories, I find it curious, given Wall's earlier stress on Matthew's priority leading into Mark, that he makes no comment concerning Mark's jumping right into Jesus' adult vo-cation. Beyond the old-style historical judgment that Mark has abridged Matthew and thus has little to contribute beyond Matthew, or a rather bland canonical judgment that Mark's readers can simply assume Mat-thew's Christmas story and move on from there, it might be useful to re-flect on the significance of Matthew and Luke's bracketing birth narra-tives around Mark's more compressed, urgent, get-down-to-business approach to Jesus' "kingdom of God is at hand" mission (Mk 1:15). (Of course, the Gospel of John's cosmic story of Jesus' origins adds a whole other dimension!) I throw out as a possible line for fruitful discussion the

---

[3]On the political dimensions of Matthew's narrative, see Richard A. Horsley, *The Liberation of Christmas: The Infancy Narratives in Social Context* (New York: Crossroad, 1989); Warren Carter, *Matthew and the Margins: A Sociopolitical and Religious Reading* (Maryknoll, N.Y.: Or-bis, 2000).

phenomena of varying twists and turns on a major "journey" motif both within Matthew and Luke's respective infancy stories and in Mark's introduction of Jesus ("In those days Jesus came from Nazareth of Galilee and was baptized . . . in the Jordan" [Mk 1:9]).

In comparing the birth accounts of Matthew and Luke, Wall admirably fulfills his goal of "resist[ing] harmonistic or historicist reductions of the two, while recognizing the common traditions they do share that help sketch a unified narrative of Jesus' beginnings" (p. 128). A narrative critic could not put it better, while a deconstructive critic would chafe at the "unified" constraint.

Probe 3: Reading Matthew 2:7-15 by the rule of faith. Wall's canonical view, unlike some others' (that of James A. Sanders in particular), makes much of the apostolic rule of faith (Irenaeus) as a "working grammar of faith" and "governor for interpretation" (Tertullian) (p. 115) of the Bible as supremely the church's Book, its Holy Scripture, shaping the universal (catholic) church's worship, character and mission. While Wall "employs all the tools of modern criticism" (p. 115), he does so in the humble service of spiritual formation or the aims of salvation and sanctification (2 Tim 3:15-16). Moreover, he hastens to clarify that the rule of faith is not meant to be a "restrictive" procrustean bed, lopping off all progressive applications of Christian faith and practice to changing situations, but allows for, within orthodox parameters, "different expressions of this same grammar, shaped by different creeds, cultures and crises, order[ing] the faith traditions of the West and East in a theological variety that extends further Scripture's revelation of God's way of ordering the world" (p. 115).

My literary/postmodern view may choose, for confessional reasons, to operate within the rule of faith, but the approach itself does not demand any particular faith commitment or theological yardstick (canon). Secular literary and historical critics may offer keen insights into biblical interpretation, but I would argue—on literary and historical grounds—that their value is limited to the extent they do not appreciate the fundamental nature of biblical texts as *religious literature* historically produced, preserved and practiced as *sacred Scripture* in the life of the church. My main discomfort with a hermeneutic driven on a rule-of-faith track comes from my postmodern view of an "open text." As I hope I have made clear, I do not endorse a free-for-all playground approach with no limits on interpretation, especially the limits imposed by the text itself. Nevertheless, I do worry about overly constricting today's third-millennial, multicultural Bible readers, Christian or otherwise, by an ancient rule of faith promulgated by Mediterranean church *fathers* (a feminist concern). I worry about who is left out and who gets hurt by oppressive rule-enforcers, as the history of the church and biblical reception history too often illustrate. Wall checks this tendency in his poignant closing call for "reading texts with a fellowship of believers that cultivates spiritual virtues . . . such as love for God and neighbor, truth-seeking, humility, patience and forgiveness"—all of which prove "critical for using Scripture in a way that targets holy ends" (p. 130). But I still worry.

However, I must say my worry is further assuaged by Wall's canonical reading of our focal text, which charts the magi's star trek and Jesus' Egypt flight not only according to exodus coordinates but also within the wider "celestial compass" and global horizon of all divinely ordered creation. Broad theological vision and liturgical "confession of the church's Creator God" as "maker of heaven and earth, and of all things visible and invisible" (p. 129) safeguard the rule of faith from imperial, provincial application.

THE REDEMPTIVE-HISTORICAL VIEW

Richard Gaffin's approach incorporates historical, canonical and literary perspectives in sharply defined ways. Though not opposed to investigating historical backgrounds of biblical texts, the redemptive-historical view is more focused on understanding God's role within history. Specifically, this view focuses on God's grand project of covenantal redemption in the history of God's people—culminating in Jesus Christ—to which the Bible gives faithful witness. In canonical-literary terms, Gaffin stresses following the entire Bible's "redemptive-historical plot as it unfolds scene by scene" within a "progressive," sweeping historical narrative, a "great epic drama" of God's interaction with humanity (p. 109). Though clearly invested in theological interpretation with a strong soteriological core, Gaffin underscores Geerhardus Vos's appraisal that "the Bible is not a dogmatic handbook but a historical book full of dramatic interest" (p. 90).

Besides its homing in on an overarching, singular plot—a major one, to be sure—across the canon as an integral part of his hermeneutical view (not simply illustrative of one unifying theme among many), Gaffin's approach differs from Wall's and mine in other key respects. First, on the matter of biblical coherence, while allowing for the Bible's "diverse" testimony to God's redemptive-historical work in Christ in "different parts or instances . . . times and places . . . modes and genres" (Heb 1:1; p. 95), Gaffin maintains a staunch conviction of God's scriptural Word as "a concordant unity," "a unified whole" whose "interests are never competitive or even independent of or indifferent to each other" (p. 96). This allows for somewhat limited canonical conversation that turns down the "full volume" of each biblical witness by tuning out any background noise that does not enhance the redemptive theme; and it seems to have little room for my postmodern interest in teasing out ambiguities and tensions among biblical texts and welcoming a wide variety of questions and concerns that readers bring to the interpretive process.

Second, Gaffin's emphasis on Jesus as the Christian Bible's *telos*, biblical "history's consummation, nothing less than its eschatological omega point," leads him to a strict "unidirectional" reading of the Old Testament as prophetic prelude to the New Testament and rejection as "illegitimate" any "disjunctive reading of the Old Testament" writings "on their own terms" (p. 101). To one degree or another, I think the rest of us in this volume would not drive our hermeneutical views down such a hard-and-fast one-way street, allowing more space for distinctive, if not necessarily disjunctive, Old Testament highways and side roads. In my view, we miss much of the rich complexity and dramatic tension of God's historic dealings with Israel in the Old Testament by making Christ its central character. To be fair, this is not Gaffin's intention. "One need not flatten out the differences between the Old and New Testaments," he contends, "in order to recognize in the [Old Testament] text . . . an incipient and seminal grasp, however otherwise shadowy and inchoate, of the messianic plant whose eventual full flowering in Christ [the New Testament] documents and explicates" (p. 108). But then again, Gaffin's robust christological hermeneutic, which unapologetically reads Christ into or, better put, out of the Old Testament—as John 8:56 ("Abraham rejoiced that he would see my [Jesus'] day") and John 12:41 ("Isaiah said this because he saw his [Jesus'] glory and spoke about him [Jesus]") claim[4]—stresses more the shin-

---

[4]I take these examples Gaffin cites as part of the distinctive Johannine portrait of Jesus, complementary to, but not representative of, the views of Matthew and other New Testament books.

ing and coherent, rather than "shadowy and inchoate," nature of the Old Testament's witness to Christ.

Third, even more than he looks to John's Gospel for hermeneutical guidance, Gaffin depends heavily on the book of Hebrews in his essay. Without question, starting with its soaring confession of Christ's historical and theological significance in Hebrews 1:1-4, the author bears eloquent witness to a thoroughgoing christological interpretation of the Old Testament. However, it also stands out as an idiosyncratic and enigmatic document within the New Testament: generically (letter or homily?), canonically (capstone of Pauline corpus or headstone of Catholic Epistles?) and theologically (for example, Hebrews takes the starkest stance on *covenantal replacement or supersession* with the statement: "In speaking of a 'new covenant,' he has made the first one obsolete. And what is obsolete and growing old will soon disappear" [Heb 8:13]). While Hebrews stimulates much provocative canonical conversation, I imagine it would also stimulate vigorous canonical debate, especially with Matthew's Jesus, who insists, "I have come not to abolish [the Old Testament law or the prophets] but to fulfill" (Mt 5:17).

I must say, however, that these general criticisms of Gaffin's redemptive-historical view do not apply to his sterling treatment of Matthew's use of Hosea. This may mean, of course, that I have missed something critical in his big picture. In any case, coming back to my "proof in the pudding" angle, I find Gaffin's serving of our focal Matthew text very delectable indeed. He strikes a sage balance between Sailhamer's literal, nontypological reading of Hosea that, in Gaffin's judgment, "overstates Hosea's own grasp of the messianic future" and McCartney/Enns's predominantly typological approach that remains "at best unclear how the literal sense intended by Hosea (the human author) is compatible with Matthew's reading" (p. 104). (A similar critique might be leveled against my reading.) Gaffin then does a better job than any of us in demonstrating that Matthew's citation of Hosea 11:1—"far from being a grammatical-historically indefensible or inexplicable textual grab" of a convenient text (p. 108)—is in fact thoughtfully engaged with Hosea's entire context. Moreover, in addition to probing the significance of the larger unit in Hosea 11:1-11 and related passages, Gaffin tracks how Matthew develops Jesus' vocation as Son (building on Hosea's depiction of Israel) beyond the birth narrative into Jesus' baptism and temptation scenes (Mt 3:13-17; 4:1-11). In other words, Gaffin displays keen narrative-critical sense, even if he does not dig as deeply as I do into the narrative fissures in the wider story of the magi's visit and Jesus' exodus to and from Egypt in Matthew 2.

THE PHILOSOPHICAL/THEOLOGICAL VIEW

It is appropriate to treat the philosophical/theological view last, since it offers broad theoretical "interpretations of interpretation," or philosophical assessments of the entire human interpretive process, in which our four other particular, biblical-textual approaches participate. In other words, Merold Westphal, with his expansive metaperspective, stands above and apart from the rest of us in this volume. However, he by no means resides aloft over us in some rarefied supercloud or aloof from us in our practical commitments to rigorous and relevant biblical interpretation. Indeed, he works with us to sharpen our thinking about what we are doing and why we are doing it: "What is going on, often behind our backs, when we interpret texts and other phenomena?" (p. 71). Most remarkably, Westphal guides us through the daunting thicket of hermeneutical philosophers like Hans-Georg Gadamer, Paul Ricoeur, Martin Heidegger, Friedrich Nietzsche, Jacques Derrida, Søren Kierkegaard and Nicholas Wolterstorff. These philosophers are indeed "strange bedfellows" to each other, and downright unsavory bedbugs to some Bible believers. Westphal guides us in a masterful and accessible way, spiced with lovely illustrations from the basketball court, music hall, dinner table and stovetop (a little "chicken soup for the soul," we might say).

Overall Westphal appeals to Gadamer and Ricoeur, who "deny to the author unilateral agency in fixing [textual] meaning" (p. 75) and insist on interpreters' "understanding [that] is necessarily plural, partial and perspectival" arising from their "inextricable embeddedness" in particular historical and traditional milieus (p. 74). These appeals prove congenial to my postmodern emphasis on textual openness to varieties of reader responses (though I reference Bakhtin's dialogism and Derrida's antidualism). Yet, with this open outlook, Westphal carefully steers a "middle way" between author and reader, between a nail-the-one-true-meaning objectivism and a "different-strokes-for-different-folks relativism." To this end, he advances three useful concepts: "legitimate prejudices" (Gadamer), "indispensable guardrail" (Derrida) and "double hermeneutic" (Wolterstorff) (pp. 73, 78-79).

First, Gadamer's notion of "legitimate prejudices" reminds us that interpretation is not a pristine process carried out in some hermetically sealed chamber. All of us bring our prejudgments or presuppositions to the hermeneutical table all of the time. The challenge is to be as open, honest and self-critical about our prejudices as we can in order "to sort out the good [legitimate] presuppositions from the bad ones" (p. 73). On the constructive side, Westphal calls for a healthy engagement with our religious traditions, both inherited and chosen: "The rehabilitation of prejudice restores to tradition its power because to a very large extent, prejudices . . . are carried and transmitted by traditions" (p. 73). We cannot and should not shed our traditional-theological skins, which hold us together. Here I see an affirming nod to the "rule(s) of faith," the "redemptive-historical" framework and other grammars of faith shaping our traditions. In the bitter fundamentalist-moderate wars in my denomination over the past two decades, it has been tempting from time to time to try and shed my Southern Baptist skin (the seminary where I serve was the first moderate spinoff after established institutions were "lost"); but a wiser path, like that which Westphal traces, encourages thoughtful rediscovering and reclaiming the best and truest forms of Baptist identity.

Continuing this critical line, Westphal's prejudicial, or "perspectival," approach emphasizes the "essential finitude of human understanding" and thus exposes the need for different perspectives to illuminate our inevitable "blind spots" (p. 74). Though Westphal does not pursue this point, I see a place here for the (pre)judicious use of the hermeneutics of suspicion. For me feminist biblical criticism—which lays its prejudicial cards full-face on the table—has been particularly salutary in correcting my patriarchal, male-centered blind spots, myopias and astigmatisms.[5]

Second, Derrida's image of the "indispensable guardrail," combined with his more familiar deconstructive views and blurring of binary oppositions alluded to in my essay, provides another dialectical perspective negotiating between the limits and liberties of interpretation. The Derridean guardrail of "critical reading" must "recognize and respect all its classical

---

[5]See F. Scott Spencer, "Feminist Criticism," in *Hearing the New Testament: Strategies for Interpretation*, ed. Joel B. Green, 2nd ed. (Grand Rapids: Eerdmans, 2010), pp. 289-325.

exigencies . . . and requires all the instruments of traditional criticism," lest interpretation flail out willy-nilly in all directions and be licensed "to say almost anything" (p. 78, quoting Derrida). Here Blomberg's stress on the foundation of historical-critical/grammatical criticism resonates most clearly. To reiterate my earlier stance, I also work within interpretive constraints, with the literary structures and patterns of the final form of biblical texts forming my primary guardrails.

Finally, Wolterstorff's "double hermeneutic" offers a somewhat different, yet equally effective, bridge between two interpretive horizons, with its focus on two questions: first, "What *did* the human author say to the original audience?" and second, "What *is* God *saying* to us here and now through these words of Scripture?" (p. 79, quoting Wolterstorff). The quest for authorial meaning is not a futile exercise in mining the psyche or internal motivation of Matthew or any other biblical writer (as Blomberg also debunks) but is rather an ascertainment of "the public speech acts of the author," that is, an "assertion, promise, request, command, question," or another action the writer might perform through the text (p. 76). The second question shifts to contemporary meaning or application as a necessary (nonoptional) hermeneutical move. In a pastoral context, we would ask, how does this text preach? However, to answer this question we would hold a firm commitment, as Westphal advocates, to drawing application *from* responsible biblical analysis (rather than mere personal musing and popular culture). We thus tightly tether the two questions to each other in practicing a *double* hermeneutic.

In my essay, I do not proceed to any substantive application of our focal text to today's church and society, partly because of space considerations, partly because the literary/postmodern view does not require it and partly because of the bias of specialization that tends to segregate New Testament hermeneutics from homiletics. However, Westphal will not let me off the hook so easily, and I should know better, since I preach regularly and carry the title of Professor of New Testament and Preaching. I will not attempt any great sermonizing here, but I suggest there is room for critical reflection on the quality of our relationships with Jesus the Christ in light of the magi's experience. Compared with the other essays in this volume, mine deals more extensively with Matthew's literary characterization of the magi and is the only one that complicates (deconstructs) the magi's "wise" reputation as spiritual model for seekers and Christ-worshipers. Matthew's Christmas story, I would argue, pushes us beyond a simple exemplar: *like* the magi we should diligently seek the Christ child and pay him due homage with the best gifts we have to offer. Yes, indeed. But also, perhaps, *unlike* the Magi or in *critical dialogue* with their experience, we *Gentiles from the West* should examine how, why and to what ends we seek this messianic "king of the Jews" today and also the ways our worship of this king, and the discipleship that flows from such devotion, resists and/ or reinforces the powers that exist in our world. As with Matthew's magi, we may unwittingly support, rather than subvert, violent and unjust "Herodian" interests in the name of Christ. In any case we should be truly wise men and women of acute political judgment as well as spiritual discernment ("wise as serpents" [Mt 10:16]).

This final nudge toward more destabilizing, "open" readings of biblical narratives aligns with Westphal's memorable cautionary word (via Ricoeur) to all of us that we not press our preferred hermeneutical views with such "methodological rigor" that they ossify into "rigor mortis" (p. 80). Our hermeneutical rigor should lead to new life (*vitae*, not *mortis*)—the very life of God, who raised Jesus from the dead that we might live and reign with him in justice and peace; it should lead to fresh drafts of new wine from old wineskins (Mt 9:17) and wondrous finds of treasures "new and old" from the cache of God's biblical revelation (Mt 13:52).

8

The Philosophical/
Theological Response

Merold Westphal

In response to the position papers of this volume, I will begin with my general response to all of the essays as a whole and then address each of the contributor's positions individually. First, I would like to point out that it was necessary for me to stubbornly decline to give a reading of Matthew 2:7-15, not just because I am a philosopher and not a biblical scholar, but primarily because philosophical hermeneutics is not a method or a strategy for interpreting texts and other bearers of meaning. Rather than giving how-to advice, philosophical hermeneutics seeks to describe what happens when we interpret, with or without our noticing. Nevertheless, I did predict that from different methods reflecting different theological and cultural traditions we would get different readings of the biblical text.

My prediction has come true, and I am both glad and grateful. Not because I have aspirations to become a prophet, but because the different readings throw different light on the text, each enriching our understanding in its own way. One need not reduce the gospel to a monochrome or monotone monotony out of fear of interpretive diversity. One can be fully aware of the danger of noxious weeds and noisy discords and still say with joy, "Let many flowers bloom; let many songs be sung."

However, my credentials as a prophet are somewhat marred by the fact that I predicted the diversity with reference to both the first and second hermeneutic; since the other essays tend to focus on one or the other, but not to thematize both in their dialectical tension, this double diversity has not occurred.

A reminder: Gadamer signifies a double hermeneutics when he says that interpretation of culturally significant texts is both reproductive and productive.[1] On the one hand, it seeks to duplicate or reproduce the original meaning, what the author intended to say and how the original readers would have understood the text. On the other hand, it goes beyond this in seeking its current possible meaning(s) for subsequent and different audiences. We can call these two moments (reproductive) exegesis and (productive) application.

Derrida signifies this double hermeneutics when he stresses the importance of "doubling commentary," the reproductive articulation of the original meaning as a necessary "guardrail" against interpretive subjectivism and anarchy, only to insist that this necessary condition is not sufficient.[2] A serious reading will of necessity be a recontextualizing, reading not from nowhere or from back then, but from here and now.

We can put this in terms of Ricoeur's regular account of discourse: someone says something about something to someone.[3] The first someone is obviously the author, while the second someone is the reader. The something-about-something is the text. For Ricoeur, as for Gadamer and Derrida, the meaning of the text is coproduced by the author and the reader. The author gives it a certain determinacy, an original meaning that erects a guardrail against "anything goes," on the part of the reader. However, if we stop with that, we have a dead letter rather than a living word, a corpse ready for autopsy (by scholars). Fortunately, the text is also sufficiently indeterminate that different readers in different circumstances will find it differently meaningful. Giving the author unilateral authority over meaning would be an excess of objectivity and determinacy; giving the reader an absolute authority over meaning would be an excess of subjectivity and indeterminacy. Balance is found in the dialectical tension between the

---

[1]Hans-Georg Gadamer, *Truth and Method,* 2nd ed. rev., trans. Joel Weinsheimer and Donald G. Marshall (New York: Crossroad/Continuum, 1989/2004). These two versions of the second edition have, unforgivably, different pagination and will be cited as TM x/y, where x = 1989 and y = 2004. In this case, pp. 296-97/296, xxxi/xxviii.

[2]Jacques Derrida, *Of Grammatology,* trans. Gayatri Chakravorty Spivak (Baltimore: Johns Hopkins University Press, 1976), p. 158.

[3]Paul Ricoeur, *Hermeneutics and the Human Sciences,* ed. John B. Thompson (New York: Cambridge University Press, 1981), pp. 108, 112-13, 132-33, 139, 198, and André LaCocque and Paul Ricoeur, *Thinking Biblically,* trans. David Pellauer (Chicago: University of Chicago Press, 1998), p. xii.

two. I concluded my essay with reflections on sermon preparation in order to focus on this tension. Exegesis provides the foundation, but only with application do the people of God gain a home in which to dwell.

Wolterstorff specifically relates this notion of a double hermeneutic—the phrase is his—to biblical interpretation. A full interpretation of the Bible (or any of its parts) would have to answer two questions: What did the human author say to the originally intended audience? What is God saying to us now through that very same text?[4] Note the change of tenses from past to present. These observations are helpful as we shift to analyzing the other contributions in this volume.

THE HISTORICAL-CRITICAL/GRAMMATICAL VIEW

Craig Blomberg is quite explicit about limiting his focus to the exegetical task. He makes constant reference to the author and the original audience. Blomberg gives a fine overview of many of what Derrida calls "the instruments of traditional criticism" as these have developed in relation to biblical interpretation. Their goal is exegetical, reproductive, doubling commentary, and Blomberg is quite explicit that the method he is describing "tends not to raise questions of contemporary significance, application or [re]contextualization" (p. 40).

Two interesting and significant passages can be read as glosses on this general policy.

> Believers with a high view of Scripture will presumably want to respond to a grammatico-historical interpretation of a biblical text by seeking to apply it in methodologically responsible ways to their contemporary lives and world. They will look for examples to imitate, commands to obey, promises to claim, dangers to avoid, truths to believe, and praises or prayers to offer to God. (p. 28)

If I am not mistaken, that is the whole of what Blomberg has to say about application, though he refers us in a note to what he has written on the subject elsewhere. Three comments follow from this. First, it seems to me that the formula "will presumably want to respond" is too weak. Rather, what needs to be said is that application of this sort is the whole purpose

---

[4]Nicholas Wolterstorff, *Divine Discourse: Philosophical Reflections on the Claim That God Speaks* (New York: Cambridge University Press, 1995), p. 185.

of biblical interpretation, that short of this goal the interpretative task is incomplete and risks reducing Scripture—however high our view—to an object to be mastered instead of a voice to be heeded. Ricoeur sees this clearly. Exegesis needs to be the handmaiden of application (at least in the church, if not in the American Academy of Religion) and should be understood in this light. If application is a supplement to exegesis, it is the dangerous supplement that undermines the autonomy of the foundational. We build foundations for the sake of buildings. A standalone foundation suggests a builder who went bankrupt.

Second, the question arises as to what it might mean to apply the biblical text "in methodologically responsible ways." It obviously means that the exegesis on which the application is based must be methodologically responsible. The great strength of Blomberg's essay is its account of the fundamental mode of such responsibility. Can it mean more? I think not. It is not clear that there is a method for getting from exegesis to application, in other words, to move from, "What did the human author say to the originally intended audience?" to "What is God saying to us today in and through this ancient text?"

It is sometimes said that Gadamer's book *Truth and Method* is best understood as truth against method. This is not quite right. He acknowledges that there is a place for method. What he denies is that method, especially under the influence of the Enlightenment's worship of natural science, deserves a hegemonic role in relation to truth. If it is in application that the truth of Scripture comes to light, and if, as I have suggested, there is no method for deriving application from exegesis, no matter how methodologically disciplined the latter is, then biblical interpretation will be a site where we can look for truth beyond method. It will be a matter of good listening, and that is more a matter of various virtues (openness, honesty, humility, fairness, etc.) than of method. The Word will have to be illumined by the Spirit, whom Jesus sent to be our teacher; and the Spirit is not a method.

Third, there is nothing wrong with restricting one's discussion of hermeneutical method to the exegetical part of the task, especially if there is no method that tells us how to build on that foundation the house of application in which to dwell. Nevertheless, it seems to me of crucial importance to be explicit about the preliminary role of that task and about the danger involved in leaving the impression that exegesis (doubling commentary, reproduction) is what biblical interpretation is primarily about. Within the church and especially where there is a high view of Scripture, the biblical scholar is servant to the preacher who, in turn, has a serious obligation to be informed by biblical scholarship as a guardrail against surrendering preaching to personal biases and collective ideologies. It is especially through the preacher's voice that the people of God hear what God is saying to them in the here and now.

A final comment: in Blomberg's essay, exegesis as the quest for the original meaning is a matter of the author and the text, and only the reader who might be said to coproduce the meaning is the original reader. The only place for a reader-response hermeneutic is in relation to the *"authorial reader's response—the intended audience's interpretation"* (p. 31).

Like many others, Blomberg seems nervous about a more general reader-response hermeneutics. His method "does not embrace those forms of postmodernism that so revel in diversity in interpretation of texts that they reject the constraints of limiting meaning to what was first intended and/or likely to have been understood in those texts' original settings" (p. 39). That is fine so long as we are only laying the foundation exegetically. However, if we are to get beyond this to application with meanings that can and should shape the lives of believers and congregations, then different readers in different historical and cultural circumstances that the human author could not anticipate will have to play a significant role, on pain of denying history and assuming that we are contemporaries of the biblical writers.

In any case, one does not have to be a postmodernist reveling in diversity to reject this constraint. One has only to be a Christian who holds, for example, that the gospel as proclaimed in the New Testament is incompatible with slavery. The constraint that needs to be honored is not limiting biblical meaning to its original meaning, thereby reducing interpretation to exegesis, but allowing original meaning to be a constraint, a guardrail, against reducing the biblical text to a Rorschach inkblot onto which we can project anything we find in our personal or collective psyche. That is a real danger, as the history of theology testifies. Nevertheless, there is no method that will protect us from this danger, no algorithm that will enable us to deduce our applications from our exegesis with guaranteed faithfulness. To walk by faith and not by sight is not to flee risk, but to face it honestly, daring to apply what methodological exegesis discovers without methodological guarantees.

THE REDEMPTIVE-HISTORICAL VIEW

The great strength of Richard Gaffin's redemptive-historical approach is its reminder of the historical character of the subject matter of biblical interpretation. Over against the essentially ahistorical systems of seventeenth-century Reformed orthodoxy,[5] it reminds us that theology seeks to articulate the *Heilsgeschichte* in the light of the *Offenbarungsgeschichte*, the history of redemption in the light of the history of revelation as the ongoing interpretation of God's redemptive acts in history. As such, theology is an interpretation of prior interpretations. The double qualification that special revelation is always in conversation with general revelation and that special revelation goes "beyond history to [God's] antecedent self-existence (aseity)" (p. 92) need not suggest a bifurcation within theology. For example, scripturally speaking, the affirmation of God as maker of heaven and earth functions as a reminder of who the God of the covenants is. The biblical witness to God as the eternal creator of the temporal world tells us who it is who says, "I will be their God, and they will be my people." We misunderstand if we make it into an attempt to satisfy our metaphysical curiosity or give us a quasi-scientific theory of the origin of the universe.

Unlike the historical-critical/grammatical method of interpretation, the redemptive-historical approach is overtly theological. This puts it in company with dispensationalism, which is also overtly theological and which also emphasizes the historical nature of theology's subject matter. Traditionally Reformed theology and dispensational theology have not been the best of friends, primarily, I suppose, because of substantive differences in their eschatology. However, if we restrict ourselves to the hermeneutical-methodological aspects, the question arises: are these two approaches two species of the same genus, redemptive-historical interpretation, or is there some more fundamental difference between them? One might also see the biblical theology movement of the mid-twentieth century as a redemptive-historical approach. It would be helpful to hear what

---

[5]For example, see Heinrich Heppe, *Reformed Dogmatics: Set Out and Illustrated from the Sources* (repr., Grand Rapids: Baker, 1978).

is distinctive of this approach generically (if indeed there is a genus here) and what the distinctives of the various species are. Are the differences methodological or substantively theological?

This leads to the question of whether the redemptive-historical approach has been sufficiently distinguished, even generically, from other methods of interpretation. If we ask various biblical interpreters what their approaches or strategies of interpretation are, many will specify something different from the redemptive-historical approach. Yet if they are Christian interpreters will they not almost without exception, and as if by instinct, interpret the Old Testament in the light of the New, whether or not the word *covenant* is prominent in their discourse, thereby implying a history of redemption and of revelation? Since it is this historical distinction that seems to be the focus of Gaffin's presentation, the question arises of whether the redemptive-historical approach has been sufficiently distinguished from others. Will theological discourse itself need to have a narrative, as distinguished from a systematic, form? What will this look like? Or will some substantive difference be more important than matters of form?

A related question pertains to the fundamental distinction between old and new covenants. The claim is that there is a *"continuity"* between the New Testament writers and contemporary interpreters in that their concern for redemption history arises "within basically the same redemptive-historical, eschatological context, bracketed by Christ's resurrection and his return" (p. 98). This is an important point. Surely we and they live between the already of Christ's first advent and the not yet of his second coming in a way decisively different from the Old Testament writers and their immediate audiences. Yet one wonders whether this theological continuity does not need to be held in tension with historical-cultural-linguistic discontinuity. Is it not the case that the desert fathers, the Geneva Calvinists, the American slaves and the contemporary Amish live in different historical-cultural-linguistic worlds that show up and should show up as discontinuities in their biblical interpretation? Should not the fact that all four, and many others, live together between resurrection/Pentecost on the one hand and second coming/final judgment on the other need to be qualified to take into account the dramatic differences of location that occur within the era signified by the words *anno Domini*? In other words, does not the historical nature of the subject matter of theology need to be doubled, as it were, by the historical nature of the theologian-interpreter? Of course, this diversity complicates the theological task, but it also makes it more realistic, since this diversity is a fact staring us in the face.

Gaffin regularly describes the parallel histories of redemption and revelation as organic and as whole, or a unity. I hope we can find a better term for speaking about a personal God as actor and speaker within human history than *organic*. Organic processes have a kind of natural necessity that is the very opposite of personal agency and speech, conscious and free. The acorn has an essence that unfolds, in proper circumstances, into an oak tree. The plan of God for the creation and redemption of the world is something of a quite different sort. This kind of language makes it sound as if the move from seventeenth-century Reformed orthodoxy to Vos is like the movement from Spinoza to Hegel. Organic metaphors like acorn/oak tree are natural to Hegel precisely because he does not have a personal, biblical God who preexists the world and cares for it as a shepherd tends the sheep. I do not think this is what Gaffin has in mind at all. Perhaps he uses organic language to signify the coherence that goes with the parallel theme of wholeness, completeness and unity. However, biblically speaking the unity of history is a narrative unity, not an organic totality.

Moreover, to speak of history as a completed whole may cause us to forget the "not-yet" aspect. I remember once hearing a theologian attempt to refute Jean-François Lyotard's notion that in postmodernity we have lost our faith in metanarratives. "Not we Christians," he insisted. "We know how the story ends." "We do?" I found myself asking myself. Yes, in a certain very general sense. We believe in the resurrection of the body and the life everlasting. Amen. But we do not know what life in resurrection bodies will be like, or what personal and social forms the life everlasting will have. We do not know the day or the hour when the present age will pass over into the age to come, nor what form the judgment of the living and the dead will take. We know "in a mirror dimly . . . only in part" (1 Cor 13:12).

Given a certain view of God's eternity and omniscience, we may want to say that God's plan for the redemption of the world was eternally in place before the mountains were brought forth. Unlike good football and basketball coaches, God does not make halftime adjustments to adapt to what the enemy is doing. But if salvation history is in some sense already completed in the mind of God, it does not follow that we can grasp it in its wholeness and unity. Our theologies, including the images and metaphors in which we seek to give them concreteness, will always be attempts from between the already and the not yet to articulate and anticipate the totality, which is anything but fully present to us. Our Old Testament predecessors who knew so emphatically how the story would end were the ones who ended up shouting, "Crucify him!"

I am not for a moment suggesting that this is what Gaffin is doing. I am only suggesting that the language of wholeness and completeness is highly dangerous and needs to come with strong warnings from theology's surgeon general. For the church, at least, I think it is far less important to have the right theory about how the whole of history is present to God eternally (if that is what we want to say) than to remember the finitude of our perspectives on the totality of God's redemptive and revealing activity, and to remember the many ways in which we do not know how the story will end. One strength of philosophical hermeneutics is its constant insistence that we remember we belong to history and thus to a finite perspective with fallible presuppositions before we try to interpret history, whether theologically or otherwise.

THE LITERARY/POSTMODERN VIEW

The explicit emphasis of the literary/postmodern approach to the final text, at least as represented by Scott Spencer, indicates a kinship with the canonical view, but as the other two approaches can and often do focus all or most of their attention on the canonical text, this is not a matter of deep disagreement. If historical-critical/grammatical interpretation includes a diachronic interest in the formation of the final text, this in no way precludes linguistic and historical analysis of the final text; nor, at least in the context of the church, should the former be privileged over the latter. There is nothing necessarily theological here. One can practice higher criticism on *The Iliad*, Kant's *Critique of Pure Reason*, or even Gadamer's *Truth and Method* and still be ultimately interested in the final text.

A more interesting kinship, I think, appears in the fact that the essay on literary/postmodern interpretation is closer to philosophical hermeneutics than its two predecessors in at least one important aspect. With the helpful schema of final text, cotext, intertext, context and open text, it explicitly articulates the double hermeneutics already discussed. Taken together, final text, cotext, intertext and context offer a not overtly theological approach to the task of exegesis complementary to the historical-critical/grammatical approach. Cotext and intertext together express a theme especially dear to Schleiermacher's heart at the "origin" of philosophical hermeneutics, namely, the importance of interpreting the parts of any text in light of the larger wholes to which they belong, understanding that our reading of these larger wholes, presupposed at the outset, will need to be revised in light of the interpretations of the parts to which they give rise. Whole and part (while these are relative terms—the book of Matthew is sometimes part and sometimes whole) take turns as the independent variable that guides interpretation of the other. This is the meaning of the hermeneutical circle.

Since the context includes not just the larger literary units to which smaller ones belong but also the historical-cultural-social setting in which the text arises, there is a significant overlap between the literary/postmodern approach and the historical-critical/grammatical approach. Blomberg argues that this latter approach should be privileged as fundamental to all the others. Insofar as the Bible is the Word of God written, we are dealing with a text composed of many texts. If our theologies are to take the textual character of the Bible seriously, it is not clear that grammatical analysis of the communication between the author and the original audience is more fundamental than the literary strategies (narrative structure, allusions, figures of speech, etc.) employed by the author to communicate to the original audience. It seems to me that grammatical and literary analysis, both in the context of the original historical-cultural-social setting, should be equally fundamental.

It becomes clear that Spencer's primary focus on the text is not at the expense of the author. We do not know who wrote *The Iliad* or who wrote and redacted the various "documents" out of which the Old Testament arose. We do not know for sure who wrote Shakespeare's plays, and we certainly do not know who wrote Hebrews. Still, we learn a lot about the authors and their strategies from the texts in question, and the "implied" author is precisely the author we infer from the text as its necessary author. Thus, for example, we take "Matthew," whoever he may be, to be especially concerned with communicating the gospel to a Jewish readership. So to speak with Ricoeur and Spencer about textual meaning is not to suppose that hermeneutics can ignore authors but simply that often most or all or the most important things we know about an author are what we find inside the text, not outside. Thus the first four moments of Spencer's hermeneutic spell out the exegetical task, discovering, as best we can, the original meaning as intended by the author and understood by the intended readers.

However, Spencer does not wish to disenfranchise all the other readers, and that is what the final moment is about: the open text. Gadamer will say that the readers of a text, including those well beyond the scope of the author's imagination, not to say also its intention, belong to the text in the sense that the fullness of its meaning needs them in order to come to light. Thus, as Gregory the Great put it, "[Scripture] grows with its readers."[6] When these readers include later readers such as ourselves, we have the double hermeneutic that asks about both what the human author was trying to say back then to the intended audience and what God is saying to us now through the same text. According to Spencer's hermeneutic, if I understand him, Scripture needs distinctively Asian, Latin American and African readings, along with feminist and postcolonial applications in order to be itself fully. This does not mean that anything goes, for the text has enough determinacy to preclude some interpretations as misunderstandings, a point essential to Gadamer's analysis as well. Exegesis functions as the Derridean guardrail for Spencer.

When Matthew applies to an individual a theme that for Hosea applied to a people, this is not doubling commentary or reproduction, but the production of a new meaning. Scary. We try to comfort ourselves by talking (quite rightly, I think) about typology, about "Matthew" as an apostolic author, about the book of Matthew as part of the canon, the inspired Word of God and so forth. Nevertheless, only if we are deliberately inattentive can we hide from ourselves the fact that postbiblical interpretations of the Bible of the sort Spencer has in mind make the same sort of moves without any of the same guarantees of authenticity.

There is a second significant affinity between Spencer's essay and phil-

---

[6]Gregory the Great, *Moralia* 20.1.1.

osophical hermeneutics. Toward the end he confesses that what he has written he has seen "through *my* eyes—my male, middle-class, middle-age, Western professorial, parental, churchly . . . eyes. Others will doubtless see things quite differently, and for that I can only be gratefully open to the fresh insights they will provide" (p. 67). I take this to apply to his account of exegesis, his account of application (using my own terms to describe his work) and his interpretation of the Matthew text. All of these are made possible through a finite perspective full of fallible presuppositions. Thus, without claiming any finality, he overtly welcomes other perspectives. This is an ecumenical hermeneutic.

THE CANONICAL VIEW

Like the redemptive-historical approach as presented by Gaffin, Robert Wall's canonical approach is overtly theological. By contrast, the historical-critical/grammatical and the literary/postmodern modes of exegesis make no theological commitments. They can be and have been practiced on biblical and nonbiblical texts (and on the biblical texts without the assumption of scriptural status). Likewise, philosophical hermeneutics is an account of how interpretation happens whether the text is scriptural or otherwise. To me this is a happy result. I think all five of us contributors are primarily interested in interpreting the Bible in the context of the church, and I expect that will be true of most of our readers. Yet precisely when we have such a purpose, it is a good thing to think about interpretation both as it occurs within the context of specific theological commitments and as it occurs across the spectrum of culturally significant texts, scriptural and otherwise. What we do is both alike and unlike secular hermeneutics. For example, I find a double hermeneutics in Gadamer and Derrida, but only with Wolterstorff is the second defined by the question, what is God saying to us now through this text?

I believe Wall's essay is the one that comes closest to thematizing the double hermeneutic of which I have spoken, though not in the language of exegesis and application. Wall makes it abundantly clear, especially in the opening paragraphs (at least five times in the first three), that the goal of biblical interpretation is what I have called application, guidance for what today's Christians should believe and how they should behave. Thus the church, as the worshiping congregation, rather than the academy, is the "legal address" of the Bible and the true home of biblical interpretation.

At the same time, exegesis has an important role to play as a "restraint" or "constraint" on application. The scholarly tasks of biblical interpretation are essential, but penultimate. I recently heard a biblical interpreter described as writing with "a scholar's eye and a pastor's heart." This is exactly the combination called for by this hermeneutic. To paraphrase Kant, that eye without that heart is arid; that heart without that eye is arbitrary.[7]

However, Wall says some puzzling things about exegesis. First, he gives strong priority to linguistic matters over historical setting. Why? I should think that grammatical, literary and historical dimensions of exegesis could and should be equally basic.

Second, he explicitly rejects the idea that exegesis has as its goal the original meaning, what the author meant to say and how the intended readers would have understood the text. Perhaps this is one reason for stressing linguistic over historical issues, but once again, why? If exegesis is to function as a constraint on application to keep it from being arbitrary and subjective, would not the original meaning be important as a "guardrail"?

Third, this disregard for the historical distance between the text's origin and contemporary readers helps to explain why Wall sees the goal of exegesis as building a consensus about what the text "says," always present tense. But he goes beyond this to speak again and again about what the text "plainly says." "Plainly" can hardly mean "immediately obvious." Otherwise we would not have so much conflict in interpretation, and it would not be necessary to speak of the consensus that exegesis seeks as a goal, presumably not yet in hand. At one place he equates "plainly" with "literal." However, many parts of Scripture are obviously or at least arguably metaphorical. Protestants do not take the words "This is my body" to be literal, as the doctrine of transubstantiation tries to make them. Nor, when the Old Testament regularly speaks of what the right hand of God has done or will accomplish, theologians do not conclude that God has hands, much less that God is right-handed. Sometimes the literal sense of the text is said to be the originally intended sense, but (1) this is frightfully mis-

---

[7]Kant writes, "Thoughts without content are empty, intuitions without concepts are blind." *Critique of Pure Reason*, trans. Norman Kemp Smith (New York: St. Martin's, 1961), A 51 = B 75.

leading, since the originally intended sense is often metaphorical (the Lord is my shepherd), and (2), in any case, Wall does not want to invoke the original sense. I cannot tell what Wall means by "plainly," and I suspect that whatever he means can be better said otherwise.

Finally, Wall says that interpretation—presumably both as exegesis and as application insofar as the two are distinguished—is subject to the rule of faith, going back to Irenaeus. However, why should any churchly summary of the gospel, an extracanonical interpretation, be the norm for subsequent interpretation? As a matter of fact, all interpretations are guided by some at least implicit creed. Should not our creeds be subject to Scripture and revisable in light of our growing, or at least changing, understanding of biblical teaching? The hermeneutical circle as articulated within philosophical hermeneutics acknowledges the prima facie authority of presuppositions in any hermeneutics but refuses to grant final authority to any. Appeal to any creed or rule of faith needs to be conscious of its human, fallible character.

In a different respect, Wall's appeal to the rule of faith is in harmony with philosophical hermeneutics. Rather than appealing to this rule for the sake of the one true theology, he finds it flexible enough to accommodate a rich variety of theological expressions. He says, in effect, "Let many theological flowers bloom; let many songs be sung." I join him in celebration and thanks for the light thrown on the tasks of biblical interpretation by this diverse set of essays growing out of a deep affinity of faith.

9

The Redemptive-
Historical Response

Richard B. Gaffin Jr.

Ivalue the other essays for the stimulus and challenge of each to
my own thinking about biblical interpretation. My response will consist
first in some brief comments on the other contributors' treatments of our
test passage, Matthew 2:7-15 (except for Merold Westphal's, whose comments in keeping with his philosophical view are minimal). I will then
make some broader observations about the hermeneutical positions presented in the essays of the other contributors.

MATTHEW 2:7-15

The variety in approaches to this passage among the five views certainly
provides ample evidence that all interpretation is partial and perspectival.
Readers will likely be struck with how differently, in the space at our dis-
posal, each of us has chosen to treat these verses.

Although the detailed conclusions reached by the other contributors
differ notably from each other, I find them frequently instructive and
compatible at a number of points with the redemptive-historical view I
represent. Keeping that generalization in mind, I limit myself to noting
some points where I have reservations or think some clarification would be
helpful.

The historical-critical/grammatical view. Craig Blomberg's historical-
critical/grammatical approach does not intend to include theological analysis but does intend to provide the indispensable foundation for it (pp. 28-29).
Nonetheless, in at least one place he is on essentially theological terrain. In

rightly noting the distinctive prominence that Matthew gives to the fulfillment of prophecy and typology in Matthew 1:18–2:23, he adds that this approach "might not seem as persuasive to us today as a straightforward prediction-fulfillment scheme," though it "should have had significant impact on a faithful first-century Jew," who would have found it "very astute" (p. 46). That generalization prompts questions. Why would this approach be less persuasive today? Should it be? Why was it astute and its impact significant for Matthew's original readers but not today? Matthew's approach, again as Blomberg rightly notes, was rooted in the conviction that "God's providence worked through recurring patterns in history, especially with respect to creative and redemptive events" (p. 46). Was that a valid conviction? Is it, with the typology it gave rise to, still valid today? Historical analysis and theological assessment are hardly separable.

The literary/postmodern view. Scott Spencer's narrative reflections on the magi brings to light a number of suggestive contrasts and juxtapositions. Some, however, seem strained. For instance, the magi may not have been "exotic dignitaries," but to characterize them "more as quixotic, wandering star chasers," while colorful, goes beyond what the text warrants, even with the ancient-world background he provides (p. 65). Similarly the stress on their foolishness, particularly implicating them as Herod's unwitting accomplices, seems overdrawn (pp. 65-67).

What could have been brought out more clearly (by the other contributors as well, including myself) is that the magi are the initial indication of what is surely a central theme in Matthew, namely, that "the king of the Jews" they seek is divinely destined to be the king of all nations. Their Gentile faith and worship—echoed subsequently, for instance, by the Roman centurion and the Canaanite woman, both of whose faith Jesus remarks on in contrast to Israel's unbelief (Mt 8:10; 15:22-28)—anticipates the time when "many will come from east and west and recline at table with Abraham, Isaac, and Jacob in the kingdom of heaven" (Mt 8:11-12; cf. Mt 21:43: the new "people producing its [kingdom] fruits").

Before Jesus' death and resurrection, the Twelve as well as Jesus himself confine their ministries to "the lost sheep of the house of Israel" (Mt 10:6; 15:24). Afterward, the situation alters dramatically. This previous limitation is now lifted. They are to make disciples not only of one but of all nations, of Gentiles as well as Jews. This shift occurs because the king of the Jews—now resurrected and invested with power over the entire creation—is king of all nations (Mt 28:18-20). The magi glimpsed this universal kingship, however indistinctly, from the outset at Jesus' birth.

With its complex interweaving of outlooks both backward and forward, communal and individual, and involving both captivity and deliverance, Hosea 11 can leave one, as Spencer says, "a little dizzy" (p. 62). However, Spencer's statement that in Matthew's use of Hosea "the dizziness all but knocks us out cold" is puzzling. This is especially puzzling when compared to some of Spencer's other statements. For example, he helpfully observes that "out of Egypt" in Matthew 2:15, which many commentators view as misplaced, "may not be so clumsy after all from a typological intertextual and narrative cotextual perspective" (p. 63).

The canonical view. Robert Wall considers our passage in terms of three "probes." My reservations are not so much about what he says under each of these headings (in that regard my questions are minor and much that he says is helpful) but rather with what he intends structurally by distinguishing probe 2 ("with other Scripture") and probe 3 ("by the rule of faith"). However, that reservation is better spelled out and addressed below.

BROADER REFLECTIONS

I now move on, first, to address some criticisms of the redemptive-historical view and, second, to consider the hermeneutical approach of each of the other contributors in light of the issue of divine authorship, with some related observations about the historical-critical method.

Craig Blomberg on the redemptive-historical view. Craig Blomberg distinguishes his view from each of the others, sight unseen. In brief response to his comments on "the redemptive-historical method," the view that I hold is not a method in the strict sense, marked by a fixed set of specific procedures. It is better characterized more loosely as a large-scale orientation or overall outlook on the revelation-historical content of the Bible. As such, it depends on the proper implementation of various interpretive methods and procedures among those that Blomberg advocates and details, procedures customarily included under the designation "grammatical-historical."

Certainly the overall outlook of the redemptive-historical view is only valid when it is supported by the careful exegesis of a specific passage and is true to the distinctive contributions of each of the biblical documents. Yet this view holds that such responsible, detailed exegesis can only take place within the back-and-forth attention from specific passages or units of text (however factored) to the whole of Scripture. That whole, in turn, is to be read in light of the particular text. (This ongoing reciprocal movement is an aspect of the hermeneutical circle or, as I prefer to view it, the hermeneutical spiral.)

Among Blomberg's reservations about the redemptive-historical method is the tendency he finds to "read New Testament meanings back into Old Testament texts" (p. 40). This is no doubt a danger. However, there is a difference between reading the New Testament *into* the Old and reading the Old Testament *in light of* the New. The former is wrong; the latter is not only legitimate but also requisite. Readers of this volume can judge, for instance, whether that distinction has been properly maintained in my handling of Matthew's use of Hosea.

Blomberg also maintains that the redemptive-historical method is among those that "too often appeal uncritically to the principle of Scripture interpreting Scripture" (p. 41). Even one such uncritical appeal is "too often"; the redemptive-historical approach properly implemented avoids such appeals when utilizing this indispensable hermeneutical principle.

Divine authorship. All five views are oriented toward considering the biblical documents as historically conditioned and culturally situated. All clearly recognize that they are to be understood in terms of their human authorship. What is not so clear, however, is how the other contributors regard the Bible's divine authorship (or inspiration, to use the classical term), in other words, how each contributor views the Bible as God's word. It seems appropriate in a symposium like this to raise this issue because it brings us into the area of hermeneutical foundations, namely, the underlying commitments inevitably present and controlling for any view of interpretation.

On this issue, there are differences between my view and the views of the other contributors, which raise matters that I believe need clarifying. My own view of divine authorship (to be taken along with some brief comments in my position essay (pp. 98, 107-8, 111), which is rooted in the self-witness of the Bible, will for the most part simply have to be asserted without being elaborated or defended. Nor will I be able to develop my comments on the other views in any full way. No doubt there is need for further consideration of these matters, for which there are no facile answers, but, given their overriding importance, there is value in drawing attention to them and indicating lines of resolution even if only in a preliminary way.

The literary/postmodern view. Scott Spencer makes no reference to divine authorship, and it is unclear what place, if any, inspiration might have within the author-text-reader triad he develops. To say anything more beyond taking note of this silence would be speculation.

The historical-critical/grammatical view. In the interests of considering Blomberg's view on the issue of divine authorship, I begin with some observations about the historical-critical method. The use of the definite article is deliberate. Recently Anthony Thiselton has opined in the introductory chapter of a multiauthored volume that there is not "a single, uniform, 'historical-critical method,'" and he continues, "In my judgment the term '*the* historical-critical method' should be banned from all textbooks and students' essays."[1] In subsequent chapters of the volume in which Thiselton's essay appears, however, we find other authors doing precisely that, talking for instance about "the historical critical approach" (Brevard Childs, p. 52); "the historical-critical method" and "the findings of historical-critical inquiry" (Christopher Seitz, p. 102); and "the historical-critical paradigm" and "this basic historical-critical perspective" (Stephen Chapman, pp. 167, 170).

Certainly, what is meant by historical-critical method has been and continues to be understood differently. Further, historical-critical method may be defined in different ways provided that the definition is made clear and functions consistently. Still, Thiselton's sharply expressed proposal notwithstanding, there is good reason why "the historical-critical method" deserves its widespread currency as best covering a broad spectrum of interpretive undertakings, despite all sorts of differences observable among them.

Craig Blomberg's appropriation and explanation of the method demonstrates both why this spectrum exists and why this definite article designa-

---

[1]Anthony Thiselton, "Canon, Community and Theological Construction," in *Canon and Biblical Interpretation,* ed. Craig G. Bartholomew et al., Scripture and Hermeneutics 7 (Grand Rapids: Zondervan, 2006), p. 4, italics original.

tion is appropriate. He intends a use of the historical-critical method that differs from its original conception and, famously, its subsequent articulation around the beginning of the twentieth century by Ernst Troeltsch (p. 27). Specifically he advocates using the method but without adopting the "antisupernaturalist worldview" or "antisupernatural presuppositions" that accompany Troeltsch's principle of correlation as a defining aspect of the method (p. 30).

However, as its most consistent and self-conscious practitioners have made clear, this antisupernaturalism, as well as Troeltsch's other two defining principles (criticism and analogy), stems from a more basic presupposition: the more deeply rooted, fundamental commitment to the autonomy of reason in the interpretation of all texts, including the Bible.[2] Whatever its precursors, the historical-critical method was birthed by the Enlightenment, with its resolute commitment to the autonomy of human reason.[3] For the historical-critical method the authority of human reason is supreme; nothing is more basic and controlling for considering and assessing any text, particularly historical texts. No authority external to reason may be recognized as final or above it, whether of the church, the state or Scripture. The integrity of the method demands this. However the Bible's uniqueness or religious importance may otherwise be affirmed, historical criticism insists that it is to be treated like any other collection of documents from the past. No exception can be made for it before the final and all-determining bar of reason. For historical-critical thinking applied

---

[2]Many works could be cited here. Two have especially shaped my own understanding: Gerhard Ebeling's programmatic essay, "The Significance of the Critical Historical Method for Church and Theology in Protestantism," in *Word and Faith*, trans. James W. Leitch (Philadelphia: Fortress, 1963), pp. 17-61, and Van Harvey, *The Historian and the Believer* (New York: Macmillan, 1966), in which on the role of autonomy see esp. chaps. 1-3. The title of the original of Ebeling's essay is "Die Bedeutung der historischen-kritischen Methode . . ." "Historischen-kritischen" would be better translated "historical-critical" (rather than "critical historical"); see Gerhard Ebeling, *Wort und Glaube*, 3rd ed. (Tübingen: Mohr, 1967), p. 1. The essay first appeared in *Zeitschrift für Theologie und Kirche* 47 (1950): 1-46.

[3]This could hardly be made clearer and more pointed than by no more representative a figure than Immanuel Kant in his 1784 essay, "An Answer to the Question: What Is Enlightenment?" beginning with its opening paragraph: humanity has emerged from its previous "minority" and now come of age is able to think for itself. "*Sapere Aude* [dare to be wise]! Have courage to make use of your *own* understanding! is thus the motto of enlightenment" (Immanuel Kant, *Practical Philosophy*, in *The Cambridge Edition of the Works of Immanuel Kant*, trans. Mary J. Gregor [Cambridge: Cambridge University Press, 1996], pp. 17-22, italics original); accessible online at www.english.upenn.edu/~mgamer/Etexts/kant.html.

to the biblical documents, "historical" carries the demand to consider them in terms of their exclusively human and historically conditioned origin and character; "critical" refers to the rational autonomy by which they are to be assessed.[4]

Essential, then, to the historical-critical method with its commitment to autonomy is *Sachkritik*, that is, criticism of content or subject matter, the requirement to judge whether what a text claims to be true or right is in fact true or right. Again, the integrity of the method demands such criticism. In the case of the Bible, even what it maintains to be true or right may not be accepted as such but is subject to critical reason, which decides whether or not it is true or right. I take it that Gerhard Ebeling is widely representative in expressing this pointedly: the historical-critical method "is—not just, say, where it oversteps its legitimate limits, but by its very nature—bound up with criticism of content [*Sachkritik*]."[5]

For the redemptive-historical view that I represent in this volume, the Bible is not a proper object of the historical-critical method. Certainly a sound and penetrating understanding of Scripture ought to take account of its historical conditioning, of both the biblical documents and their subject matter, and do so in a careful, methodologically reflective and responsible fashion. However, the Bible is not properly assessed by human reason understood as autonomous, nor are its truth claims subject to *Sachkritik*. The divine authorship and consequent authority of Scripture, on the one hand, and the historical-critical method, with its commitment to autonomy, on the other, exclude each other.

According to its self-witness the Bible provides documents that more properly have God as their author than the fully engaged human authors and editors integrally involved in their production. Unlike any other texts, God is ultimately accountable not only for their content but also for their

---

[4]In Craig Bartholomew et al., eds., *"Behind" the Text: History and Biblical Interpretation*, Scripture and Hermeneutics 4 (Grand Rapids: Zondervan, 2003), Alvin Plantinga provides a helpful survey treatment in his essay titled "Two (or More) Kinds of Scripture Scholarship," pp. 19-57. In discussing the use of the historical-critical method, "Historical Biblical Criticism" (HBC), he distinguishes "Troeltschian" HBC from its other "non-Troeltschian" forms (e.g., p. 55). My comments above about rational autonomy apply across this distinction (as well, apparently, to his own understanding of the role of reason, p. 56).

[5]Ebeling, "Significance of the Critical Historical Method," pp. 42-43 ("Die Bedeutung der historischen-kritischen Methode," p. 29); cf. p. 47 (German, p. 34), where he elaborates further on *Sachkritik* as "the really decisive and revolutionary thing about the critical historical method."

syntactic-semantic form and the plurality and specificity of the words used. The mind of Paul that his letters exhibit, for instance, is more ultimately the mind of God.[6] Thus to subject Scripture to *Sachkritik* is necessarily to place human reasoning and the human mind above the mind and reason of God. The use of the historical-critical method cannot but "place the interpreter above Scripture."[7]

With all the factors that need to be considered—the historical, cultural and linguistic distance between our present and the times of the Bible's origin—its in-depth understanding is challenging enough without the added burden of the unnecessary and inappropriate demand for *Sachkritik*. There are difficulties in understanding the Bible and, without losing sight of the pervasive clarity of Scripture, at points these difficulties are considerable (cf. 2 Pet 3:16, "some things hard to understand"). But interpretation with a proper view of divine authorship is able to address them, confident that God is speaking through the text in the sense that the text is God himself speaking in a way that condescends to our creatureliness yet is commensurate with who he is as God, including his omniscience and truthfulness, and without that speaking being limited or rendered ineffective by the sinfulness and personal and cultural limitations of the human author involved.[8] Divine authorship guarantees the unity of the Bible's teaching, its doctrinal coherence as a redemptive- and revelation-historical record, in its diverse human authorship and literary genres, and in its historically differentiated subject matter.

I find Blomberg unclear about the commitment to autonomy and the attendant *Sachkritik* of historical-critical thinking, and so likewise unclear about divine authorship. His overall conclusion does state that his historical-critical/grammatical approach "is critical in the sense of being analytical, not in the sense of criticizing" (p. 46). Yet earlier he says, "Such analysis can also lead to judgments about the reliability of the document being assessed" (p. 39). Among other things, the approaches to the text of Scrip-

---

[6]See, e.g., Paul's overstatement for emphasis, "Not as the word of men but as what it really is, the word of God" (1 Thess 2:13), which fairly applies not only to his (oral) preaching but also to his writings as an apostle (see, e.g., 2 Thess 2:2, 15), in form as well as content.

[7]Contra Blomberg, p. 37.

[8]Accordingly, the Bible's infallibility and inerrancy (its entire truthfulness) is to be affirmed because of its divine authorship, not, as Blomberg appears to suggest, on the basis of the probable determinations of historical criticism (Blomberg, p. 37 n. 40).

ture that he advocates "allow us to adjudicate . . . the probability of its historical trustworthiness" (p. 37). In fact, his method, he says, "must have this 'critical' dimension to it— that is, a dimension that is both analytical and evaluative, based on common ground shared with the skeptic" (p. 37).

It is difficult not to conclude, particularly from this last statement—especially based on its immediate context—that this "common ground" is a shared commitment to the autonomy of reason. It seems clear, then, that the "chastened forms of historical criticism" (p. 37) he approves of are chastened in the sense that they allow for the supernatural and the presence of transcendence in history, but not because they have abandoned the claim to rational autonomy. Autonomy, however chastened, tempered or otherwise attenuated, is still autonomy, and its allowance for the supernatural and for divine transcendence will be determined on its own terms and by its own criteria.[9]

The canonical view. Robert Wall says that "divine inspiration" is among several terms to be "defined in functional rather than in dogmatic terms" (p. 121). Why this disjunction? What does it mean and entail? These are questions prompted in the face of the classic text, 2 Timothy 3:16, where Scripture is said to be "profitable" (functional) because and as it has been "breathed out by God" (a dogmatically disposed affirmation).[10] Scripture indeed may be said to be "God-breathing," "living and active" (Heb 4:12), in its functioning today as always. However, Scripture has this function only because it is "God-breathed" and remains so by virtue of its origin. The dynamic is grounded in the static. The ever-fresh quality of Scripture is rooted in its fixed and abiding stability as God's Word.

I very much appreciate the concern of the canonical view to find and

---

[9] As I judge it, these observations also apply to the "tempered" use of the historical-critical method advocated by Donald Hagner (in otherwise helpful articles), which Blomberg cites with approval in n. 5, as well as to the critical realism of N. T. Wright, also cited with approval in n. 41; see also Wright's *The New Testament and the People of God* (Minneapolis: Fortress, 1992), pp. 31-46 (the term "critical" in critical realism is not unrelated to the different sense it has in "historical-critical").

[10] *Theopneustos* is a passive verbal adjective ("God-breathed"); here it describes a permanent quality as a result of their origin, referring to documents that are "Scripture." Recently Craig D. Allert (*A High View of Scripture?* [Grand Rapids: Baker Academic, 2007], pp. 153-56) has argued that the specific meaning of this adjective is so indeterminable that it has little weight for deciding how we should view the biblical documents, especially their origin. That is hardly the case. Its meaning has been well established in the works of those such as B. B. Warfield, among others, whom Allert cites and attempts to refute (quite unsuccessfully in my view).

maintain a role for the Bible as a whole in the life of the church today and to counter the fragmenting and disunifying consequences of so much historical-critical interpretation since the Enlightenment. It appears to me, however, that this approach lacks an adequate understanding of the divine authorship of Scripture essential for accomplishing what it intends.

As far as I can see the canonical position views the Spirit's activity in producing the biblical documents as being on the same level with his activity within the church in the formation and ongoing use of the canon. This view does not recognize or effectively denies the unique order of the Spirit's working in the origin of these documents and does not distinguish this from the order of his work in forming and utilizing the canon in the church. In contrast the redemptive-historical view holds that inspiration, with its "God-breathed" result, is not predicable of the church's use of Scripture or even of the process through which the church came to recognize the canon.[11]

These observations are further borne out by what Wall says about the rule of faith in relation to Scripture, especially on pages 116 (including n. 11), 121, and 128-29. In his view this rule, elicited in the early church from Scripture, is not an analogy of Scripture but Scripture is analogical of it (n. 11). I cannot understand this other than that the rule of faith is to function in effect as a "canon above the canon," in which the locus of final authority shifts from Scripture to the church in its ongoing appropriation of Scripture in accordance with the rule. For the redemptive-historical approach the sound view of this relationship and the authority involved are provided by a classic distinction: the canon of Scripture is the sole and sufficient supreme "norming norm"; the church's creeds and confessions, including the rule of faith, while hermeneutically important, even necessary, for the church's well being, are "normed norms," subordinate to Scripture, as they derive from Scripture.[12]

---

[11]According to 2 Pet 1:20-21, the Spirit's "bearing" or "carrying" the biblical authors in what they wrote ("prophecy of Scripture") is an originating order of his working ("not by human will"—ultimately the human author's will, though integrally engaged, does not come into consideration; cf. again, "not as the word of men but as what it really is, the word of God," 1 Thess 2:13). This action of the Spirit goes well beyond providential control and oversight or the "leading" (e.g., Rom 8:14) subsequently experienced in the church.

[12]This distinction *(norma normans—norma normata)* functions, for instance, within Lutheran and Reformed orthodoxy from the late sixteenth century on; see, e.g., Richard A. Muller,

The philosophical/theological view. Merold Westphal affirms "God's role in producing the text such that God is the ultimate author of it" (p. 86). However, earlier on the same page he says that the hermeneutic he espouses "does not presuppose any particular theory of the inspiration of the Bible." This is at best unclear. If God is said to be the Bible's ultimate author, does that not suggest incipiently a theory (doctrine) of inspiration capable of some further measure of reasoned articulation and clarification? I raise this question because I find the way Westphal speaks in various ways on this page and elsewhere of God "speaking through Scripture" or speaking "through the words of Scripture" (p. 87) problematic.

The problem is not with such language. Questions arise, however, from the way this language functions within Westphal's "double hermeneutic" that as much as anything appears to be at the heart of his philosophical/theological view. The task of this hermeneutic is defined by the two decidedly different questions it has to answer: "What *did* the human author say to the original audience?" and "What *is* God *saying* to us here and now through these words of Scripture?" (p. 79). As Westphal notes, "The [second] question is no longer what Isaiah or Matthew or Paul were trying to say to their contemporaries, but what God is saying to us now through the words they wrote" (p. 85).

The disjunction in view between these two questions, highlighted by the original italics, is evident, as are the potentially divergent answers they anticipate. The contrast lies in what the human author, not God, said *then* with what God, not the human author, is saying *now* through the human author. On this construction, it does not seem to be over-reading to say that what the text said/says and what God is presently saying through the text are not identical. The text, qua text, is not God's Word; the text as such is not God speaking but God speaks through the text.

Confirming this reading, as a consequence of this now-then disjunction between the human author and God, Westphal goes on to maintain a further disjunction. The answer to the first question above is "reproductive" (reproducing as faithfully as possible the original meaning of the

---

text/the human author), while the answer to the second question (what God is saying through the text today) is to be "productive." Because interpretation depends on the interpreter's (ever-changing and varying) context, it is given a constitutive or creative role in determining the meaning of the contemporary speaking of God through the text. Interpretation is not only necessary for understanding God's speaking through the text; it is also necessary for constituting the meaning of that speaking.

However, one should note that the "God-breathed" of 2 Timothy 3:16 is an abiding, perduring predicate of *the text* of Scripture; it is not descriptive of an ongoing speaking activity of God "through the text," and with its interpreter contributing productively to its meaning. It is difficult to see how Westphal's double hermeneutic squares with this predicate or how his affirmation that God is the ultimate author of the text of Scripture reflects an adequate view of divine authorship and what it entails. Despite his disclaimer, noted above, Westphal, after all, appears to have a rather developed theory of inspiration and of what it means that the Bible is God's Word.

Westphal has aligned himself with the postmodern turn in philosophy as an important ally of Christian faith in refuting modernism's pretentious, Godlike claims to transcendent objectivity and universal validity of reason.[13] The final sentence of his essay reads, "Then theology can remain a matter of Word and Spirit and not of Word and Method" (p. 88), a sentence that follows from his concluding accent on the importance of his philosophical hermeneutics for unmasking the mindset of modernity disposed toward methodological "arrogance . . . as if we were God" (p. 88).

As far as I can see, however, despite postmodernism's stress that all human reasoning is less than absolute, fragmentary and situated, it shares with modernism the critical exercise of reason that stems from the Enlightenment's commitment to autonomy. As already noted above, autonomy, however circumscribed or apparently humble in its claims, is still autonomy. I surely agree with Westphal when he says that we are not God is "good news" (p. 88). But postmodernism appears to differ from modernism only by being less overtly Godlike in its use of reason. I wonder if Westphal does not end

---

[13]This is a major emphasis in his writings, see Westphal, p. 73 n. 14. Nathan D. Shannon provides a thoughtful review article of *Whose Community? Which Interpretation?* in *WTJ* 72 (2010): 415-25.

up with an opposition between the Spirit and method in biblical interpretation, because for him there is an inherent tension between *any* exercise of
human reason as such and the work of the Spirit.

In contrast, the redemptive-historical approach proceeds on the conviction that human reason, properly understood, is creaturely. *Creaturely* here
is not merely a synonym for *finite* or *limited*, generally or abstractly considered, but includes its full biblical sense. The word describes human beings
created in the image of God. Reason and language are gifts among those
image-bearing capacities, reflective of their origin in God. They are given
to be used in absolute, creaturely dependence on him and his self-revelation in the creation at large and in Scripture. To be sure, these capacities
can be abused and, in fact, have been and continue to be misused sin-
fully—though image-bearing creatures, we are sinners. But reason and
language are not inherent barriers to fully engaged fellowship with the
triune God and others that need to be offset by the Spirit's work. By divine
design, reason and language are to function for the purpose of personal
fellowship in receptive dependence on the Spirit's working—in a completely positive, nondialectical fashion—with Scripture in its entire truthfulness and supreme authority.

Our use of reason is inevitably context-embedded, and all our uses of
language are situation-bound. That certainly ought to keep us aware that,
whether as individuals or collectively, our understanding and perceptions
are limited, partial and for now "in a mirror dimly" (1 Cor 12:12). Nevertheless, this does not preclude that they and their expressions can be true,
even certain. Nor is this limited creaturely state of affairs necessarily a
barrier to mutual understanding and authentic interpersonal relationships.
Because language and reasoning are image-bearing capacities common to
all human beings, they have the potential for constructive communication
across differences in gender, ethnicity, language and culture, even as they
are context-qualified, personally and communally situated, and culturally
embedded. This is especially true for Scripture, God's Word for all image-
bearers, and for its interpretation.

Methodology and doxology are not at odds, at least not necessarily. In
interpreting Scripture, the Spirit's working is not limited to compensating
for defects in our methods or shortcomings in our implementing them
(though he does do that). Rather, sound hermeneutical method functions

to facilitate true worship and praise. The arresting example set by Jesus in Luke 24 shows that when he "opened" existing Scripture to his hearers—with the rationally reflective, methodological aspects undoubtedly involved in doing that—their response was not somehow in spite of these aspects. Nor was it merely notional, but rather fully engaged, as their "hearts burned" within them (Lk 24:25-27, 32). Such a response ought to be the final aim of all methodology concerned with the interpretation and eventual proclamation of Scripture.

This prompts me also to say finally that sound methodology ministers certainty. An instance of this certainty is found in Luke 1:1-4, where the Evangelist indicates with some specificity the rational-reflective process he followed in examining eyewitness reports and other sources with the ultimate end that on the gospel matters under consideration his reader might have "certainty" (Lk 1:4). The all-absorbing hermeneutical turn that has taken place in theology over the last half-century or so has brought to light in an unprecedented fashion the complexities of language and the functioning of texts and their interpretation. Nevertheless, biblical interpretation has lost its way if, in considering this undeniable complexity, it fails to move beyond it to the singular simplicity of Scripture in its entirety: its pervasive and concordant focus on Jesus Christ as the full and final revelation of the triune God as Creator and Redeemer for the salvation of sinful human beings and the consummate restoration of his creation.

"I wouldn't give a fig for the simplicity on this side of complexity, but I would give my right arm for the simplicity on the far side of complexity."[14] Whatever the individual limitations of those who adopt it and however it could be better articulated than I have in this volume, the redemptive-historical view is an approach that, without evading the complexities of biblical interpretation—whether in the text or on the part of the interpreter—does so in a way that takes us through them to their far side, to the manifold and unsearchably rich (Eph 3:8, 10) Christ-centered simplicity of all of Scripture.

---

[14]This unsourced quotation, attributed to Oliver Wendell Holmes, is apparently from Holmes Sr. (1809–1894), a physician, writer and poet, and father of Holmes Jr., the United States Supreme Court chief justice.

10

The Canonical Response

Robert W. Wall

The other four contributors to this volume and I all agree that biblical interpretation has four loci: (1) the world(s) external to the biblical text, (2) the biblical text itself, (3) the author(s) of the text and (4) its current reader(s). I agree with Scott Spencer that there is "considerable fluidity" in how these four are interrelated.[1] What remains contested is the level of play between them and how each is defined and mined for its contribution to the full meaning of a biblical text. However, it is precisely these differences between us that invite the question: what determines "good" interpretation of Scripture?

Most would respond that a good interpretation is one constrained by the text's context, for any reading of a text out of its context is the pretext for its misuse as a proof text. The authors of the five different views of interpretation collected together in this book understand a text's context somewhat differently, and we tend to rank its common elements differently. Even though Richard Gaffin rehearses and applies the Reformation's rubric that "Scripture interprets Scripture" to the intended meaning of biblical authors, surely even he would agree that a text's full meaning is not inherent to it or easily accessed by means of its author(s); nor would we expect Craig Blomberg to reduce a text's meaning to what it originally meant for its first auditors/readers, or Spencer to its current readers. Rather, textual meaning is

---

[1]This rubric is similar to the "hermeneutical triangle" mentioned by Spencer in his essay on the literary/postmodern view but adds the world of antiquity behind the text as another location of evident interest to biblical scholars and the church's clergy. To this world behind the text we might also add the different social locations of Scripture's readers, past and present, in front of the text.

illumined over the course of a very long history when it is picked up and performed again and again for use in a variety of roles to hear the word of the Lord God Almighty in ever-changing ecclesial contexts.

Additionally, even though often counterproductive to the church's use of Scripture as a trusted witness to God's self-communication, the academy's reception of Scripture has also elaborated its meaning in powerful and enriching ways. A good interpretation must engage all these sources with prayerful attentiveness to search the Scripture under the Spirit's direction and by the church's confession to teach, to reprove, to correct and to train God's people for the ministry of reconciliation.

THE PHILOSOPHICAL/THEOLOGICAL VIEW

I consider Merold Westphal's philosophical/theological view first because his concerns are logically prior to the tasks of biblical exegesis and interpretation. For this reason, his essay is difficult to engage from the perspective of a canonical approach. On the one hand, the structure he provides for considering any interpretive strategy is helpful to us all, yet he offers no interpretive strategy in particular or a set of conditions that might help explain or guide one's interpretation of Matthew 2:7-15. He evades a reading of this passage based on his philosophy of hermeneutics. While he anticipates what interpreters should find in a biblical text and then applies this to the preparation of a sermon, his reflections are highly provisional and often made from the perspective of a sermon's auditor rather than a sermon's preparer-presenter. For this reason, it is not entirely clear to me how Westphal's philosophy of hermeneutics shapes the habits of good interpretation and, in turn, the preparation of a good sermon. While I find his comments in this regard enriching, I take them as matters of personal preference and common sense.

Nonetheless, his essay prompts me to ask what role hermeneutical "theory" has in biblical interpretation. I am reminded of John Webster's comment that "the most fruitful way of engaging in theological interpretation of Scripture is to do it," further suggesting that "especially academic conventions change more often by subversion than by high theory."[2] Certainly the bias of the canonical approach is to favor Bible practices and their effect in forming a people belonging to God, and to detach this more functional in-

---

[2]John Webster, "Editorial," *International Journal of Systematic Theology* 12, no. 2 (2010): 116.

terest from any particular hermeneutical theory. But is this always smart? Westphal reminds us that an interpreter's self-criticism should be framed by an account of why she reads sacred texts the way she does, which includes both epistemological and theological reasons. As Gaffin points out, Jesus provided his disciples with a "hermeneutical theory" (Lk 24:44) before opening their minds to understand Scripture in light of it (Lk 24:45-47)!

For this reason, we should welcome Westphal's helpful definition of self-criticism—those rules that regulate right interpretation—which recognizes the epistemic bankruptcy and practical impossibility of scientific neutrality while allowing for the core beliefs of a faith tradition. Any approach to Scripture, whatever its chief interests, should be made with passionate faith rather than passive agnosticism. The fair-minded interpreter will be ever alert to prejudices that exclude her from engaging other readers in a robust conversation over what the text plainly says or that prejudge its full meaning. Unlike God, a catholic community of diverse but faithful readers cannot know the full meaning of a biblical text, but such a community can better approximate the full meaning (or God's intended meaning) of a text than any single interpreter, no matter how intellectually competent and spiritually mature.

In this regard, Westphal could have paid more attention to the authority of the good *interpreter*. While much has been said about Scripture's authority and the authority of its author, both human and divine, relatively little has been said, including by Westphal, about the role of the prepared interpreter in right interpretation.[3] Michael Fishbane, in commenting on the phenomenon of Jewish exegesis, observes that biblical interpretation responds to a practical crisis—the incomprehensibility of a text or its perceived irrelevance by its audience—that requires an "individual talent" to clarify that text for the present day.[4] Such a "talent" is intellectually engaged: she must know the Bible well. Moreover, a talented interpreter must also be spiritually mature: she must also know and love God and God's people intimately. It strikes me that misguided interpretations, however sincerely given, are sometimes the result of ignorance of a text's grammatical or linguistic makeup; however, just as often mistakes are made because of sinful dispositions.

---

[3]See N. Clayton Cloy, *Prima Scriptura* (Grand Rapids: Baker Academic, 2011), pp. xxxviii-xli, 1-12.
[4]Michael Fishbane, *The Garments of Torah* (Bloomington: Indiana University Press, 1992), pp. 16-18.

THE HISTORICAL-CRITICAL/GRAMMATICAL VIEW

Joel B. Green has recently argued that the theological interpretation of Scripture problematizes the idea of "history" and the role it performs in contemporary biblical studies.[5] Following his lead, let me again emphasize that the canonical context of biblical exegesis is in part cobbled together with materials retrieved from a postbiblical historical moment, when the church recognized and received a text as canonical for future generations of believers. Because of Scripture's sacred nature and for mostly theological reasons, the canonical approach mines this location as more useful (even if no more difficult) to excavate than the origins of its production, which remain the prolegomena of modern critical orthodoxy.

Moreover, it should be clear that biblical exegesis is not a history of religions discipline in which the text is mined for a matter-of-fact description of how, say, the anonymous Evangelist of Matthew's Gospel and his first readers/auditors once thought about the past of Jesus. Quite apart from the practical difficulties and contested assumptions of doing this kind of historical spadework, the effect of this criticism is to create a vast distance between the text and its current readers. More importantly, historical criticism often results in replacing the narrative of Jesus' life with a plotline and purpose different from the canonical Gospel, which the church has recognized and received as Scripture.

Blomberg's persistent interest in authorial intent, also expressed by the other contributors to this volume, is of a piece with a historian's interest in the biblical text. The practical problem of reconstructing what the original author may have meant or how his first audience may have understood what he wrote them, for lack of evidence, should make us nervous about pressing this interest beyond its limits. At the very least the interpreter should seek the author's purpose or his audience's occasion in what is plainly stated in the text itself rather than in circumstances hidden from view. Missing in Blomberg's discussion is the question raised by the canonical approach regarding the connection between the author's intentions in writing a text and the intentions evinced during its postbiblical history, which includes the editing of the text into its final form as part of a canonical collection (e.g., fourfold Gospel) and the

---

[5]Joel B. Green, "Rethinking 'History' for Theological Hermeneutics," *Journal of Theological Interpretation* 5, no. 2 (2011): 159-74.

church's reception of the collection as canonical.

No one denies the importance of careful linguistic analysis of the biblical text to discern what it plainly says. This remains the heartbeat of good exegesis, as Blomberg rightly notes. Of course, determining the precise meanings of ancient words and carefully assessing their grammatical/syntactical relationships within a text are hardly a precise science. Our exegetical decisions typically reflect theological and methodological biases and at the very least prompt us to check our decisions with others.

Nor does anyone deny the importance of settling on which "critical text" to use—and one supposes this extends to which translation to use in our worshiping communities. However, Blomberg does not hint at the enormous problems in assigning foundational importance to the recovery of a single "original document." Not only are there multiple textual witnesses to almost every biblical writing to sort out, including to Matthew's Gospel, but there is also evidence that multiple written and oral versions of this Gospel circulated within the early church before a fourfold Gospel was fixed toward the end of the second century. That is, there was no single original document. However, these historical matters aside, the canonical approach questions whether this quest for the best text to translate or exegete should target its point of composition (the so-called autograph) rather than its point of canonization. While the distinction has no bearing on an uncontroversial text such as Matthew 2, it does in the instance of the second Gospel, whose "longer ending" is not original to the autograph but was received by the ancient church as canonical and should be read as such today.[6]

A theological reading of Matthew's Gospel is not very interested in the factual accuracy (or inaccuracy) of the Jesus "event" or in the original circumstances of its telling, but in the theological shape of Matthew's narrative of Jesus' life, which enables the Spirit to draw disciples into loving communion with the risen one. In this sense the central character of the Gospel narrative is not the historian's Jesus but the living Jesus. Matthew's narrative world is shaped not only by the first-century Palestinian world of Jesus, which must also be studied, but must also be understood in such a way that allows current readers to travel in and experience it so that they can reenter and reinterpret their own worlds, now from God's perspective.

---

[6]See Robert W. Wall, "Response to Thomas/Alexander, 'And the Signs Are Following' (Mk 16.9-20)," *Journal for Pentecostal Theology* 11, no. 2 (2003): 171-83.

In making this observation, Blomberg's treatment of our set text from Matthew 2 surprises me. One would expect the historian's work to include a greater interest in testing the factuality of the events narrated, especially of the Herodian infanticide, for which there is no record in antiquity. I welcome his inattention! Modern historical criticism typically rules out this event and rewrites the narrative accordingly. Blomberg's interest to vest the narrated events with theological significance, even if in dialogue with source-, form- and redaction-critical conjectures, which are hardly determinate of textual meaning, is appreciated. While biblical narrative is interested in real events, it is more interested in how those events bear witness to God's way of salvation. Blomberg gets this!

Perhaps because of space limitations, Blomberg pays only passing attention to the historical background of the Matthean story. Although one should be careful not to fill in a story's gaps with more information than is required to follow its plotline, more background information could be supplied to help readers "place" the Herodian court, the magi and the practice of astrology within the social, cultural and religious contexts of Second Temple Judaism, especially its contact with Hellenism. My sense is that this information would help thicken Matthew's sparse narration of various exchanges that are of extraordinary theological importance in the telling of the Gospel: between Herod and the magi (as well as Jewish interpreters of Scripture), the magi and Jesus, and even the oration of Joseph's dream and the circumstances of his flight to Egypt.

THE LITERARY/POSTMODERN VIEW

Spencer provides us with a stunning example of the many benefits of a literary/postmodern approach to biblical narrative (as opposed to Scripture's more didactic literature, where the benefits of Spencer's literary approach are less exciting). He does so while carefully avoiding several pitfalls of postmodern literary approaches to biblical interpretation. For example, he speaks of the importance of rendering a "final text" of a biblical writing and laments that Matthew's Gospel is often studied by bits and pieces rather than as a literary whole. The turn toward literary strategies in recent years has often occurred as a substitute for the indeterminacy of a historical approach to the biblical text: at least we have a real text with which to work! Spencer, however, understands that a literary approach to

Matthew is an alternative way of recovering some historical sense of the anonymous Evangelist's communicative intention for writing his story of Jesus. Finally, he is fully aware of the invincible relativism that often attends a postmodern interpretation of an "open text," when all sorts of readers with competing agendas from all kinds of places gather around a common biblical text to deconstruct competing messages from it in support of their own cultural experience rather than the church's Christian gospel.

The critical issue in this regard, as Spencer rightly puts it, is how "to arbitrate fairly between different viewpoints" (p. 57). While this same question may also extend to the interpreter's facilitation of the "dialogue" between the Bible's two testaments and its cotexts, Spencer suggests that we negotiate between different biblical interpretations by placing emphasis on "common experience" and "seasoned exegesis" of the text according to the intentions of its author. Were more space allowed him, one might ask for a much fuller explanation of the kind of agreements this "common experience" attests to and also for a justification of why textual meaning should be constrained by the author's intentions when this information is not readily available in the text itself (see above). In any case, he does not mention either the canonical shape of Matthew's "final text" or readings that interpret its narrative of Jesus within an ecclesial setting that requires theological coherence with the apostolic witness of Jesus and performances that align with certain roles and results that are constitutive of the biblical canon.

For example, what might be gained from Spencer's highly suggestive literary reading of the opening of Matthew's Gospel, which he extends to include the focal text, if this text were viewed as the canonical seam between Old Testament and New Testament? That is, within its full canonical context, given the priority of Matthew's placement within the fourfold Gospel, the highly allusive character of its opening narrative, which resounds with a vibrant array of Old Testament references, suggests that Matthew plays a role in framing the church's christological reading of the Old Testament as Christian Scripture beyond the more limited role Spencer gives his reading by enclosing it within the first Gospel. Not only are connections made within the composition that underwrite the church's claim that this Son of God Messiah is the "true representative of God's people," but the adumbration of Old Testament citations in the Gospel's opening chapters (1:23; 2:6,

15, 18, 23) also targets the historical events of Jesus' beginnings as revelatory of God's redemptive purpose for Israel (1:21). In this sense, Matthew's repeated use of Old Testament texts brings the story of Jesus to bear on the story of Israel. Yet the reverse is also true: the story of Israel impresses itself on the plot line in defining the very shape of the Gospel narrative.[7]

THE REDEMPTIVE-HISTORICAL VIEW

The ecclesial location of Scripture's principal practices is a condition of the canonical approach to biblical interpretation: Scripture was formed by and for the church.[8] I am not interested to continue here my long-standing (and mostly failed!) effort to extricate the church from the academy's grip in hermeneutical matters, but welcome Gaffin's firm commitment to locate his biblical hermeneutics within the Reformed communion of the Protestant church. Westphal's important reminder of the significance Gadamer grants to religious traditions as carriers of a culture's truth helps to secure this interest. Simply put, if the endgame of Scripture's interpretation is to bring the church catholic into loving communion with the triune God, then all its reading strategies, whether scholarly or devotional, must accommodate this end and not the reverse. An ecclesiology of Scripture must complement a theology of Scripture; and if the latter relates to how God uses Scripture, then the former concerns how the church uses its Scripture as the second element of an integral whole.

An ecclesiology of Scripture may also compare the differences of interpretation formed at particular theological locations within the church catholic. For example, for more than a decade I have asked whether a reading of Scripture shaped by the worship practices and theological grammar of the Wesleyan communion helps to form distinctively Wesleyan readings and applications of the biblical word. My evaluation is ongoing, but my hunch is that the differences between Christian interpreters are often less a matter of methodological or epistemological disagreements and more a matter of their confessional differences. The different theological grammars that find and articulate Scripture's meaning are shaped within

---

[7]Cf. Brevard S. Childs, *The New Testament as Canon* (Philadelphia: Fortress, 1984), pp. 69-71.
[8]Especially helpful for illumining the theological implications of this observation is the collection, coauthored by A. K. M. Adam, Stephen E. Fowl, Kevin J. Vanhoozer and Francis Watson, *Reading Scripture with the Church* (Grand Rapids: Baker Academic, 2006).

a variety of Christian communions by a version of the apostolic rule of faith and worship practices apropos to each.

To a large extent the influence that a particular tradition exerts on its Bible teachers is intuitive and hard to explain in formal ways. Yet I am fully aware that a routine of reading John Wesley's sermons and a love for his brother's magisterial hymns have decisively shaped my theological reading of Scripture, even as Gaffin's Reformed heritage and its greatest teachers, such as Calvin and Vos, have shaped his. As teachers of different theological traditions, we should make no effort to remove this bias from our interpretation of Scripture, since modernity's warning that biblical criticism must protect the Bible from self-interested interpreters is directed specifically at the confessing church! Self-criticism requires awareness of theological prejudice and ethical preference, but it need not dismiss them if they cohere to the content and intended effects of the apostolic rule of faith.

I also appreciate Gaffin's insistence on setting out the theological commitments that underwrite his approach to Scripture. His Reformed doctrine of Scripture as a revealed and revealing canonical text that discloses trustworthy information about God's redemptive plans for creation is implicit in his hermeneutical program. The plot line of God's redemptive history worked out in Israel continues into the New Testament, so that the prophecy narrated by the Old Testament is realized in the New Testament story of Jesus and his apostolic witnesses. The result is a robust and dynamic intertextuality that is highly suggestive, nicely illustrated in this volume by Gaffin's expansive reading of the quotation in Matthew 2:15 of Hosea 11:1.

According to Gaffin's view of salvation history, Scripture is a "book of history" that documents divine revelation; in fact, he assumes that Scripture's narrative of the core events of God's salvation (*Heilsgeschichte*) is a factually accurate account of what happened (*Historie*). He asserts this belief, but he never demonstrates it; and in this sense he collapses the two, the history of revelation with human history, thus securing it as a dogmatic category that is not subject to the suspicions of modern historical criticism. At the very least, this claim would have benefited from a fuller discussion prompted by moving his dependence on Vos forward to later Reformed scholars such as Oscar Cullmann and Gerhard von Rad, who more carefully distinguish their understanding of Scripture's narrative of the history of redemption from what actually happened on the ground. I would quickly add, however, that the construction of a critically chastened biblical history of salvation, put forward as modernity's alternative to Scripture's witness to it, should be rejected as subversive of theological interpretation.

Gaffin's emphasis on a plot line of saving *events*, which on the one hand brings Old Testament and New Testament into fruitful dialogue, on the other hand fails to engage the particulars of each testament. For example, Scripture (both Old Testament and New Testament) includes not only narratives of events but also bears inspired witness to God's revelation. Additionally the New Testament interpretation of Old Testament texts sometimes rewrites them or alters their communicative intention.

Gaffin relates Scripture's intertextuality to the Reformation's rubric, "Scripture interprets Scripture," rather than to more recent literary studies that explore an author's creative use of antecedent texts (see Spencer's study). More importantly Gaffin supposes that these intertexts supply a line of evidence for a continuously unfolding revelation of God's salvation history, documented by Scripture, which concentrates on the dying and rising of Jesus. In effect the study of New Testament intertexts is the means by which interpreters can track down Christ in the Old Testament. In this sense the human authors of both New Testament text and Old Testament cotext cohere to God's intended meaning, the one elaborating the other as revelatory of God's salvation. The assumed simultaneity of biblical texts allows the interpreter to exegete each text within its particular "God-given context" as an uncomplicated unity.

Progressive revelation tends to define intertextual practices unidirectionally. In fact, I do not see how Gaffin's reading of Hebrews 1:1-2 (which is more sharply contested than he admits) can avoid the effect of supersessionism. At the very least, a fuller exploration of the relationship between Old Testament and New Testament within a single biblical canon is needed. From a canonical perspective that upholds each testament as a discrete yet integral witness to God, which agrees with what the apostles saw and heard of Jesus, the relationship between the two is mutually glossing and bidirectional. Not only is Matthew's story of Jesus interpreted by Hosea's oracle of divine love, but the response of Hosea's God is better understood by God's sending Messiah Jesus on a mission to "save his people from their sins" (Mt 1:21).

Finally, Gaffin routinely speaks in material terms of Scripture's "special revelation" as reporting, documenting and testifying to historical events in which God discloses and reveals God's redemptive plans. While I think this confuses epistemic categories, since the evidence of theology (revelation) is not the same as the evidence sought after by historians,[9] I want to comment on his use of "witness" to distinguish his conception of biblical theology from the one currently in play. Gaffin believes Scripture is divine revelation and that in this sense its witness to God is depositional of hard evidence in the court of inquiry. For the most part, advocates of the canonical approach follow Karl Barth's typology of biblical witness, which carefully makes the distinction that Scripture is not identical to the divine revelation but bears witness to the divine revelation.[10]

CONCLUSION

The canonical approach is a species of *theological* interpretation. What one believes about the Bible is the most important condition of its interpretation; all other historical, literary and philosophical considerations are ancillary to a theology of Scripture. While the Bible is also a human production from beginning to end and so its interpretation must include every biblical criticism, the central feature of a canonical approach to study of the Bible is confessional and employs a theological grammar of core beliefs about the sacred nature of the biblical text and its practices and holy effects at an ecclesial address.[11]

Because what one believes about the Bible follows from what one believes about divine revelation, every method and intended result of biblical interpretation must cohere to what one believes about the triune God and the manner of God's self-communication to humankind. Sharply put we read the canon with the creed. In this sense the change of rubrics from

---

[9]For this clarification see William J. Abraham, *Crossing the Threshold of Divine Revelation* (Grand Rapids: Eerdmans, 2006), pp. 58-78.

[10]Karl Barth, *Church Dogmatics* I/2, ed. Geoffrey W. Bromiley and T. F. Torrance (Edinburgh: T & T Clark, 1936–1975), pp. 457-537.

[11]This point is now broadly developed in Daniel Castelo and Robert W. Wall, "Scripture and the Church: A Précis for an Alternative Analogy," *Journal of Theological Interpretation* 5, no. 2 (2011): 197-212. There is no such thing as Christian "Scripture" apart from the church. They are of a piece. This is true in a historical sense: Scripture was written, edited, collected and canonized for the spiritual benefit of Christians. While there are surely other "addresses" where the Bible is found, the church remains its principal residence. But this claim is also true in an existential sense: the Spirit is God's gift to the church, whose worship, evangelism, study and fellowship enliven the Spirit's work in forming the faith and witness of its members.

"Bible" to "Scripture" by practitioners of theological interpretation is purposeful and heavy-laden with theological freight. To speak of the Bible as Scripture recognizes "its role in God's self-communication, that is, the acts of Father, Son and Spirit which establish and maintain that saving fellowship with humankind in which God makes himself known to us and by us."[12] The Bible's authority at its ecclesial address, then, is not predicated on the identity and intentions of its inspired authors, on the divine nature of its inerrant propositions or on the artfulness of the biblical text understood in its original historical setting. Rather, the Bible's authority as God's Word for the church is predicated on God's persistent use of the Bible to bring to realization God's redemptive purposes for the world. In this sense the Bible's authority is defended by a long history of evident usefulness as an auxiliary of God's Spirit in reordering its faithful readers according to the Creator's holy intentions for them—what Paul names in 2 Timothy 3:15-17 as wisdom for salvation and maturity for good works.[13]

Assuming this orienting belief as a primary condition of theological interpretation recognizes that the primary referent of Scripture is not a plot line of ancient historical events but the living God who desires *koinōnia* with every human. Such a deeply personal relationship is predicated on knowing God, whose presence—the nouns that decline God's transcendent existence and the verbs that conjugate God's actions in the world—is rendered by Scripture's many diverse witnesses, prophetic and apostolic, all of whom testify to the truth incarnate in Jesus, God's Son. The Holy Spirit's purpose for Scripture is to mediate God's self-communication to the church, whose ignorance of God will lead them into sin and self-destruction. Thus in recognition of this sacred trust the church meditates on Scripture day and night to learn the ways of our triune God, with whom we work out our salvation from sin and from whom the meaning of eternal

---

[12]John Webster, *Holy Scripture: A Dogmatic Sketch* (Cambridge: Cambridge University Press, 2003), p. 8.

[13]It is one of the principal theses of William J. Abraham's "canonical theism" that the church's epistemic criterion is divine revelation, most especially in the Son, and not in Scripture. Scripture and all other auxiliaries of the Spirit function first and foremost soteriologically. These earthen vessels are transformed under the Spirit's direction into a "complex means of grace that restores the image of God in human beings and brings them into communion with God and with each other in the church" ("Canonical Theism: Thirty Theses," in *Canonical Theism: A Proposal for Theology and the Church*, ed. William J. Abraham et al. [Grand Rapids: Eerdmans, 2008], p. 8).

life is disclosed. Every interpretive strategy and performance of Scripture is measured by this holy effect rather than, say, some hermeneutical theory.

Scripture's pluriform witness to God's self-revelation also guides the formation of the community's holy practices in the world so that God's redemptive purpose to put the world to rights will be achieved. The formation of a single biblical canon in the past and its functions for a present ministry of reconciliation target a future when God's promise of a new creation will be realized for Christ's sake. Then, when the Torah of God will be inscribed on everyone's heart, there will be no need for Scripture. In the present age, however, faithful readers are sanctified by God's grace through practicing the church's Scripture, especially in Spirit-led worship and catechesis, where a "right-handling of the word of truth" (2 Tim 2:15) cultivates cooperation with God's providential reordering of all things.[14]

The practice and reception of theological interpretation that is formative of Christian discipleship depends on a certain kind of faith community in which the Spirit is set free to inspire Scripture's teaching as a means of grace. The community must ready itself for God's address in Scripture. This encounter not only requires the disposition of faith over skepticism but also the formation of a theologically literate community that is able to distinguish good from bad theology in order to respond obediently to the hearing of God's Word.

This is also to say that Scripture is received in community, to whom the Lord's Spirit is given, rather than for private meaning. For this reason the solidarity of its membership, who "believe with one heart and soul" (Acts 4:32) and love one another, is an unconditional virtue of Scripture's reception. To hear Scripture together in loving communion will make it impossible for the body of Christ to divide over disagreements of interpretation. In fact, freedom will be granted for the Spirit to lead its members into truth, especially when an admission of the truth disclosed through Scripture requires repentance and restoration. This is another, more existential layer of the "hermeneutical circle": a spiritually mature community seeks the truth from Scripture that will enable the Spirit to make it ever more wise and understanding.

---

[14]In his commentary on Philippians (THC; Grand Rapids: Eerdmans, 2005), Stephen E. Fowl restates and then demonstrates this commitment in a more organic way by defining a theological reading of Scripture as the very shape of its faithful exegesis. That is, retrieving the theological goods from a biblical text for the church is not a hermeneutical end but an exegetical means.

Interpreting Together

Synthesizing Five Views of Biblical Hermeneutics

Stanley E. Porter and Beth M. Stovell

The five contributions to this volume have ably and incisively demonstrated the diversity of views in the field of contemporary biblical hermeneutics. In viewing the proposals and responses, one can see many of the points of tension and even disagreement that animate and illuminate the discussion among these contributors. However, as all of the contributors have also noted, all of the hermeneutical approaches share four major foci of discussion, around which their treatments take place: "(1) the world(s) external to the biblical text, (2) the biblical text itself, (3) the author(s) of the text and (4) its current reader(s)."[1] These foci provide a set of orienting features for discussing the mutual help that each method lends to the others. Their terminology will appear and reappear in our discussion below regarding the common elements of our five views of hermeneutics.

LEARNING FROM FIVE VIEWS OF BIBLICAL HERMENEUTICS

This conclusion to the discussion of biblical hermeneutics presented in this volume will suggest three major ways that elements of these five views of biblical hermeneutics—in terms of the four foci noted above—might work together to provide helpful insights into hermeneutics and for interpreting

---

[1] While Robert Wall provides this helpful list in his response essay (p. 188), all of the contributors address these issues in their position papers and their response essays in a variety of ways.

the biblical text. These three major avenues of understanding are (1) identifying the role and context of the author, the text, the readers both ancient and modern, and the biblical interpreter; (2) allowing for literary integrity and diversity, as well as interpretive integrity and diversity, by identifying literary features of the text and acknowledging the larger narrative of the overall biblical account, while balancing this with awareness of the specificity of the biblical culture(s); and (3) acknowledging the vital role of faith in interpretation, both as influential for our interpretation and as constructive for theological and ethical implications.[2] With these three avenues of exploration adumbrated, we now attempt a constructive hermeneutical analysis and synthesis of them, taking into account the similarities and differences in the five hermeneutical models discussed in this book.

CONTEXT AND COMMUNICATION

We begin with the important notions of context and communication. Scott Spencer's literary/postmodern view has rightly shown us that any piece of literature is a form of communication.[3] Craig Blomberg's historical-critical/grammatical view reminds us that this communication takes place in a historical context. Merold Westphal's account of philosophical/theological hermeneutics has brought to the fore that complete epistemological neutrality and certainty are equally mythical, nudging us toward a greater sense of hermeneutical humility.[4] Thus recognizing this insight of postmodernism, as we approach our biblical text, we must contextualize each part of the communication process. In fact, postmodernism has also

---

[2]Using Merold Westphal's terms (following Hans-Georg Gadamer), one might describe these as "reproductive" and "productive" (p. 77). These suggestions engage with many of the concepts put forward by Stanley E. Porter in "Literary Approaches to the New Testament," in *Approaches to New Testament Study*, ed. Stanley E. Porter and David Tombs, JSNTSup 120 (Sheffield: Sheffield Academic Press, 1995), pp. 120-28.

[3]Linguistic models have much to offer here. The list of four foci reflects a simplified version of Roman Jakobson's basic theory of communication ("Linguistics and Poetics," in *Style in Language*, ed. Thomas A. Sebeok [Cambridge, Mass.: MIT Press, 1960], pp. 350-77), built upon in the narratological model of Seymour Chatman, *Story and Discourse: Narrative Structure in Fiction and Film* (Ithaca, N.Y.: Cornell University Press, 1978). Norman R. Petersen presents this model by way of presenting literary theory as a helpful addition to the tools of biblical scholarship. See Petersen, *Literary Criticism for New Testament Critics* (Philadelphia: Fortress, 1978), p. 37.

[4]In their own ways, each of the other four contributors has praised Westphal for highlighting the need for humility through his approach to philosophical hermeneutics.

led, in an ironic way, to greater hermeneutical precision.[5] We can no longer speak of the implications of author or text without also being keenly aware of the reader/critic. This is an important contribution for developing a constructive interpretive dialogue, ready to listen to other viewpoints with a realization that we, as individual readers/interpreters, do not have complete knowledge within ourselves and that any approach we take will only provide a part of the larger picture. Thus the resultant model of communication includes author, text, original reader and modern reader/interpreter.[6] Each of these merits further, if only brief, discussion to place it within its respective hermeneutical context and in relation to the contributions to this volume.

Author. In the history of literary criticism, the author has held a special position of authority and as the origin of intentionality for many years, ever since and under the influence of romanticism. This view also had an important and abiding influence on biblical hermeneutics (as we see in Friedrich Schleiermacher's progeny).[7] As our five hermeneutical proponents have shown, while one should not subjugate every part of the text and its interpretation to authorial intent, we must rethink the move in narrative critical (New Critical/formalist) and poststructuralist approaches, as well as in forms of biblical hermeneutics (the New Hermeneutic),[8] that remove the author entirely from the equation. As we consciously bring back into the interpretive equation the author's role, we must, in turn, also be explicit in placing the author in his or her historical context. First, following more traditional models such as those represented by Blomberg, we should attempt to gain access (to the best of our ability) to the biblical author. Barring this, we should at least attempt to place an author (whoever that author might be) in their social context, for example, placing a New Testament biblical author within the world of Hellenistic

---

[5]This is ironic in so far as much postmodernist theory denies the ability to gain precision.

[6]Our use of this approach is designed to deal with both the "history in the text" and the "history of the text," using the language of John H. Hayes and Carl R. Holladay. Thus, our contextualization of author and reader is devoted to attention to the "history of the text," while our discussion of textual context will address the "history in the text." See Hayes and Holladay, *Biblical Exegesis: A Beginner's Handbook,* 3rd ed. (Louisville: Westminster John Knox Press, 2007), pp. 56-57.

[7]See Stanley E. Porter and Jason C. Robinson, *Hermeneutics: An Introduction to Interpretive Theory* (Grand Rapids: Eerdmans, 2011), pp. 24-33 and following.

[8]See ibid., pp. 237, 279.

Judaism,[9] assuming his postresurrection experience and recognizing his goal of sharing the message of Jesus Christ. (These latter two contexts are well-explored by the redemptive-historical view provided by Richard Gaffin.)

Text. Traditional and modern models of interpretation have both shown that the biblical texts do not exist as independent documents. As with their authors, the biblical texts are informed by and connected to their contexts. This textual context includes their relationship to other texts within the biblical canon (as affirmed by Robert Wall's canonical approach)[10] and their relationship to texts of a similar genre within the historical context. As with issues of authorial context, issues of textual context—such as what constitutes a suitable context, how one determines a context in the ancient world in light of sometimes limited evidence and the role of context in interpretation—have developed in both literary and biblical circles.[11]

Reader(s). As we address the question of readers, traditional criticisms such as those represented by Blomberg remind us that the twenty-first-century reader does not read the same way as the ancient reader. While

---

[9]We should ask if this author would be more likely to use Greco-Roman perspectives as a Gentile, on the one hand, or Jewish ones, on the other, though one may agree with Martin Hengel's premise that Hellenistic Judaism makes this division much less precise. Nonetheless, a Gentile would stress particular factors in different ways than would a Jew. See Hengel, *Hellenism and Judaism: Studies in Their Encounter in Palestine in the Early Hellenistic Period*, 2 vols., trans. John Bowden (Philadelphia: Fortress, 1974); and with Christoph Markschies, *The 'Hellenization' of Judaea in the First Century after Christ*, trans. John Bowden (London: SCM Press, 1989).

[10]In recent times, much discussion has focused on "intertextuality." While the literary/philosophical term *intertextuality* is not without its problems, the concept of texts existing in some relationship to other texts is necessary for understanding much of the use of Scripture within Scripture. For example, in order to understand much of the New Testament, it is important to understand its relationship to the Old Testament. For the strengths and weaknesses of this field of study, see Stanley E. Porter, "Further Comments on the Use of the Old Testament in the New Testament," in *The Intertextuality of the Epistles: Explorations of Theory and Practice*, ed. Thomas L. Brodie, Dennis R. MacDonald and Stanley E. Porter (Sheffield: Sheffield Phoenix Press, 2006), pp. 98-110; and Porter, "The Use of the Old Testament in the New Testament," in *Early Christian Interpretations of the Scriptures of Israel: Investigations and Proposals*, ed. Craig A. Evans and James A. Sanders, JSNTSup 148, SSEJC 5 (Sheffield: Sheffield Academic Press, 1997), pp. 79-96.

[11]One such interdisciplinary question concerns genre. The question of genre has been approached by disciplines throughout the humanities, including literary, biblical, sociolinguistic, cultural-material and film studies, with varying results. See David Duff, ed., *Modern Genre Theory* (London: Longman, 1999), for a selection of significant opinions, and Garin Dowd, Lesley Stevenson and Jeremy Strong, eds., *Genre Matters: Essays in Theory and Criticism* (Portland: Intellect, 2006), for contemporary essays.

this insight is incredibly important for a correct understanding of the impact of the Bible on the early church, we should also balance this observation with the equally important realization that the Bible, with its continuing revelation, is also intended for today's reader (a point affirmed by both Wall and Gaffin, if in different ways). Further, postmodern literary theories point to the role of the modern reader in the act of interpretation (as both Westphal and Spencer affirm). While we cannot accept the more radical positions of poststructuralist theory, which at their most extreme place the author's role and text's roles in communication entirely in the hands of the reader, we must be aware of what we as interpreters bring to the interpretive process. Thus our goals in contextualizing the "reader" are threefold: seeking the context of the original ancient reader, determining the context for today's reader and understanding our own context rightly.

The context of the original reader includes using archaeological, anthropological/sociological, historical and linguistic information, among other possible avenues of insight, as Blomberg's approach affirms. Such study will also, and perhaps especially, involve the careful analysis of ancient sources, with the realization that we may only gain access to this history in part (as Westphal's view demonstrates).

As Spencer's approach demonstrates, the context of the twenty-first-century reader will imply a good deal of diversity as well. Our goal in gaining this awareness is to realize both the difference and similarity between the original reader and today's reader. Our interpretations should have relevance historically, academically and theologically; but as Westphal, Spencer and Wall all agree, these interpretations should also aim to be intelligible in our modern context.

Finally, we must be aware of ourselves as interpreters. This points to the necessity of reading in community to realize our own presuppositions.[12] As Christian interpreters we are parts of multiple communities, some academic, others ecclesiastical. Any method we develop for interpretation must include an element of reexamination as part of its continuing development. In this vein Westphal's approach demonstrates the need for an awareness of our own presuppositions, while Wall adds the sobering re-

---

[12]Spencer provides a description of his specific personal and theological context (p. 67), which Westphal approves in his response (p. 171). Spencer identifies himself as one interpreter among many diverse possible interpreters.

minder that each of us as *Christian* interpreters is capable of sin, and we should reflect on this truth as we approach any biblical text.

LITERARY AND INTERPRETIVE INTEGRITY AND DIVERSITY

Identifying the various contexts of each point of communication allows us to address the issue of what is behind the text without completely dismantling the text itself. This concept of unity within the text (and within the grander overarching narrative of the Old Testament and New Testament) could be one of the greatest shared strengths that literary approaches and theological approaches such as the redemptive-historical and canonical viewpoints offer.

The redemptive-historical approach and the literary/postmodern approach provide for the possibility of reading and interpreting the story of the Old Testament and the New Testament as one coherent story. Pointing to the unity of Scripture points to the unified grand story, or metanarrative, that underlies the entire Bible. The key to our understanding of this grand story is that this is a story of God's faithfulness and humanity's (our) response of faith. Yet in dealing with the unity of the story, we must not overlook the uniqueness of the specific individual stories that constitute this grand narrative. This attention to parts within the whole is particularly important in discussing the relationship between the Old Testament and the New Testament, where there is a good deal of diversity between the two testaments, to say nothing of differences between particular Old Testament passages and their specific uses in the New Testament (a point made by both Blomberg and Spencer in their responses).[13]

Related to this issue of literary integrity and diversity is the issue of interpretive integrity and diversity. The approaches in this volume demonstrate the tension (and at times surprising joy) of seeking and even finding interpretive consensus while constantly being faced with interpretive difference. None of the contributors advocates a free-for-all approach to interpretation, yet each contributor offers a different amount of space for

---

[13]While the relationship between the Old Testament and the New Testament is a difficult one, it is a very necessary one as well. Porter offers some critique and insight for possible ways forward in the discipline. See Porter, "Further Comments," and Porter, "Use of the Old Testament in the New Testament."

interpretive difference in the translation and transition of Old Testament to New, alongside the question of what is meant by continuing revelation.

To navigate these difficult waters, this volume demonstrates ways to build on recognizable continuity, and at the same time to incorporate at least the awareness of diversity, by engaging in careful and purposeful interaction with this diversity. How do we deal with difference without sliding into meaninglessness? From a theological standpoint, we must honor the uniqueness of persons within the overarching story of Scripture. In giving his Scriptures to us, God chose to mediate his message through unique persons at specific times to better portray the *imago Dei*. Postmodernism can, if nothing else, teach us that diversity has a purpose. By attending to more of Scripture's individual, if diverse, elements, we are capable of seeing more of the grand story, the story God is telling about himself and the potential for Scripture to transform the lives of its original audience and of our lives today. While each contributor to this volume would express this truth in different ways, we believe that each would agree with it, at the very least in part.

ROLE OF FAITH IN INTERPRETATION

One of the goals of postmodern theorists was the reintroduction of interpretive elements modernism had attempted to remove. Yet many have critiqued elements of postmodernist theories of interpretation and philosophy as merely the logical conclusion of modernism, or at least the next logical stage, thereby suggesting that postmodernism itself is another form of modernism or its alter ego.[14] Poststructuralism, with its literary/philosophical theoretical progeny deconstruction, has pushed increasingly toward the dissolution of meaning.[15] Some have argued that, within modern and especially postmodern hermeneutical models, humanity has been lost. In the overemphasis on the critic's interpreting the text, the text and its meaning have indeed at times been lost. Scholars in various hermeneutical circles, including literary and biblical, have looked to the past longingly,

---

[14]This argument is present in this volume in Gaffin's critiques of Spencer and Westphal, alongside his critique of Blomberg. For other scholars discussing similar issues, see David J. A. Clines, "The Postmodern Adventure in Biblical Studies," in *Auguries: The Jubilee Volume of the Sheffield Department of Biblical Studies*, ed. David J. A. Clines and Stephen D. Moore (Sheffield: Sheffield Academic Press, 1998), pp. 276-93.

[15]See Porter and Robinson, *Hermeneutics*, pp. 190-213.

hoping to reach back to a period before the taint of the Enlightenment, modernism and postmodernism. Such an attempt, however, is not only impossible but also unwise.[16] However, postmodernism is not the end of the story, nor has it left us completely bereft of hermeneutical and interpretive hope. Instead, as Christian interpreters, postmodernism has in part opened the way for a new means to acknowledge and incorporate our own faith convictions within our hermeneutical agenda. Here we have an opportunity to bring back the experience and instruction of the Holy Spirit that modernism bracketed out with its closed materialism (a point made in varying ways by Blomberg, Wall and Gaffin); we can also learn from the extremism of postmodern theory that, when we remove history and authorship, reading the text with only our experience to guide (or create) our interpretation, we are left only with a reflection of ourselves, losing the text, which is other, and verging on hermeneutical solipsism (a correction noted by Spencer and Westphal).

As scholars respond to what many are deeming the end of postmodernism, the question is often asked, what now?[17] This is an important question for scholars across the hermeneutical spectrum. With Paul Ricoeur, one may answer that between the *cogito* of Descartes (the assertions of modernism) and the anti*cogito* of Nietzsche (the antiassertions of postmodernism) is a "credence without guarantee, but a trust greater than any suspicion."[18] Ricoeur rightly sees we cannot be guaranteed that all our

---

[16]As Jens Zimmermann points out, "Recovering theological hermeneutics cannot mean a simple return to presuppositions of premodern theology, as if centuries of philosophical development had never occurred. . . . [The insights of premodern theology] must be recovered by working through modern and postmodern hermeneutic philosophies rather than by circumventing them." Zimmermann, *Recovering Theological Hermeneutics: An Incarnational-Trinitarian Theory of Interpretation* (Grand Rapids: Baker Academic, 2004), p. 317. The same is equally true of biblical hermeneutics. Valentine Cunningham presents a similar position upon reflection on past literary theory in his chapter, "The Good of Theory," in Cunningham, *Reading After Theory* (London: Blackwell, 2002), pp. 38-53.

[17]Cunningham describes this dilemma in his chapter, "What Then? What Now?" in Cunningham, *Reading After Theory*, pp. 1-2. Another equally fitting description comes from a special session of the Modern Language Association in 2008 titled "What Is Post-Post-Modernism?"

[18]Paul Ricoeur, *Oneself as Another*, trans. Kathleen Blamey (Chicago: University of Chicago Press, 1992), p. 23. Here Ricoeur speaks of the role of the self rather than narrative specifically, but in this work the role of the self is intimately connected to the role of narrative. Further, this statement of credence and trust beyond suspicion is Ricoeur's response to his own "hermeneutic of suspicion" held earlier in his academic career. Many scholars (whether literary or biblical), based on Ricoeur's early views of interpretation, especially his famous "hermeneutic of suspicion," have situated Ricoeur as a liberal or in line with deconstruction.

findings will be correct; therefore, we approach interpretation humbly; but our trust is greater than our suspicion.[19] This trust allows us to come again to the Bible and believe that we will find a disclosure of God's truth. This truth comes through the true story of a real person, Jesus Christ, who was both human and divine. Thus we come seeking the historical reality of the event and person (what is behind the text, as Blomberg affirms); we come seeking the meaning of this true story (what is within the text, as all contributors would affirm); and we come seeking the transformative power of this text in the lives of those who believe (what is in front of the text, as Westphal, Wall and Gaffin emphasize in their different ways).

FROM FAITH TO ACTION

This leads to the final movement of our hermeneutics of interpretation: the movement to theology and to action. Amid the many responses to the demise of postmodernism, there has been a trend among some scholars to suggest a reaffirmation of humanity.[20] Ricoeur's theories of self and narrative challenge us to view self-awareness firmly in relationship to the other. In *Oneself as Another*, Ricoeur, faced with his son's suicide, posits that we only truly gain identity through our interconnection with others.[21] This view of self-other has ethical implications that are consistent with the recurring ethical implications of the biblical narrative itself, as we are encouraged in both the Old Testament and the New Testament to love our neighbors,[22] and this love is described as "not in words or tongue, but with

---

Yet this is a misrepresentation of Ricoeur's overall position, which is typically mediating and often conservative in comparison to the French theories of his time. Charles Reagan discusses Ricoeur's view of the self in relation to others as it relates to personal identity and ethics. See Reagan, "Personal Identity," in *Ricoeur as Another: The Ethics of Subjectivity*, ed. Richard A. Cohen and James L. Marsh (New York: SUNY Press, 2002), pp. 6-9.

[19]Richard B. Hays follows elements of Ricoeur's idea of hermeneutics here in his advocating of a "hermeneutic of trust." Hays does not fully explain how he balances his hermeneutic of trust with the hermeneutic of suspicion, but he rightly notes our need to have a hermeneutic of suspicion regarding our own interpretation, rather than credence in our own experience and suspicion in the biblical text. Hays, "A Hermeneutic of Trust," in *The Conversion of the Imagination: Paul as Interpreter of Israel's Scripture* (Grand Rapids: Eerdmans, 2005), pp. 190-201.

[20]This is apparent in several "after theory" writings, including Denis Donoghue, *The Practice of Reading* (New Haven: Yale University Press, 1998), and Cunningham, *Reading After Theory*.

[21]While this theme permeates the entire book, Ricoeur particularly focuses on this in *Oneself as Another*, pp. 240-96.

[22]Lev 19:18; Mt 19:19; 22:39; Mk 12:31, 33; Lk 10:27; Jas 2:8.

actions and in truth."[23] This relationship, however, is not limited to self-other in our neighbor, but only truly becomes possible through the I-Thou relationship with God.[24] Thus, if we wish to understand ourselves in relationship to Scripture, we must reassert relationality with both the other and God (the ultimate other) in biblical interpretation as well. As we read the biblical account, we are drawn into the continuing story of God's relationship to us and are encouraged to be in relationship to others. Further, this interpretation extends from us as we share it with our community. In different ways, each contributor has asserted the Bible's continuing impact on our everyday lives and the lives of others. When we examine biblical hermeneutics in light of this self-other relationality, we see that our interpretations are *informed by* our faith commitment, *inform* our faith commitment, and *transform* our relationships within the faith community and with the world. This faith commitment joins the diversity of biblical hermeneutical theories (and their proponents) together in a unified purpose. Through reading carefully, contextually and in community, we are able to be transformed by what we read and help to transform others.

---

[23]1 Jn 3:18. James uses both the love of neighbor and the need to show this through deeds in Jas 2, esp. Jas 2:14-17.

[24]Zimmermann explains (in terms strikingly similar to Ricoeur): "Selfhood is understood as person in relation, a subjectivity that neither begins with, nor is defined as, solitary, independent consciousness but is brought to life by the call of the other. Here theological hermeneutics is close to the theologically inspired thought of [Emmanuel] Levinas: the self cannot found itself by itself. . . . Yet incarnational subjectivity is richer. . . . The origin of subjectivity is ethical in a qualified sense, qualified as love in the concrete act of God's self-abnegation in the incarnation and the cross." Zimmermann, *Recovering Theological Hermeneutics*, p. 319. For further discussion of the "I-Thou" relationship between us and God, see the classic work of Martin Buber, *I and Thou*, ed. Walter Arnold Kaufmann (New York: Scribner, 1970).

Contributors

Craig L. Blomberg is distinguished professor of New Testament at Denver Seminary in Littleton, Colorado. Among his publications are *The Historical Reliability of the Gospels* (IVP), *Interpreting the Parables* (IVP), *From Pentecost to Patmos: An Introduction to Acts through Revelation* (B&H), *Neither Poverty nor Riches: A Biblical Theology of Material Possessions* (IVP) and *Contagious Holiness: Jesus' Meals with Sinners* (IVP). Blomberg has also written commentaries on Matthew (B&H), 1 Corinthians (Zondervan) and James (Zondervan).

Richard B. Gaffin Jr. is professor of biblical and systematic theology emeritus at Westminster Theological Seminary in Philadelphia, Pennsylvania. He is the author of *Resurrection and Redemption: A Study in Paul's Soteriology* (P&R Publishing), *Perspectives on the Pentecost: Studies in New Testament Teaching on the Gifts of the Holy Spirit* (P&R Publishing), *Calvin and the Sabbath: The Controversy of Applying the Fourth Commandment* (Focus) and *By Faith, Not by Sight: Paul and the Order of Salvation* (Paternoster).

Stanley E. Porter is professor of New Testament at, and president and dean of, McMaster Divinity College in Hamilton, Ontario, Canada. He is the author or coauthor of eighteen books, and the editor of over seventy volumes, and has published over three hundred journal articles, chapters, and other contributions on a wide range of New Testament and related topics. His authored volumes include *Verbal Aspect in the Greek of the New Testament* (Lang), *The Paul of Acts* (Mohr Siebeck/Hendrickson), *The Criteria for Authenticity in Historical Jesus Research* (Sheffield/Continuum), *New Testament Greek Papyri and Parchments* (De Gruyter) and *Hermeneutics: An Introduction to Interpretive Theory* (Eerdmans). He is currently coauthoring a book on understanding biblical languages with Beth Stovall (IVP).

F. Scott Spencer is professor of New Testament and preaching at Baptist Theological Seminary in Richmond, Virginia. He is the author of *Journey Through Acts: A Literary-Cultural Reading* (Hendrickson), *The Gospel of Luke and Acts of the Apostles* (Abingdon) and *Spirited Mothers, Salty Wives, and Savvy Widows: Capable Women of Persistence and Purpose in Luke's Gospel* (Eerdmans).

Beth M. Stovell is assistant professor of biblical studies at St. Thomas University in Miami Gardens, Florida. She is the author of *Mapping Metaphorical Discourse in the Fourth Gospel: John's Eternal King* (Brill) and is a contributor to several edited volumes, including *Global Perspectives on the Bible* (Pearson Prentice Hall), *The Undead and Theology* (Wipf & Stock), *The New Testament in Its Hellenistic Context* (Brill) and *The Language of the New Testament* (Brill). She is currently writing a commentary on Hosea-Micah (Zondervan), and cowriting a book on interpreting biblical languages with Stanley E. Porter (IVP).

Robert W. Wall is the Paul T. Walls Professor of Scripture and Wesleyan Studies at Seattle Pacific University in Seattle, Washington. He is coeditor of *The Catholic Epistles and Apostolic Tradition* (Baylor) and the New Testament coeditor of the *Wesley Study Bible* (Abingdon). Wall has published commentaries on the *Pastoral Epistles* (Eerdmans), *Acts* (Eerdmans and Abingdon), *James* (T & T Clark), *Colossians and Philemon* (IVP) and *Revelation* (Baker). His canonical approach can be found in numerous journals and collections, as well as in his coauthored book, *The New Testament as Canon* (T & T Clark).

Merold Westphal is distinguished professor of philosophy emeritus at Fordham University in New York, adjunct professor at Australian Catholic University in Australia, and guest professor at Wuhan University in China. Among his writings are *Suspicion and Faith: The Religious Uses of Modern Atheism* (Fordham), *Overcoming Onto-theology: Toward a Postmodern Christian Faith* (Fordham) and *Whose Community? Which Interpretation? Philosophical Hermeneutics for the Church* (Baker Academic). He has also written extensively on Hegel and Kierkegaard.

Name and Subject Index

Abraham, William J., 198n, 199n
Acts, book of, 23, 41, 51, 120
Adam, A. K. M., 12n, 19, 39n, 55n, 56n, 57n, 195n
Adams, James L., 27n
Alexander, T. Desmond, 106n, 140n
Alexandrian school, 13
Alexandrov, Vladimir E., 58n
allegorical embellishment, 84
Allert, Craig D., 182n
Allison, Dale C., 13n, 45n, 61n, 106n
analysis, analyses, investigation of ancient sources, 205
   biblical, 145
   comparative, 52
   contextual, 64
   discourse, 50
   of grammar, 37
   grammatical, 37, 169
   hermeneutical, 202
   historical, 30, 34
   historical-critical/ grammatical, 145
   historical-cultural, 29-30, 36
   historical-linguistic, 50, 168
   linguistic, 112, 192
   linguistic and conceptual, 85
   literary, 109, 151, 169
   narrative, 58, 147
   recent literary, 49, 59
   sociological, 135
   theological, 175
   theological or literary, 31
   traditional-critical, 36
ancient biographies, 33
Anderson, Janice Capel, 55n, 57n
anthropological values and customs, 30, 205
antidualism, 156
Antiochene school, 13
antisupernatural presuppositions, 46, 179
antisupernaturalist worldview, 30, 179
apostolocity, 113
application (practical; productive; contemporary; etc.), 10, 40, 47, 85, 112, 152, 161-64, 170-73, 195

approach(es). *See* criticism, hermeneutics
archaeology, archaeologists, 49, 205
aseity, 92, 165
audience(s), addressees, 39, 123, 141, 147, 161
   ancient, original, intended, 27, 30, 39, 41, 77-80, 86, 114-15, 158, 162, 164, 169, 170, 184, 207
   occasion, 191
   specific/particular, 46, 138, 145
Augustine, 124
Aune, David E., 36n, 122n
author(s), authorial intent, 17-18, 20, 27, 31, 39, 49, 57, 75, 76-77, 79, 134, 141, 146-147, 156, 161, 164, 169-170, 184, 191, 202-3
   apostolic, 170
   authority (of the), 75-76, 81
   biblical, 29, 145, 188
   captivity, 19
   divine, 96, 102, 105, 176-78, 180-81, 185, 190
   final, 34
   historical, 31
   human, 96, 102, 104-5, 155, 158, 162-64, 170, 177, 180, 181, 184, 190
   identity and intention, 48, 199
   implied, 39, 169
   intention(s) of, intended, 19, 113, 138-39, 161, 170, 194
   mind of, 14
   of a New Testament text, 40
   Old Testament, 142
   original, 20, 30, 191
   particular, 38, 115
   perspective of, 11
   psyche, 76
   purpose of the, 72, 191
   real, 39
   relation(ship) between, 14, 78
   role, 205
   speech acts of the, 76
   text or the mind of, 20
   textual strategies, 134
   understanding of the, 72
   world of the, 77, 86
authorial discourse, 78

author-text-reader triad, 133, 178
Ayayao, Karelynn Gerber, 11n
Bailey, Kenneth E., 32n
Baird, William, 9n, 14n, 90n
Bakhtin, Mikhail M., 51, 51n, 113n
Barbour, Robin S., 36n
Barth, Gerhard, 123n
Barth, Karl, 198
Bartholomew, Craig, 178n, 180n
Barton, John, 11n, 14n, 15n, 16n, 113n
Barton, Stephen, 30n, 54n
Bauckham, Richard, 60n
Bauer, David R., 58n, 61n, 66, 66n
Beale, G. K., 42n, 105n, 142n
Beardsley, Monroe C., 31n
Bellinzonni, Arthur J., 124n
Berding, Kenneth, 104n
Berger, Peter, 81
Betti, Emilio, 82, 82n
Bible, Scripture(s), 19, 22, 29, 32, 34, 37, 40, 45, 54, 56-57, 70, 80, 86, 97, 105, 109, 111-12, 130, 140, 143-45, 153, 158, 162, 164, 171, 173, 177, 179-81, 183, 184, 187, 190, 195, 199, 209
   actual effects of the, 115
   antecedent, 135, 144
   authority of, 121, 180, 190, 199
   background, 15
   battle for the, 116
   a book of history, 196
   canonical function of the, 118
   as the church's text, 121, 189
   diversity of, 96
   divine authorship of, 183
   ecclesiology of, 195
   Hebrew, 42
   humanity of, 96
   impact on the early church, 205
   inerrancy of, 37
   inspiration of, 85, 90, 182, 184
   interpreting the/ interpretation of, 24, 79, 84, 93, 98, 116, 196
   Israel's, Jewish, 52, 99, 124

literal or plain sense of, 114
meaning of, 80, 196
method of interpreting the,
    46
nature of, 113
pluriform witness, 200
real task of, 115
revelation historical content
    of, 176
role for the, 183
sacred nature, 112, 114,
    152, 191
as a sacred text, 114, 143
as a shaped text, 117, 143
as a single text, 116, 143
tenor of, 113
textual character of, 169
theological interpretation
    of, 191
theological pluriformity of,
    113
theological use of, 115
theology of, 195, 198
translations of the, 83
unity of, 206
Black, Clifton C., 124n
Black, David Alan, 11n
Bleicher, Josef, 82n
Blomberg, Craig L., 10n, 11n,
    21, 21n, 28n, 30, 31n, 33n,
    38n, 44n, 102n, 133, 137n,
    139n, 140n, 146, 147, 148,
    149, 158, 162, 163, 164, 169,
    174, 175, 176, 177, 178, 181,
    182n, 188, 191, 192, 193, 202,
    203, 204, 205, 206, 207n,
    208, 211
Bock, Darrell L., 10n
Bockmuehl, Markus, 40n
Boda, Mark J., 13n
Bornkamm, Günther, 123n
Boyles, Craig C., 10n
Brenner, Athalya, 60n
Brodie, Thomas L., 204n
Bromiley, Geoffrey W., 198n
Brook-Rose, Christine, 58n
Brooks, Stephenson H., 45n
Brown, Jeannine K., 11n
Brown, Raymond, 58n, 61n,
    63n,
Broyles, Craig C., 34n
Bruce, F. F., 14n
Bruner, Frederick D., 144n
Buber, Martin, 210n
Burns, R. M., 13n
Byrskog, Samuel, 32n
Calvin, Calvinists, 103, 107,
    166, 196

canon, canonization, canonical,
    18, 21, 23, 29, 41, 47, 68, 90,
    93, 97, 99, 101, 111-12, 114,
    118-20, 122-27, 130, 143,
    144-45, 149-51, 153-55, 170,
    183, 191-92, 194, 197,
    199-200, 204
Carey, Haley J., 36n
Carson, D. A., 31n, 38n, 40n,
    89n, 142n, 149
Carter, Warren, 56n, 64, 64n,
    65n, 66n, 136
Cartesian thought, 13
Castelo, Daniel, 198n
Catchpole, David, 15n, 34n
Catholicism, 74
centrifugal motion, 68
Chapman, Stephen, 178
character, characters, 22, 50, 51,
    59, 60, 138, 147
Chatman, Seymour, 202n
Childs, Brevard, 22, 22n, 41n,
    111, 111n, 112n, 114, 119n,
    122, 122n, 125n, 126n, 128n,
    178, 195n
Chilton, Bruce E., 36n
Christ. See Jesus
christocentric unity, 95
christological, 61, 104, 142,
    154, 194
Chronicles, book of, 35
Clarke, Andrew D., 54n, 148n
class, 57
classical philology, 70
Clayton, Charles, 11n
Clines, David J. A., 207n
cogito (anticogito), 208
Cohen, Richard A., 209n
coherence and unity, 51, 56, 96,
    100, 167
coherence
    biblical, 154
    internal, 136
    theological, 194
Collini, Stefan, 58n
communication event, 54
communication, intercultural,
    54
communication network, of
    polyphonous and heteroglot, 55
communicative act, 31, 39, 46
communicative intentions, 31
community, communities, 81
    ancient, 20
    Christian, 150
    continuing, 20
    interpretive, 136
    modern, 20

composition(s)
    biblical, 115
    of the first written sources,
        34
    history of individual
        biblical, 113
    original, 21
    original Gospel, 50
Conn, Harvie M., 93n
consistency or coherence, 41, 59
context, contexts, contextual,
    38, 53, 64, 68, 78, 82, 85, 91,
    97, 98, 105, 109, 130, 135,
    139, 149, 168-69, 188, 202,
    204-5
    canonical, 111, 122, 134,
        194
    and communication, 202
    ecclesial, 189
    eschatological, 166
    God-given, 197
    hermeneutical context, 203
    historical, 41, 134, 146,
        166, 202-3
    historical and cultural,
        47
    immediate, 37-38, 182
    Jesus', 66
    legal and theological,
        80
    literary, 141
    original, 18
    original historical, 27, 139
    pastoral, 158
    principal, 149
    prophetic, 127
    recontextualization, 162
    social, 64, 203
    symbolic spatial, 64
    textual, 204
    theological, 111, 171
Corley, Bruce, 11n
cotext(s), cotextual, 50-51, 59,
    68, 127, 134, 151, 169, 176,
    194, 198
Cotterell, Peter, 39n
covenantal redemption, 153
covenantal replacement, 155
criteria, 11, 182
    of authenticity, 36
    for distinguishing between
        fact and fiction, 33
    for a good interpretation, 41
criticism, critics, approach,
    approaches
        author-oriented, 48
        biblical, 196
        canonical, 17-18, 23, 29, 93,

111-12, 115-16, 119, 121-22, 125-26, 130, 143, 149, 171, 189, 191-92, 195, 198
  classic literary criticism, 134
  composition, 16
  of content or subject matter, 180
  form, 15, 20-21, 33-36, 46, 49, 51, 139, 147
  free-for-all playground, 152, 206
  grammatical, 47
  higher, 29
  historical, 21, 28-31, 36-37, 135, 150, 179, 182, 191
  historical-critical/ grammatical, 28, 46, 47, 133, 158, 169, 181
  historical-evolutionary, 49
  historically oriented, 49
  literary, 16, 28-29, 48, 54, 57, 61-62, 70, 134, 137-138, 144, 193, 203, 206
  literary-focused, 48
  literary-oriented, 49, 54, 59, 64
  literary/postmodern, 22, 49, 68, 133-34, 147, 168-69, 193, 206
  lower, 29
  modern, 114-17, 119, 123, 152, 193, 196
  narrative, 16, 17, 51, 54, 59, 147
  New, 16
  New Critical/formalist, 203
  philosophical/theological, 23, 40
  postmodern, 134, 137
  poststructuralist, 203
  psychological biblical, 138
  reader-centered, 17-18
  reader-oriented, 18, 48, 57-58
  reader-response, 17
  redaction, 16, 20-21, 33-36, 46, 49, 58, 134, 147
  secular literary, 16
  social-scientific, 16, 30
  socio-rhetorical, 16
  source, 20-21, 33-36, 46, 49, 58, 59, 147
  text-centered, 112
  text-oriented, 48
  textual, 21, 29, 41, 46, 50, 156

  theological, 28, 169, 206
  tradition/traditional, 14-16, 21-22, 31, 36, 46, 78, 79, 158, 162
Crossan, John Dominic, 41n
Crouch, James E., 61n
Crouter, Richard, 14n
Croy, N. Clayton, 190
Culler, Jonathan, 19n, 58n
Cullmann, Oscar, 196,
culture(s), cultural, 53, 68
  ancient Near Eastern, 35
  biblical, 31-32, 202
  modern, 31
  oral, 32, 146
Cunningham, Valentine, 208n
Cyprian, 124
Davids, Peter H., 36n
Davies, W. D., 45n, 61n
deconstructionism,
  deconstructed,
  deconstructive, 18, 56-57, 152
Derrida, Jacques, 18, 18n, 56, 57n, 77, 78n, 79, 79n, 84, 85, 156, 157, 158, 161, 161n, 162, 170, 171
Descartes, René, 208
deSilva, David A., 53n
diachronic, 22, 49, 52, 54, 68, 168. *See also* synchronic
dialogism, Bakhtinian, 54, 156
Dillard, Raymond, 106n
Dilthey, Wilhelm, 14, 19, 23, 70-71, 75, 82
dispensationalism, 140, 165
Dockery, David S., 11n
doctrine of the covenants, 90
document(s), books, manuscripts, 30, 35, 50, 54, 93, 96, 101, 179, 181
  actual, 34
  ancient, 29
  author of the, 39
  autograph, 50
  best available, 48
  biblical, 109, 177, 180, 183
  collection of authoritative, 29
  composition of ancient, 34
  congressional-record-like, 147
  context of the, 106
  formation of, 39, 46
  hypothetical, 49
  idiosyncratic and enigmatic, 155
  narrative world internal to a, 148

  original, 29, 46, 50, 192
  reliability of the, 39
  written, 31
Dodson, Derek S., 46n
dogmatic system, 90
Donoghue, Denis, 209n
double (doubling) commentary, 81, 85-86, 161-63
Dowd, Garin, 204n
Dube, Musa, 56n, 136
Duff, David, 204n
Duke, James O., 9n
Dunn, James D. G., 32n
Ebeling, Gerhard, 179n, 180, 180n
Eco, Umberto, 30n, 57, 58n
egalitarian, 136
Eliot, T. S., 60n,
Ellis, Earle E., 32n, 36n,
Emerson, Caryl, 113
English deism, 13
Enlightenment, 13, 19, 21, 73, 87, 90, 163, 179, 183, 185, 208
  post-, 103
  scholars, 13
  tradition, 14
Enns, Peter, 63n, 104, 104n, 105n, 155
Enuwosa, J., 67n
epistemological neutrality, 18-19
epistles
  Catholic, 119, 155
  Pastoral, 119
  Pauline (corpus), 119, 155
Erickson, Richard J., 10n
ethnicity, 57
etymologies, 38
Eusebius, 118
evangelical, evangelicalism, 9, 21, 37, 54, 114, 140, 143
Evans, Craig A. 34n, 204n
event(s), 21, 193
  creative and redemptive, 46
  historical, 27, 91, 127, 195, 198, 199
  historical reality of the, 209
  interpretive, 54
  narrated, 193
  original, 34
  past or present, 39, 106
  redemptive, saving, 151, 197
evidence
  archetypal, 106
  external, 42
  historical and biblical, 21

lack of, 191
   manuscript, 42, 122
   new, 114
   of theology, 198
exegesis, exegetical, exegete,
   9-10, 79, 82, 86, 97-98, 109,
   112-15, 119, 121, 127, 130,
   137-38, 143, 147, 161-65, 169,
   170-73, 176-77, 189, 190-92,
   194
extremism, 208
eyewitness interviews, 33-34
fallacy, fallacies, 19
   intentional, 30
   lexical, 38
Fanning, Buist M., 10n
Farnell, David F., 37n
Fee, Gordon D., 10n, 30n, 134n
feminism, feminist (criticism),
   55-56, 153, 157, 170
Fetterly, Judith, 55n
Fishbane, Michael, 190, 190n
Floyd, Michael H., 13n
Foucault, Michael, 19, 19n
foundationalists, 18
foundations, 11, 163
   historical, 28
   historiographical, 58
   necessary, 47, 146
Fowl, Stephen E., 12n, 116,
   116n, 195n, 200n
Fowler, Robert M., 55n
France, R. T., 42n, 61n, 63n,
   102n, 141n
Freitheim, Terence E., 129n
Freud, Sigmund, 19
Gabler, J. P., 90
Gadamer, Hans-Georg, 18,
   18n, 23, 24n, 70, 70n, 71,
   71n, 72, 72n, 73, 73n, 74n,
   75, 76, 76n, 77, 77n, 79, 80,
   83, 84, 85, 156, 157, 161,
   161n, 163, 168, 170, 171, 195,
   202n
Gaffin, Richard B., Jr., 22, 22n,
   89, 89n, 140, 141, 143, 153,
   154, 155, 165, 166, 167, 168,
   171, 174, 188, 190, 195, 196,
   197, 198, 205, 207n, 208, 209,
   211
Galatians, book of, 79
Gamble, Harry Y., 124n
Garland, David E., 31n
Garrett, Don, 15n
Gempf, Conrad H., 33n
gender, 57, 136
genre, 33, 46, 72, 96, 123, 134,
   181, 204

George, Mark K., 57n,
Gnuse, Robert, 46n
Goldsworthy, Graeme, 11n, 28n
González, Joaquín, 43n
Goppelt, Leonhard, 46n, 102n
Gospel, Gospels, 34, 36, 48-51,
   53, 102, 118, 120, 122-25,
   128, 143, 147, 150, 194
government, 57
grammar
   and history, 41
   study of, 30
   and syntax, 27
   theological, 195, 198
   of theological agreements,
      130
grammar(s) of faith, 115, 152,
   157
grammatical construction, 146
grammatical/syntactical
   relationships, 192
Green, Barbara M., 55n,
Green, Gene L., 36n,
Green, Joel B., 11n, 12n, 13n,
   30n, 36n, 49n, 50, 50n, 54,
   54n, 56n, 58n, 68n, 191, 191n
Gregory, Andrew A., 120
Gregory the Great, 170
Grieg, Josef A., 89n
Gundry, Robert H., 46n
Gurtner, Daniel M., 61n
Habermas, Jürgen, 82, 82n
Hagner, Donald, 28n, 42n,
   102n, 107n, 182n
harmonistic or historicist
   reductions, 127, 152
Harrisville, Roy, 15n
Harvey, Van, 179n
Hayes, John H., 10n, 52n, 56n,
   203n
Haynes, Stephen R., 51n
Hays, Richard, 61n, 98n, 209n
Hebrews, book of, 155
Hegel, G. W. F., 167
Heidegger, Martin, 70-72, 156
Heilsgeschichte, 89, 165, 196
Held, Heinz Joachim, 123n
Helmer, Christine, 14n
Hemer, Colin J., 33n
Hengel, Martin, 122n, 204n
hermeneutic(s), hermeneutical,
   9-11, 18-19, 71, 82, 137, 170,
   187
   anarchy, 57
   approaches, 11, 12, 176
   of authorial discourse, 76
   biblical, 9-11, 12-13, 19-24,
      137, 195, 201, 203, 210

canonical, 141
circle/spiral, 71-72, 74, 81,
   138, 145, 169, 173, 177,
   200
communications model of,
   17
conservative, 80
deregionalization of, 71
double, 79-80, 84, 157-58,
   161-62, 169, 170-71,
   184-85
ecumenical, 171
evolutionary model of, 17
form of, 14
foundations, 177
framework, 20
humility, 202
issues, 11-12, 22
literary, 19
model, models, 14, 17, 18,
   202
modern, 14
New Testament, 13, 158
New, 17, 203
Old Testament, 13, 99
phenomenological, 18-19
philosophical, 18-19, 23,
   70-72, 75, 81-86, 88, 138,
   160, 168-71, 173, 185
poststructuralist, 19
radicalization, 71
reader-oriented, 17
reader-response, 164
romantic, romanticism, 14,
   19, 75-76, 138, 203
secular, 171
solipsism, 208
stances, position(s), 12, 21,
   23, 146, 174
   of suspicion, 55, 157
synthesis, synthesizing,
   201-2
task, 85
taxonomies of, 28
theological, 23
topics of, 10
triad, 49
hierarchy, hierarchical, 19, 56
Hirsch, E. D., Jr., 77n, 79, 79n,
   82, 82n, 138, 139, 139n
Historie, 196
historiography, 33, 147
history, histories, historicity,
   historical, 19, 28, 46, 73-74,
   91, 94-95, 129, 168, 180, 182
   ahistorical systems, 165
   ancient, 33
   anti-, 54

and authorship, 208
background(s), 17, 36, 40, 43, 123
behind the text, 21, 30
of biblical hermeneutics, 12-13
of biblical interpretation, 81, 143
biblical reception, 153
Christ-centered, 95
context, 16
distance, gap, 78, 80, 172, 181
exegesis, 13
exodus-exile, 63
forward-looking, 108
God's mighty acts in, 140
God's role within, 153
good and bad, 33
human, 167
idea of, 191
inquiry, 37
of a/the language, 37-38
material, 46
of miracles, 13
orientations, 16, 20
phenomenon, 94
positions, 20
postbiblical, 191
purposes for, 33
of reception, 116
reconstruction(s), 14-15
recurring patterns in, 46
of redemption, 165-67, 197
research, 53
of revelation, 90, 166, 196
of salvation (salvation-history), 89, 109, 168, 197, 198
study of, 27
of theology, 164
unity of, 167
writing of, 71, 81
Holladay, John R., 10n, 203n
homiletics, 158
Horsley, Richard A., 45n, 151n
Hosea, book of, 22, 103-6, 127, 141, 149, 151, 170
Howard, Tracy L., 44n, 142n
Hubbard, Robert L., Jr., 11n, 31n, 33n, 140n
Hughes, Paul E., 34n
human sciences, 72
Hutzwit, J. R., 14n
ideological
    bias, 33
    emphases, 47
    spin, 33, 147

tent, 56
Idhe, Don, 18n
idiolect, 38
imperialism, 136
implication, author and text, 203
implications, theological and ethical, 202, 209
Instone-Brewer, David, 61n
interpretation, interpreting, interpretive, interpreter(s), 9-10, 18-19, 21, 28, 30, 41, 48, 73, 74, 79, 82, 86, 94, 120, 135, 144, 157, 169, 171, 173-74, 178, 181, 185, 189, 203, 205
    act of, 205
    of the biblical canon, 17
    biblical text, 135, 156, 162-64, 172, 187, 202
    biblical, scriptural, 9-11, 13, 20-21, 23, 38, 48, 54, 56, 68, 84, 93, 96, 109-10, 112, 114-16, 118, 121, 138, 141, 188, 190, 193-95, 210
    canon for, canonical, 23, 114, 122, 150
    of the Catholic Epistles, 23
    Christian, 206
    christological, 155
    conflict in, 172
    consensus, 206
    conservative biblical, 37
    constraints on, 79, 83, 158
    constructive/deconstructive lines of, 67
    correct, 41
    disagreements of, 200
    diversity of, 145, 164
    exhaustive or inerrant, 135
    extracanonical, 173
    faithful, 121, 130
    form of, 14
    goal of, 75, 76, 80, 163, 171
    of the Gospels, 23
    grammatico-historical, 28
    guide to, 11
    guided, 72
    hermeneutics of, 209
    historical situation of the, 77
    historical-critical, 183
    historical-critical/grammatical, 168
    integrity and diversity, 202, 206
    intended audience's, 31

interpretations of, 70, 93, 156
    limits on/of, 57, 79, 152-53
    literary and historical, 152
    literary and legal, 80
    literary-centered, 49
    literary/postmodern, 22, 168
    methods of/in, 10, 73, 166, 176, 186
    models for, 83, 111
    modern, 20
    movement, 17
    nature of, 11
    of the New Testament, 98, 206
    objectivity of, 74-75, 81
    of the Old Testament, 206
    of the Pauline Epistles, 23
    orthodox, 145
    oval, 52
    phenomenological biblical literary, 16
    postbiblical, 170
    postmodern, 20, 194
    practice(s), 112, 115-16
    presuppositions of the, 73
    principal concern, 121
    principles, 36
    process of, 75, 156, 205
    psychological, 138
    psychological dimensions of, 72
    purpose of, 75
    rational autonomy of, 90
    relationship between author and text, 14
    relativity of, 81, 83
    role of faith in, 202, 207
    role of the subject, 18
    spiritual authority of the, 115-16, 121
    strateg(ies), 50, 52, 130, 166, 189
    subjective, subjectivism, 19, 161
    text-, 76
    theological, 22, 153, 197-200
    topics of, 10
    traditional, 117
    traditions of, 19
    variety of, 83-84
intertext, intertexts, intertextuality, 51-53, 61, 62, 68, 127, 129, 134-35, 149, 150, 169, 196-97
intratext, 128

Irenaeus, 122, 124, 128, 173
Israel, Israel's
    biblical story, 125
    history of, 92
    story of, 13
Jakobson, Roman, 202n
Jesus, Christ, 52, 58-60, 62, 65,
    92-93, 98-101, 108-9, 117-18,
    120, 124-25, 128, 152-55,
    187, 191, 197, 199, 209
    authentic words and deeds
        of, 49
    authenticity, 15
    baptism and temptation
        scenes, 156
    earliest sayings of, 15
    event, 21
    gospel of, 55
    historical, 13, 36
    historical and theological
        significance, 155
    message of, 204
    role of, 22
    saying or deed attributed to,
        36
    trial, life, death, and
        resurrection of, 13, 60,
        99-100, 108, 166, 175
    types of, 103
John, Gospel of, 41, 124, 144,
    150-51, 155
Jude, book of, 36
Juhl, P. D., 136, 136n
Kaiser, Otto, 10n
Kaiser, Walter, 144n
Kant, Immanuel, Kantian, 70,
    72, 168, 172
Kaufmann, Walter Arnold,
    210n
Keener, Craig S., 33n, 43n, 105,
    105n
Kelber, Werner H., 32,
Kierkegaard, Søren, 74, 156
Kille, Andrew D., 138,
Kings, Book of, 35
Klein, William W., 11n, 31n,
    33n, 140n
Koester, Helmut, 124n
Krentz, Edgar, 14n, 27n, 40n
Kümmel, Werner G., 10n
LaCoque, André, 79n, 161n
law, 70
Lehmann, H. T., 97n
Lemcio, Eugene, 17n, 23n
Lemke, Steve W., 11n
Lemon, Joel M., 57n
letters, New Testament, 36
Levenson, John D., 113,

Levinas, Emmanuel, 210n
Linemann, Eta, 37n
linguistic discontinuity, 166
literary integrity and diversity,
    202, 206
literature
    biblical, 149
    didactic, 193
    Greco-Roman, 53
    Hellenistic-Jewish, 52
    hermeneutical, 139
    historical and biographical,
        32
    prophetic, 107
    religious, 152
logical positivism, 17
Longenecker, Richard N., 13n,
Longman, Tremper, III, 31n,
    106n
Love, Stuart L., 136
Lovejoy, Grant I., 11n
Luckmann, Thomas, 81
Luke, Gospel of, 34-35, 41, 50,
    53, 57-58, 120, 123-24,
    127-28, 144, 150-52
Lunde, Jonathan, 104n
Luther, Martin, 74
Luz, Urich, 45n, 61n, 125n
Lyotard, Jean-François, 167,
Maalouf, Tony T., 43n
MacDonald, Dennis R., 204n
Machen, J. Gresham, 45n
Maier, Gerhard, 11n
Makkreel, Rudolf A., 14n, 70n,
    81n
Malina, Bruce, 16, 16n
manuscript(s). See documents
Mark, Gospel of, 35, 123-25,
    143, 150-52
Markley, Jennifer Foutz, 10n,
    21n, 28n, 30, 38n, 139n
Marsh, James L., 209n
Marshall, Donald G., 23n, 161
Marshall, Howard I., 14n, 15n
Martínez, Aquiles Ernesto,
    67n-68n
Marx, Karl, 19
Massaux, Édouard, 124, 124n
Matthew, Matthew's, first
    Gospel (of), 35, 45-46, 48-49,
    52, 56, 58-64, 66, 84, 104-5,
    120, 122-28, 136, 141,
    147-48, 150-52, 158-59,
    169-70, 175, 191-94
    audiences, 142
    birth and death narratives,
        60-61
    birth narrative, 42, 58

dating of, 42
depiction of Christ, 22
historical background of,
    144, 193
intended aim for, 48
literal-critical
    interpretations of, 48
narrative strategies in, 49
normative authority of, 144
oral versions of, 192
text, 48
use of Hosea, 103, 108, 155,
    176-77
use of typology, 141
Matthews, Kenneth A., 11n
McCartney, Dan, 11n, 63n,
    104, 104n, 155
McDonald, Lee Martin, 124n,
    150
McKenzie, Stephen L., 51n
McKim, Donald K., 89n
McKnight, Edgar V., 15n
McKnight, Scot, 10n
meaning, meanings, sense, 18,
    20, 27, 30, 55, 81, 161, 185,
    194
    assumptions and
        foundations for, 19
    author's, authorial, 46, 158
    basis or foundation of/for,
        20
    bearers of, 160
    distinctive, 38
    of earlier texts, 143
    from texts, 54
    fuller, 31, 117, 142, 149,
        190
    intended, 30, 188, 197
    of later texts, 143
    limiting, 39, 148, 164
    literal, 103-4, 155
    narrative-critical, 156
    New Testament, 40, 148
    original, 14, 41, 79, 82, 143,
        145-46, 161, 170-71
    perception of a text's, 114
    private, 200
    pure, objective, 138
    source of a text's, 76
    textual, 121, 156, 189,
        193-94
    transmitting, 17
    of words, 37, 47
mental processes, 31
method, methods,
    methodological, 10, 48, 73
    canonical, 41, 144
    grammatical, 37

grammatico-historical,
    27-28, 103, 176
historical, 20, 29
historical group of
    hermeneutical, 28
historical-critical, 21, 27,
    29-30, 46, 90, 103,
    178-81
historical-critical/
    grammatical, 30, 33,
    37-41, 135, 145, 165
literary and postmodern,
    39, 41, 68, 133
philosophical/theological, 41
Second Temple interpretive,
    104
traditional, 16, 18
of typology, 44
methodological doubt, 27
Metzger, Bruce M., 29n
Meyer, Ben F., 136n
Mickelsen, Berkeley A., 11n
Millard, Alan, 33n
Milton, Terry S., 11n
modern science, 71
modernity, modernism,
    modern, 33, 87, 96, 103, 140,
    185, 191, 196-97, 207-8
Moo, Douglas J., 31n
Moore, Stephen D., 16n, 17, 17n,
    19, 19n, 55n, 57n, 135n, 207n
moral dilemma, 121
moral discipline, 112
Morgan, Robert, 14n
movement, movements
    biblical theology, 165
    intellectual, 21
    interpretive, 17
    literary-philosophical, 18
    redemptive-historical, 144
    religious, 114
    women's equal rights, 55
Mueller-Vollmer, Kurt, 12n
Muller, Richard, 183n
Murray, John, 105n
mutual illumination, 62
myth, modern myth, 33, 76
narrative cotextual perspective,
    63
narrative, narratives, narrators,
    narratees, 17, 22, 33, 53, 125,
    147, 176, 193
    behind and within the, 50
    biblical, 34, 134, 159, 193
    birth, 45
    complex, 51
    critic, 152
    epic, 35

final, polished, 49
Gospel, 51, 53-54
historical, 61, 114
implied, 39
larger, 68
Lukan, 50
memory, 32
meta-, 135, 167, 206
Old Testament, 35, 150
outside the, 53
overall, 50
plotline or thematic
    developments, 120
reflections, 175
structure, 169
Synoptic and Johannine, 52
themes across the, 50
unity, 167
written, 35
Naselli, Andrew D., 31n,
natural science(s), 72-73, 82,
    163
naturalist universe, 27
Neill, Stephen, 11n, 15n
neutral deep structures, 18
New Testament, 13, 14, 17,
    22-23, 52, 94, 98-102, 108,
    119-20, 144, 150, 154-55,
    164, 194, 196-97, 206, 209
Newsom, Carol A., 55n
Neyrey, Jerome, 16, 16n, 53n
Nietzsche, Friedrich, 19, 74,
    156, 208
Nolland, John, 44n, 45n, 58n,
    61n, 63n, 126n, 127n
norming norm, 183
objectivism, 135, 156
O'Day, Gail R., 52n
Oeming, Manfred, 12n
Offenbarungsgeschichte, 165
Olbricht, Thomas H., 32n
Old Testament, 13-14, 17,
    22-23, 35, 42, 52, 61, 63,
    98-102, 104, 106, 108,
    119-20, 149-50, 154, 168-69,
    172, 194, 196-97, 206, 209
organic
    language, 167
    metaphors, 167
    totality, 167
Osborne, Grant R., 11n, 18n,
    138n
Oswald, H. C., 97n
patriarchy, patriarchal, 136, 157
Pelikan, J. J., 97n
Pellauer, David, 18n
Penny, Robert L., 98n
Perdue, Leo G., 9n

Perrin, Norman, 16n
perspectivism, perspectivist,
    perspectival, 74, 156-57, 174
Pervo, Richard I., 134n
Petersen, Norman, 14, 14n, 16n,
    17n, 202n
phenomenology, 18
philosophy of hermeneutics,
    189
philosophy, philosophers,
    philosophical, 16-18, 21, 23,
    32, 40, 71-73, 156, 160, 185
Pixner, Bargil, 43n
plot, 50-51, 59-60, 109, 140,
    148-49, 153
poetics, 17
Pokorný, Petr, 9n
polyglot perspectives, 56
polymerōs, 95
polytropōs, 95
Popkin, Richard H., 15n
Porter, Stanley E., 9n, 10n, 12n,
    13n, 14n, 16n, 17n, 18n, 23n,
    24n, 32n, 34n, 36n, 38n,
    117n, 118n, 201, 202n, 203n,
    204n, 206n, 207n, 211
postcolonialism, postcolonial,
    22, 55-56, 170
postmodern, postmodernism,
    postmodernity, 18-19, 33, 39,
    48, 56-57, 87, 135, 137, 148,
    154, 156, 164, 167, 185, 193,
    202, 207-9
post-Reformation, 89, 90
post-structuralism, 18-19, 22,
    207
Powell, Mark A., 39n, 43n, 48,
    48n, 49n, 51n, 53n, 56n, 64,
    64n, 65n, 66n
power, 19
practical results, 24
premodern, 103
presupposition pool, 39
presuppositions, 11, 72-73, 81,
    84, 136, 157, 168, 171, 173
pretext, 188
principle, aesthetic, 118
principle of analogy, 27
principle of correlation, 27, 179
principle of criticism, 27
principle of Scripture, 41
prooftext, proof-texting, 52,
    188
Prophets, 13, 35
Protestant
    evangelicalism, 91
    orthodoxy, 90
Proverbs, book of, 35

Psalms, book of, 13
psychic
    facts, 75
    life, 75-76, 80
    reality, 75
psychologism, 75-76
psycho-sociological conditions,
    77
public recitation, 32
Pyrrhonian skepticism, 13
Quelle (Q), source (M, L), 35,
    44
Rad, Gerhard von, 196
reader(s), reader's, reading(s),
    18, 20, 32, 49, 50, 52, 54, 56,
    68, 78-79, 113, 125, 130,
    136-38, 145, 147, 153, 161,
    164, 170-71, 177, 188,
    191-92, 194, 203-5
    act of, 77
    activity, acts, work, 93, 154,
        165, 168, 196
    ancient, 22, 202
    approach, method(s), 22,
        40-41, 47, 89, 91-94,
        96-98, 101, 104, 109-10,
        157, 165-66, 177, 186,
        206
    competent, 53
    contemporary, today's, 17,
        22
    context, 98, 109
    continuity, 98
    correct, 20
    dominant, 55
    engagement, 20
    experience of, 21
    faithful, 111, 117, 130, 190,
        199
    helpful or harmful, 20
    hermeneutic, interpretation,
        140, 165
    highly textured, 129
    historical context, 81
    history, 92-93, 95, 97-98
    implied, 39
    intended, original, 17, 29,
        48, 161, 164, 172, 175
    modern, 22, 202
    New Testament, 55
    non-traditional, 55
    non-typological, 155
    panoply of, 57
    presuppositions and
        traditions, 81
    real, serious, 39, 48, 161
Reagan, Charles, 209n
realism

critical, 135, 138
    naive, 135
reason and language, 186
reason(ing), rational, 73, 82,
    179-82, 185-87
redemption, theme of, 22
redemptive-historical (or
    biblical-theological)
    resistant, 55
    response(s), 31, 134, 156
    scholars, 13
    significance, 106, 109
    variety of, 83
reductionisms, 122-23
Reformers, Reformation,
    Reformed, 21-22, 89-91, 97,
    109, 165, 167, 188, 195,
    196-97
Reid, Daniel, 123n
relativism, 156, 193
religionsgeschichtliche Schule, 15
Resseguie, James L., 39n, 51n
Revelation, book of, 36
revelation, revelatory, 90-98,
    109, 140-41, 152, 159, 165,
    187, 197-98, 200, 205, 207
Reventlow, Henning Graf, 9n
Rhoads, David, 16n
Richards, Kent Harold, 57n
Richardson, Kurt Anders, 13n
Richards, Randolph, 32n
Richardson, Peter, 43n
Ricoeur, Paul, 12n, 18, 18n, 23,
    70, 70n, 71n, 72, 75, 75n,
    76n, 77, 77n, 79, 80, 86, 156,
    161, 161n, 163, 170, 208,
    208n, 209, 209n
Ridderbos, Herman N., 93n
Riesner, Rainer, 43n
Risser, James, 77n
Robinson, Jason C., 9n, 12n,
    14n, 17n, 18n, 23n, 24n,
    203n, 207n
Rodi, Frithjof, 70n, 81n
Rorty, Richard, 58n
Rosner, Brian S., 106n, 140n
Rowe, C. Kavin, 120
rule of faith, 41, 52, 115-16,
    121, 128-30, 143, 150,
    152-53, 173, 176, 183, 196-97
Sachkritik, 180-81
Said, Edward, 56n
Sailhamer, John H., 93n, 104,
    104n, 155
Sanders, James A., 112n, 152,
    204n
Schertz, Mary H., 10n
Schippers, R., 142n

Schleiermacher, Friedrich, 14,
    70-72, 75, 169, 203
scholar(s), 17
    biblical, 15-17, 19, 160, 164
    conservative, 133
    conservative legal, 82
    interdisciplinary, 139
    modern, 16
    New Testament, 16
    Reformed, 196
    traditional, 16
scientific neutrality, 190
scribal copying, 29
scrolls, 32
Seeley, David, 57, 57n
Segovia, Fernando F., 56n
Seitz, Christopher, 111n, 178
semantic
    anachronism, 38
    obsolescence, 38
setting(s), milieu(s),
    circumstance(s), 59
    canonical, 41
    geographical, 59
    historical, 39, 134, 172, 199
    historical and cultural, 31,
        46, 112, 164
    historical and traditional,
        156
    historical-cultural-social,
        169
    literary, 53
    native, 146
    original, 39, 164
    social, 130
    sociocultural, 139
    sociohistorical, 14
Shannon, Nathan D., 185n
Sloan, Robert B., 11n
Soares-Prabhu, George M., 63n
social sciences, 72
socio-cultural conditions, 77
sociological, 48
    values, 30
sociology of the Gospels, 135
socio-political relations, 57
sola scriptura, 97
speaker, speakers, writers, 31-32
    dead, 31
speech act(s), 76, 78, 85, 139,
    145, 158
Spencer, Scott F., 22, 22n, 48,
    52n, 53n, 54n, 56n, 60n, 67n,
    133, 134, 135, 146, 148n,
    157n, 168, 169, 170, 175, 176,
    178, 188, 188n, 193, 194, 202,
    205, 205n, 206, 207n, 208,
    211-12

Spinoza, Baruch, 15, 167
Stanton, Graham N., 122n
Stein, Robert H., 15n, 123n
Stendahl, Krister, 43n
Stenger, Werner, 10n
Stevenson, Lesley, 204n
Stott, Douglas W., 10n
Stovell, Beth M., 201, 212
Strecker, George, 33n
Strong, Jeremy, 204n
structuralism, 17-19
Stuart, Douglas, 10n, 30n, 134n
studies
    biblical, 21, 56, 191
    canonical, 23
    historical, 68
    historical and grammatical,
        143
    literary, 21-22, 29, 197
    Matthean, 56
    redaction-critical, 127
    social-scientific, 21-22
    source, 127
style, 22
Sundburg, Walter, 15n
supernatural, 27
supersession(ism), 155, 197
synchronic, 10, 22, 50, 52, 54,
    68, 134. *See also* diachronic
Synoptic Gospels, 123
Synoptic Problem, 123
Old Testament, 35
Tate, W. Randolph, 9n, 10n
Taylor, Charles, 75
Tertullian, 115, 152
text and reader, 133, 191
text, texts (biblical texts),
    textual, 14-15, 18, 20, 22,
    27-31, 34, 36-37, 47, 49, 51,
    56-57, 71, 76, 79, 81, 85-86,
    88, 94, 111, 113, 115-17, 121,
    126, 130, 134, 138-39,
    141-42, 145-47, 153-54, 158,
    160-61, 163-64, 169-71, 181,
    184, 188, 190-92, 194, 201,
    203, 206
    after-life of, 40
    allusions and quotations of
        parallel, 126
    ancient, 18, 163
    antecedent, 197
    approaches to the, 36-37
    around the, 68
    authenticity of, 15
    background of, 14
    behind the, 12-13, 16-18,
        59, 68, 76, 80, 209
    canonical, 114, 117, 168

captivity to the, 19
close reading of the, 50
comparative, 54
constructs created by the, 20
critical, 192
current, 15
diversity in the
    interpretation of the, 39
earlier, 16
final, 49-50, 54, 58, 68,
    134, 168-69, 193-94
final Greek, 58
foci/focal, 49, 51, 54, 58-59,
    61, 67-68, 149-150, 153,
    158, 194
in front of the, 12, 17, 68,
    76, 80, 209
God's role in producing the,
    86, 184
grammar of, 21, 190
historical trustworthiness,
    37
historically remote, 82
human, 112, 143
inscribing the, 76
inside and outside of the, 46
interpretation of/
    interpreting, 30, 41, 71,
    116, 148, 160, 179
itself, 16
literal/plain sense of a/the,
    115, 122, 129-30, 172-73
meaning from, 14
meaning of (a/the), 42,
    75-77, 113, 119, 146, 161,
    188, 190
meaning resides within, 18
nature of, 152
nature of transmission, 37
new, 52
New Testament, 54, 142,
    177, 197
non-biblical, 135, 171
objective reading of the, 19
Old Testament, 40, 61, 102,
    144, 177, 197
open, 54, 66, 68, 134-35,
    152, 169-70, 194
origin, 37
original, 146, 172-73
original meaning of a/the,
    15, 135-36
outside the, 54
preached, 135
preferred, 42
prior, 52
reading/readers (of) the, 20,
    72, 134

reconstructed Greek, 50
relationship between, 14,
    52, 135
role, 205
sacred, 114, 119-21, 130,
    190
scriptural, literary, legal,
    85-86
secure, 42
set, 193
sociological/grammatical
    reading of, 137
sources, 13
stories behind the, 15
theological or ethical sense
    of the, 115
translating the, 37
transmitted, 76
types of, 13
unity, 17
within its context, 16
within the, 15-18, 56, 209
world of (a/the), 77
wrong, 42, 145
theology/ies, theological,
    theologians, 15, 21, 29, 40,
    70, 85, 98, 129, 165-68,
    171-72, 174, 185, 191, 193,
    196, 200
    art, 50
    assessment, 175
    biases, 192
    biblical, 22, 40, 89-90, 109,
        137, 140, 198
    conception, 111
    confusion, 121
    content, 118
    continuity, 166
    covenant, 140
    emphases, 35, 40, 47, 151
    historical nature of, 165
    illumination, 129
    perspicuity, 114
    role of, 20
    standpoint, 207
    systematic, 22, 40, 109,
        110, 137
    truth, 88
    understanding, 111-12, 117,
        120
    vision, 153
theory, theories, theorists
    expressivist, 75
    French literary, 56
    goals of postmodern, 207
    hermeneutical, 138, 189-90,
        200
    historical-critical, 14

of inspiration, 184-85
literary, 16, 17, 51
postmodern hermeneutical,
    18
postmodern, 208
postmodern-literary, 205
poststructuralist, 205
reader-response, 22
of *religionsgeschichtliche
    Schule*, 15
of self and narrative
    challenge, 209
variety of, 18
Thiselton, Anthony, 9, 9n, 10n,
    11n, 12n, 13n, 17n, 18n, 24n,
    178, 178n
Thomas, Robert L., 37n
Thompson, John B., 70n
Tombs, David, 16n, 34n, 202n
Torah, 13
Torrance, T. F., 198n
traditio, 117
tradition, traditions, 39, 49, 73,
    111, 147, 196
    apostolic, 119, 145
    biblical, 63
    Calvinist, 140
    collections of, 35
    common, 152
    covenantal and royal, 61
    cultural and theological, 54,
        160
    exodus, 63
    faith, 152
    Gospel, 123
    hermeneutical, 17
    Herod and magi, 59
    hypothetical, 49
    methodological and
        theological, 84
    oral, 15, 33, 35, 147
    political, social and
        cultural, 74
    postmodern, 72
    Protestant or Christian, 54,
        140
    religious, 74, 157, 195
    stories and, 32

theological, 196
traditum, 117
translation(s), 83, 207
Treier, Daniel J., 40n
Troeltsch, Ernst, 27, 179
Tuckett, Cristopher A., 11n
Tull, Patricia K., 51n
Turner, David L., 44n
Turner, Max, 39n
typological intertextual
    perspective, 63
typology, typologies,
    typological, 46-47, 62, 102,
    104, 106-8, 118, 126, 128-29,
    140-42, 148, 150-51, 155,
    170, 174, 176, 198
use of the Old Testament (in
    the NT), 20, 31, 52, 98-99,
    101, 103, 141, 148, 166, 177
van Bruggen Jakob, 108n
Vanhoozer, Kevin J., 12n, 24n,
    57, 58, 58n, 139n, 195n
Vickers, Jason, 116n
view (position), views,
    viewpoints, perspective
    canonical, 102, 107, 111,
        142-43, 149, 152-53, 168,
        171, 176 182, 188, 206
    historical, 153
    historical-critical/
        grammatical, 21, 27, 146,
        162, 174, 178, 202
    literary, 153
    literary/postmodern, 48, 68,
        133, 146-50, 152, 158,
        168, 175, 178, 193, 202
    maximalist, 21
    minimalist, 21
    narrative-critical, 59
    philosophical/theological,
        70, 137, 156, 160, 184,
        189, 202
    political or religious, 33
    redemptive-historical, 22,
        89, 102, 137, 140, 153,
        155, 165, 174, 176, 180,
        183, 187, 195, 206
    revelation-historical, 107

sociological and
    psychological, 77
symphonic-choral, 149
traditional Western, 55
variable, 147
Virkler, Henry A., 11n,
Vos, Geerhardus, 22, 22n, 89,
    89n-90n, 90, 90n, 91, 91n,
    92n, 93n, 97n, 153, 167, 196
Wall, Robert W., 17n, 23, 23n,
    68n, 111, 117n, 118, 119n,
    120n, 141, 142, 143, 144, 149,
    150, 151, 152, 153, 171, 172,
    173, 182, 183, 188, 192, 198,
    201n, 205, 208, 209, 212
Warfield, B. B., 182n
Watson, Francis, 12n, 195n
Watts, Rikki E., 106n
Weaver, Dorothy Jean, 65n
Weaver, Walter P., 13n
Webster, John, 189n, 199n
Wegner, Paul D., 29n
Weinsheimer, Joel, 161
Wenham, David, 102n
Wesley, Wesleyan, 23, 195, 196
Westminster Confession of
    Faith, 100
Westphal, Merold, 9n, 23, 23n,
    70, 73, 137, 138, 156, 157,
    160, 184, 185, 185n, 189, 190,
    195, 202, 202n, 205, 207n,
    208, 209, 212
Wilkins, Michael J., 44n
Wimsatt, William K., 31n
Winter, Bruce W., 54n, 148n
Witherington, Ben, 16, 16n,
    33n, 44n
Wolterstorff, Nicholas, 75, 76n,
    78, 79, 79n, 80, 81, 84, 85n,
    117, 118n, 156, 157, 158, 162,
    162n, 171
Woodbridge, John A., 40n
Wright, Tom, 11n, 13n, 15n,
    39n, 86, 86n, 182n
Yarbrough, Robert W., 89n
Yoder, Perry B., 10n
Zimmermann, Jens, 208n, 210n

Scripture Index

Genesis
1:31, *91*
3, *91*
32:30, *86*
37–50, *63*

Exodus
2:15, *126*
4:22, *61*, *107*
8:18-19, *65*
9:29, *129*
15, *129*
19:5, *129*
20:2, *106*

Numbers
22–24, *65*
23:22, *107*
24:8, *107*, *126*

Deuteronomy
4:19, *129*
18:9-14, *65*

2 Samuel
7, *126*
7:14, *61*

1 Kings
14:19, *35*
14:29, *35*

Psalms
2:1-7, *61*
2:2, *107*
2:6-7, *107*
2:12, *107*
80:15, *107*
80:17, *107*
89:26-27, *107*
94, *96*

Isaiah
14:13-14, *82*
42:1-4, *107*
47:12-15, *65*
49:1-13, *107*
49:6, *107*
52:13–53:12, *107*
55:9, *93*
57:15, *92*
60:2, *107*

Jeremiah
31, *96*
31:9, *61*

Daniel
2:1-24, *64*

Hosea
1:1, *106*
2:15, *106*, *127*
5:13, *106*
7:11, *106*
7:16, *106*
8:9, *106*
8:13, *106*
9:3, *106*
9:6, *106*
10:6, *106*
11, *62*, *176*
11:1, *20*, *44*, *47*, *61*,
 62, *64*, *67*, *84*, *98*,
 102, *103*, *104*, *105*,
 106, *107*, *126*, *127*,
 140, *141*, *142*, *148*,
 150, *151*, *155*, *196*
11:1-11, *107*, *151*, *155*
11:2-4, *107*
11:2-7, *62*
11:5, *62*, *106*
11:5-7, *107*
11:8-11, *107*
11:11, *62*, *106*, *107*,
 108
12:1, *106*
12:9, *106*, *127*, *151*
12:13, *106*, *127*, *151*
13:4, *106*, *127*, *151*

Micah
5:2, *43*

Habakkuk
3:2, *107*

Zechariah
9–14, *13*

Matthew
1, *42*, *127*, *128*
1–2, *43*, *45*, *59*, *125*,
 127, *137*
1–7, *45*, *61*, *125*
1–13, *42*, *102*
1:1, *42*, *43*, *61*, *126*
1:1-2, *60*
1:1-17, *42*, *52*
1:3, *60*
1:5, *60*
1:5-6, *43*, *60*
1:6, *61*
1:8, *43*
1:13-15, *43*
1:17, *59*, *61*, *148*
1:18, *43*
1:18-25, *102*
1:18–2:23, *42*, *46*,
 102, *175*
1:19, *128*
1:20, *61*
1:21, *63*, *126*, *128*,
 151, *197*
1:23, *42*, *43*
2, *43*, *59*, *60*, *61*, *65*,
 67, *89*, *102*, *127*,
 136, *138*, *147*, *148*,
 156, *192*, *193*
2:1, *45*, *59*
2:1-2, *67*
2:1-6, *102*
2:1-12, *43*, *45*, *58*
2:1-23, *58*, *59*, *68*
2:2, *44*, *45*, *60*
2:4-6, *61*
2:5-6, *61*
2:6, *42*
2:7, *129*
2:7-8, *65*
2:7-15, *20*, *43*, *47*, *49*,
 58, *59*, *61*, *64*, *65*,
 68, *98*, *102*, *126*,
 128, *134*, *135*, *139*,
 140, *144*, *149*, *150*,
 151, *152*, *160*, *174*
2:8, *44*, *45*, *66*
2:9, *43*, *44*, *45*, *67*,
 139
2:9-13, *43*
2:10, *129*, *139*
2:11, *60*, *66*, *127*, *139*
2:12, *67*, *139*
2:12-14, *126*
2:13, *66*, *139*
2:13-14, *127*
2:13-15, *43*, *44*, *63*
2:13-23, *102*, *151*
2:14, *139*
2:15, *42*, *44*, *47*, *61*,
 62, *63*, *67*, *98*, *99*,
 100, *102*, *104*, *105*,
 126, *139*, *140*, *142*,
 176, *196*
2:16, *59*, *60*, *65*, *66*,
 67
2:16-18, *46*, *64*, *102*
2:17-18, *61*
2:18, *42*
2:19-21, *62*, *63*
2:19-23, *102*
2:21-22, *62*
2:23, *42*, *59*, *61*
3–4, *127*
3:13-17, *63*, *108*, *156*
4:1, *63*
4:1-2, *63*
4:1-11, *108*, *156*
4:3-11, *63*
5:3, *144*
5:17, *155*
5:17-20, *117*
7:1-5, *69*
7:24-27, *66*
8:10, *175*
8:11-12, *175*
8:17, *63*
9:17, *159*
10:6, *175*
10:9, *65*
10:16, *66*, *67*, *159*
10:23, *63*
13, *45*
13:17, *105*
13:52, *159*
15:22-28, *175*
15:24, *175*
19:19, *209*
21:1-9, *59*
21:10-11, *59*
21:33-46, *60*
21:43, *175*
22:39, *209*
23:37-39, *60*
24:45, *66*
25:1-10, *66*
25:14-30, *60*
26–28, *59*
27:19, *61*

27:22-23, *59*
27:54, *61*
28:9, *60*
28:16-20, *60*
28:17, *60*
28:18-20, *176*
28:19-20, *60*, *127*

Mark
1:9, *152*
1:15, *151*
2, *45*
12:31, *209*
12:33, *209*
16, *192*

Luke
1:1, *147*
1:1-4, *34*, *187*
1:3, *51*, *147*
1:4, *187*
1:38, *128*
1:48, *128*
2:1-20, *43*
2:29-32, *128*
3, *45*
4:16-21, *55*
6:20, *144*
8:1, *51*
10:24, *105*
10:27, *209*
24, *101*, *142*, *187*
24:1-43, *99*
24:25-27, *187*
24:27, *99*
24:32, *99*, *187*
24:44, *99*, *142*, *190*
24:44-45, *99*
24:44-47, *99*
24:44-49, *99*
24:45, *99*

24:45-47, *190*
24:46-47, *99*
24:50-53, *99*

John
1:1, *95*
5:46, *95*
8:56, *108*, *154*
11, *45*
12:38-40, *100*
12:41, *100*, *154*
20:30-31, *118*

Acts
1:3, *99*
3:24, *51*
4:32, *200*
8:9-24, *65*
11:4, *51*
13:6-12, *65*
16:7, *101*
18:23, *51*
19:18-19, *65*

Romans
1, *120*
1:18, *74*
5:12-19, *92*
8:9-10, *101*
8:14, *183*
10:4, *95*
12:3-8, *118*
12:4, *118*
12:5, *118*

1 Corinthians
10:4, *101*
12, *118*
12:7, *118*
12:11, *118*
12:12, *186*

12:17-21, *118*
12:20, *118*
13:12, *167*
15:3-4, *92*
15:21-22, *92*
15:44-49, *92*
15:45, *101*

2 Corinthians
3:17, *101*
4:7, *113*

Galatians
3:28, *77*
4:4, *92*

Ephesians
1:4, *92*
3:8, *187*
3:10, *187*
3:16-17, *101*

1 Thessalonians
1:9-10, *98*
2:13, *181*, *183*

2 Thessalonians
2:2, *181*
2:15, *181*

2 Timothy
2:15, *200*
3:15-16, *152*
3:15-17, *115*, *130*, *199*
3:16, *141*, *182*, *185*

Hebrews
1:1, *95*, *154*
1:1-2, *94*, *197*
1:1-4, *155*
2:2, *95*

2:2-3, *94*
2:3, *95*
2:5, *95*
3, *101*, *142*
3:5, *142*
3:5-6, *94*, *95*, *101*
3:7, *96*
3:16, *94*
4:3-5, *96*
4:7, *96*
4:12, *182*
8–10, *94*
8:13, *155*
9–10, *97*
9:8, *96*
9:28, *95*
10:15, *96*
11:1–12:2, *105*

James
2, *210*
2:8, *209*
2:14-17, *210*

1 Peter
1, *101*, *142*
1:3-9, *100*
1:10, *100*
1:10-11, *105*
1:10-12, *99*, *100*
1:12, *100*

2 Peter
1:20-21, *183*
3:16, *181*

Revelation
1–5, *36*
22:16, *129*